HUMAN RIGHTS AND JUDICIAL REVIEW

A COMPARATIVE PERSPECTIVE

International Studies in Human Rights

VOLUME 34

The titles published in this series are listed at the end of this volume.

HUMAN RIGHTS AND JUDICIAL REVIEW

A COMPARATIVE PERSPECTIVE

edited by

DAVID M. BEATTY
Professor of Law,
University of Toronto

MARTINUS NIJHOFF PUBLISHERS
DORDRECHT / BOSTON / LONDON

Library of Congress Cataloging-in-Publication Data

Human rights and judicial review : a comparative perspective / edited
by David M. Beatty.
p. cm. -- (International studies in human rights ; v. 34)
ISBN 0-7923-2968-6 (acid-free paper)
1. Human rights. 2. Judicial review. I. Beatty, David M.
II. Series.
K3240.6.H8587 1994
342'.085--dc20
[342.285] 94-21317

ISBN 0-7923-2968-6

Published by Martinus Nijhoff Publishers,
P.O. Box 163, 3300 AD Dordrecht, The Netherlands.

Sold and distributed in the U.S.A. and Canada
by Kluwer Academic Publishers,
101 Philip Drive, Norwell, MA 02061, U.S.A.

In all other countries, sold and distributed
by Kluwer Academic Publishers Group,
P.O. Box 322, 3300 AH Dordrecht, The Netherlands.

Printed on acid-free paper

Printed in the Netherlands

TABLE OF CONTENTS

PREFACE

This book is very much the product of its times. In the last decade of this century, people all over the world are turning to the courts and the process of constitutional review to protect what they regard to be their most basic human rights. With the collapse of communism and the surge for self determination given free reign, societies everywhere are opting for systems of government in which judges and constitutional bills of rights are given the job of ensuring the powers of the state are not abused. Human rights are a defining characteristic of our age.

By coincidence, this resurgence and revival of interest in constitutionalism and the rule of law is taking place on the occasion of two significant anniversaries in the history of human rights. It is now just over two hundred years since the Americans first experimented with the idea of the judiciary reviewing the way the other two branches of government exercise the powers of the state and we are just about to celebrate the fiftieth anniversary of the first major wave of constitutionalism that swept the world at the end of the second world war.

The idea of this book is to take advantage of the historical moment in which we are living; to draw on our past so that those who have just decided to subordinate the sovereignty of the people to the rule of law will better understand the choice they have made. Its modest ambition is to allow those who have had the most experience enforcing constitutional bills of rights to share their learning with those who have just or are just about to acquire the powers of judicial review.

The courts whose jurisprudence is the focus of the book include the Supreme Courts of India, Japan, Canada and the United States, the Constitutional Courts of Germany and Italy and the European Court of Human Rights. These are the courts with the longest and most extensive history of protecting human rights. In each chapter the most important decisions of these courts will be described and analyzed with a view to identifying the extent to which and explaining the way in which those entrusted with the powers of the state are made to conform to the most basic precepts and principles of constitutional law.

As a practical matter, the collection of essays is intended to familiarize readers with the basic principles and methods and analysis that are used by the major courts around the world in deciding whether a law, or some other activity by an official of the State, violates someone's constitutional rights. This is not a volume which tries to provide a comprehensive and exhaustive account of constitutional law around the world. Rather the essays have been organized in such a way as to highlight both the principles and doctrines which are common to all systems of judicial review as well as those which are particular to and idiosyncratic of individual courts. Nor is this a book which pretends to have all the answers. Read collectively, the essays reveal that, notwithstanding the similarity in the analytical tools they employ, there is considerable variation among the courts in the extent to which and the vigour with which they defend people's constitutional rights. At the end of the volume, readers and those just exploring nuances of constitutional bills of rights will be left with the choice of deciding which model or precedent serves their purposes and circumstances best.

While the primary purpose of this volume is a very practical one, and has quite a specific and immediate readership in mind, it has a wider, more theoretical, ambition as well. Even though we are living through an epoch in the development and protection of human rights, it happens that ideas like constitutionalism and the rule of law are very much under seige in those very societies in which judicial review and bills of rights have been in place the longest. It is one of the paradoxes of our time that constitutional bills of rights are flourishing precisely when, within the legal community itself, the integrity of law is most open to doubt.

In the first and last essays different parts of the academic debate that contests the idea of constitutional bills of rights and judicial review are introduced and assessed as a prelude and postscript to the specific case studies which constitute the core of the book. The essay which introduces the studies of the individual courts takes the doubts and concerns of those who are sceptical about the integrity of law as its point of reference while the concluding essay focuses on the ideas of those who believe that we have not, as yet, exhausted the protection which constitutional bills of rights can provide. Both have been written with a view of putting the essays which describe how bills of rights are actually enforced around the world in the context of the larger theoretical debate about the desirability of relying on the law and third branch of government to ensure the powers of the state do not trample people's most fundamental human rights. Reciprocally, the studies of how each of the major courts have addressed and enforced their respective bills of rights are designed to shed light on the academic controversy over the legitimacy of what the courts have done so far and what it is appropriate to ask them to do.

The circumstances in which we find ourselves has had as much influence on the style of this book as on the substantive law and legal reasoning which it analyses. Only in very recent times would it have been possible to find judges on each of the major courts which exercise the powers of constitutional review who had both an academic interest in and a willingness to talk about the analytical methods and doctrinal artifacts their courts use in deciding whether some law or other activity by an official of the state is constitutional or not. The unique combination of academic and judicial experience on which each of the authors of the country profiles is able to draw is itself one of the striking features of the way the process of constitutional review has developed around the world and gives this book a credibility which it would not otherwise enjoy.

In the course of organizing a collection of essays of this kind the debts one incurs are both more basic and more numerous than usual. The contributors who have written essays for this volume are already burdened with workloads which demand more of their time than the public has a right to expect. To have so willingly agreed to participate in this project goes well beyond the standard definitions of public service.

In addition to those who have shared their experience and ideas in this volume, numerous others extended kindnesses and introductions without which the book would have never materialized. Professors Hata, Murakami and Kamyia in Japan, Rajeev Dhavan in India, Ronald Macdonald of the European Court of Human Rights all were instrumental in helping move the project along at critical moments. Others including Ernie Weinrib, David Dyzenhaus, and Piet Akkermans read portions of the book and made valuable suggestions for its improvement. Merril Randell and Chris Black oversaw all of the technical and administrative details in the organization and transcription of the book. Selma Hoedt, at Martinus Nijhoff displayed a measure of patience and support without which this project would never have been completed.

Special thanks are also owed to Bertil Cottier and the Swiss Institute of Comparative Law, Hugh Corder and the Department of Public Law at the University of Cape Town where much of the book was written and organized, and to my family who cheerfully endured being uprooted again. The Social Science Research Council of Canada provided generous support to defray the administrative and research costs associated with the publication.

HUMAN RIGHTS AND THE RULES OF LAW

David Beatty*

The Rise of Constitutionalism and the Rule of Law

Ours is an age of constitutionalism. Never before have so many people of such radically different cultures and histories put so much faith in constitutional law in general, and written bills of rights in particular, as a way of trying to ensure a measure of integrity and legitimacy in how their Governments work. In the slightly more than one hundred years that have passed since 1885, when the English constitutional lawyer Albert Venn Dicey published his famous book, The Law of the Constitution, there has been an unmistakable shift, all over the world, in the importance people attach to the incorporation of written bills of rights into the constitutional framework of their governments. Especially following the liberation of Europe and Asia from the horrors of fascism and militaristic rule, and again after the emancipation of eastern Europe from the tyranny of communist cliques, country after country has embraced the idea of protecting what it regards as its most cherished human rights and freedoms by incorporating a written bill of rights into its constitution.[1] In terms of the two great principles Dicey identified as distinguishing the British method of organizing the powers of the State, one could say that the conventional wisdom of ordinary people all over the world, in the second half of the twentieth century, has been to subject the principle of democratic rule and popular sovereignty to a more demanding definition of the rule of law. Human rights and the rules of law have increasingly become the instrument of choice to reconcile the competing interests of individuals who share a common physical and social space. They have replaced earlier ideas and ideologies about absolute sovereigns, the general will of

---

*Faculty of Law, University of Toronto

[1] For brief introduction to the historical antecedents see M. Cappelletti *Judicial Review in the Contemporary World* 1971, Bobbs-Merrill, Indianapolis

D.M. Beatty (ed.), Human Rights and Judicial Review, 1-56.

the people, invisible hands, bureaucratic elites, the dictatorship of the proletariat etc as the fairest and most effective way of reconciling the interests of each individual with the interests of the larger community within which s/he lives.

Entrenching a written bill of rights into the constitutional framework of government constitutes a major extension in the reach of the rule of law. Guaranteeing basic human rights and freedoms in a constitution means, more than anything else, that Governments' power to pursue the social agenda they believe is in the best interest of their communities must meet new standards of justice and fairness. Adopting a constitutional bill of rights means that all three branches of government - legislative, executive and judicial - must exercise their powers in accordance with the fundamental precepts and principles which underlie the rule of law. Whereas in Dicey's England, Parliament's authority to "Act" was virtually unfettered, today constitutions all over the world insist Governments and their officials respect the most fundamental rights and freedoms of those they are elected to represent. As a practical matter the recognition of constitutional rights means politicians as well as the bureaucrats have new duties and standards of lawmaking to meet.

For most people, the broad outlines of the story of how different societies have come to embrace constitutional bills of rights are familiar enough. At the end of the second world war, largely at the insistence of the Americans, all of the major defeated powers - Japan, Germany and Italy - as well as countries like India which were escaping imperial rule[2] - incorporated constitutional bills of rights into their new orders of government. At the end of the century, states in eastern Europe, the former Soviet Union and the third world, escaping the legacy of arbitrariness that characterized communist and colonial rule, needed no prodding from outside forces and they sought out, at the moment of their liberation, the protection of written bills of rights on their own.

---

2 Note P.K. Tripathi's article "Perspectives on the American Constitutional Influence on the Constitution of India" in L. Beer (ed) *Constitutionalism in Asia: Asian Views of the American Influence*, School of Law, University of Maryland, 1988.

Nor, I suspect, is it difficult for most people to understand why those who have endured the excesses of colonial, fascistic and /or communist rule would be attracted to the courts and the idea of law to protect those aspects of their lives which they cherish the most. In the public's mind, the rule of law and written bills of rights have long been associated with guaranteeing a measure of legitimacy and fairness in Government. For ordinary people, invoking the authority of the law would be one of the most obvious ways of ensuring the power of the state would not be abused in the way which made colonial, fascistic, and communist Governments so notorious in the past. The expectation would be that it would significantly reduce, even if it could not completely eliminate, the possibility of some group capturing the offices of Government and using them oppressively again.

Law's Detractors: Populists and Sceptics

While the motivation which lies behind the impulse to impose greater constraints on the power of legislators is not difficult to understand, for many people there is something quite odd, if not positively perverse, in the fact that so many countries have turned to law in general and to written bills of rights in particular to fulfill that role. Indeed, for a large number of people who give over their lives to the study of law and government, relying on legal instruments to minimize the risk of history repeating itself seems like a very regrettable and even regressive development.[3] The most basic concern of people who think this way is that whatever protection the rule of law and constitutionalism may provide for human freedom, it comes at too high a cost to the power of people to govern themselves and to the principles of democratic or popular rule. They worry that whatever check a written bill of rights is able to provide against the danger of the

---

[3] See e.g. M. Tushnett *Red White and Blue: A Critical Analysis of Constitutional Law*, 1988, Harvard University Press, Cambridge; M. Mandel *The Charter of Rights and the Legalization of Politics*, 1989, Wall and Thompson, Toronto.

"sovereignty of the people" being abused, it is secured only by augmenting the power of the courts. Enhancing the power of the judges as a way of guarding against the possibility of tyranny and state despotism is not seen as a particularly attractive solution because the judiciary is generally regarded as being the branch of government which is least accountable and responsible to the people.

In a word, the problem with written bills of rights is that they come attached to courts and for many people judicial supervision of the other two, elected branches of government is the antithesis of people governing themselves. Law is pictured as something quite alien and inaccessible to the public at large and as the domain of a very small legal and social elite. It is not something ordinary people can easily understand or do on their own. Handing over the power to define the limits of legitimate Government and popular rule to a very few people trained in law, - and precisely at the moment when a community is able to regain its sovereignty and enjoy the freedom of democratic rule, - seems exactly the wrong kind of move to make.

If the lessons of history are not to be repeated, it would be far better, on this view, to enhance the opportunity of people to participate in the political processes and so increase the accountability of the elected officials rather than reduce our commitment to the principle of democratic rule by strengthening the power of the courts. On the latter course there seems a very real danger that the political, social, bureaucratic elites of the past will be replaced by a new judicial cadre which will dictate the ways in which and the extent to which people can govern themselves. For democrats, the lesson we should learn from our immediate past is to enhance not compromise the democratic character of government. Promote popular sovereignty, guarantee more participation, make the institutions more responsive to and representative of those whose lives they control etc. These are the methods democrats recommend to ensure the abuses of the past will not be repeated again.[4]

As one might expect, this view attracts a good deal of support among populists and political theorists who see themselves as among democracy's staunchest defenders. Typically, it finds favour with politicians across the whole range of the political spectrum. More surprisingly perhaps is the fact that this is a view which is also likely to have considerable support within the legal community itself. Indeed, for anyone who is familiar with the developments in law over the past fifty years, there is something anomalous in the fact that the public has chosen to put its faith in a legal device, such as a constitutional bill of rights, precisely at a time when the very meaning of law seems most unsettled and open to dispute. For many in the legal community, what is so striking about the worldwide popularity for constitutional bills of rights is not just that it has coincided with the emergence of more democratic forms of government, but also that it has surged precisely during periods when, within their own ranks, the very legitimacy of law has been under sustained attack.

For example, the proliferation of written bills of rights at the end of the second world war in Europe and Asia occurred immediately after a period of twenty five years in which some of the most respected legal academics in America, - where the idea of constitutional rights was conceived, - had dedicated their lives to exploding the myth that law is made up of a series of fixed and settled rules which are capable of producing 'correct' answers in every case. In place of the image of judges mechanically searching for and then applying the rule of law that was appropriate to each case, these scholars showed that judges had an enormous amount of discretion in deciding what rule or principle would govern a case and how, in the end, it should be resolved. Known as the Legal Realists, these academic lawyers and judges unmasked the

---

4 P. Russell "A Democratic Approach to Civil Liberties..." 29 UTLJ 109 (1964); M. Walzer, "Philosophy and Democracy" (1981) 9 Political Theory 379.

traditional perception of judges relying on formal, abstract, legal concepts like rights as little more than a transparent attempt to shield the fact that it was their own personal, subjective instincts and moral beliefs which usually determined how the most difficult and controversial cases would turn out.[5] It was the same again in the seventies and eighties when their descendants, known as the Critical Legal Studies movement, invoked slogans like "law is politics" to convey their claim that law really did not have any independent, objective, existence of its own but rather was a tool, or a device, which could be manipulated to suit the personal predilections of practically any judge.

The message from this group of theorists over the last fifty years has remained the same. Their claim is that law does not have fixed and finite parameters. Interpreting and settling on the meaning of the law is a very subjective - highly creative - task. Law is not made up of a specific number of settled, self applying principles or rules. There are no words whose meaning is absolutely settled and free of all ambiguity. In virtually all cases that make it to court there will be a significant element of choice on how a rule or standard should be interpreted and applied. What is a "reasonable rate", or "just cause", or "negligent" behaviour, no law can conclusively decide. In other cases, - often the most difficult and controversial ones, - judges are forced to choose or even change the rule which will settle the outcome of a case. Either because the relevant body of law is inherently uncertain (e.g. two principles overlap) or unavoidably incomplete, (e.g. there is no principle right on point) judges are forced to rely on their own subjective opinions and ideas in deciding which way they will rule. In the words of one critical scholar: "judges decide as they presently do in large part because of their ... political

---

5 Robert Summers *Instrumentalism and American Legal Theory* 1982, Cornell University Press, Ithaca.

assumptions"[6] On this view "with imagination and industry, legal materials can be organized to support and justify incompatible outcomes."[7] To a realist, law is nothing more or less than what each judge says it is - unless of course he or she says it in dissent.

It is this uncertainty and indeterminacy which permeates all areas of law which is so unsettling to the legal sceptics. In the area of constitutional law, it means that in deciding what human rights will be read into a constitution and where the limits of popular government will be drawn, the judges' powers will be much less fettered than they might otherwise be thought to be. On questions as fundamental as whether laws which criminalize abortion or sodomy, prescribe the death penalty, treat women differently than men, limit the right to strike or to advertise, prohibit election contributions and expenditures beyond certain limits, etc are constitutional or not, every judge will be able to read the law or find some principle or precedent which will allow their personal feelings to govern the outcome of the case. For those who think in this way, and believe that judges' personal views will effectively control how much sovereignty people will enjoy, the implications of entrenching a written bill of rights are profoundly disturbing. Rather than reducing the possibility of the powers of the State being abused in the future, they allow the courts, as well as the elected branches of governments, to act arbitrarily.

Law's Acolytes

In addition to the attack mounted by those who have disputed the claim that law has some independent, objective existence of its own, there has also been considerable controversy about the basic nature and character of law even among those who continue to defend in its integrity. These are people who believe in the

---

6 A. Hutchinson, "The Three 'R's: Reading Rorty Radically" 103 Harv. L. Rev. 555,582 (1989).

7 A Hutchinson, "Democracy and Determinacy", (1989) 43 U. of Miami L. Rev. 541, 555

legitimacy of law but who argue very vigorously over what it is that gives law its validity. In the areas of constitutional law these people would be committed to the integrity of written bills of rights but would differ sharply on how they operate and what values they promote.[8]

Even though many, indeed I suspect the majority, of those with training in law fall into this second group, and remain quite committed to the idea that law is made up of principles and rules which can restrain judges and produce just results, the way they have gone about defending their faith has only contributed to the controversy and uncertainty which surrounds the legitimacy of the law. Indeed, so many different arguments and ideas about law have been advanced to resist the charge that law is inherently subjective and indeterminate that it would be natural for anyone not trained in the law to think law's supporters had unwittingly provided further grist for the sceptics' mill. The fact is, the disagreement among those who believe in the legitimacy of the law is just as deep and intense as the debate in which they are engaged with their more sceptical colleagues.

"Believers" are hopelessly divided on virtually all of the most basic issues in law. They can not even agree on what law is or whether and/or how law differs from other social and cultural phenomena like politics or morality. They argue about what role judges and courts should and do play in our system of government. Indeed, there is not even a consensus among those who have faith in the law as to how one can determine when a law is valid and must be obeyed and when it is not and should be ignored.

---

[8] The disagreement is especially sharp in the United States where interpretivists (see e.g. R. Bork *The Tempting of America: the Political Seduction of the Law*, Free Press 1990, N.Y.) argue both with non interpretivists (see e.g. M. Perry, *Politics, Morality and the Law*, 1988 Oxford Press) and among themselves (cf R. Dworkin *Law's Empire* 1989 Harvard University Press and J. Ely *Democracy and Distrust: A Theory of Judicial Review* 1986 Harvard University Press) while positivists and pragmatists stake out independent positions of their own. See e.g. R.A. Posner *The Problems of Jurisprudence* 1990 Harvard University Press.

POSITIVISTS AND PRAGMATISTS

For some, law is essentially a system of rules whose validity lies in their pedigree or source; in how the rules come to exist. Known as "positivists", these people think that it is essential for any theory of law to have tests which determine its existence and identify its content in terms of human behaviour rather than as moral or ethical concepts. Emphasizing the fact that law is something which is made by human beings, positivists argue that conformity with particular social values is neither a necessary nor a sufficient condition of being law. Positivists think that the essence of law consists of rules which have emerged from special, designated procedures - like an Act of Parliament or a judgment of a court, - which are widely recognized as being legitimate and valid sources of law. For them it is more the process by which a rule has been formalized than its substance which determines its standing as law. Some of the most outstanding legal scholars in the United Kingdom and Europe including Jeremy Bentham, John Austin, Hans Kelson, H.L.A. Hart and Joseph Raz have understood law in this way.[9] In addition, the idea that law is essentially the pronouncements of persons and institutions who have been licensed to make law has been embraced by many Americans including Holmes, Pound, Cohen, and Lewellyn who espoused a theory which came to be known as pragmatism and which some would regard as America's most distinctive contribution to legal theory.[10]

In the view of all of these theorists, questions about what law is and what it should be are entirely different and must be kept separate and apart. However, positivists and pragmatists also

---

9 See J. Austin, *Lectures on Jurisprudence of the Philosophy of Positive Law* 1989, J. Murray, London; H. Kelsen, *General Theory of Law and State* 1945, Harvard University Press, Cambridge; H.L.A. Hart *The Concept of Law* 1961, Oxford University Press; J. Raz *The Authority of Law* Oxford University Press, 1979

10 See R. Summers *Instrumentalism and American Legal Theory* supra note 5; R.A. Posner *The Problems of Jurisprudence supra* note 8

believe that there are limits as to how far the law can reach. In difficult cases positivists and pragmatists point out that the law is often silent or unclear. In such cases, they would say the law just runs out. When that happens, these theorists would agree with the sceptics and realists that judges must act on their own. Moreover, although they would concede that in such moments the domains of law and morality may overlap, (and judges would be expected to turn to whatever moral, political, sociological, scientific material they think would assist them), positivists and pragmatists would continue to insist that whatever the moral worth of the judges' choice in such cases, it will have the status of valid law. Just because it is law does not guarantee it will be morally or ethically attractive.

NORMATIVISTS

Notwithstanding its attraction to some of the most respected scholars the law has known, for many others, positivism is seen to be afflicted with a fatal deficiency. In the view of many, positivism is inadequate and incomplete because it can not explain or capture the idealism which is an essential part of what the public generally think is embraced in the idea of the rule of law. The positivist's account of law is seen to be defective precisely because it lacks any normative bite. It is, by its own terms, morally bankrupt. On a positivist's account, even though a law may be very abusive and unjust, it must be recognized as valid nonetheless.

Critics of legal positivism have attempted to redress what they perceive to be its moral vacuity in a variety of ways. Traditionally, theories of natural law posited a set of natural, moral entitlements which every human being is assumed to enjoy and which Governments' rules and regulations would have to respect if they were to enjoy the status of law. Today "rights" theorists probably come closest to this approach although few still attempt to justify these legal entitlements as flowing from the natural or spiritual condition of human rights. More commonly, contemporary exponents of rights theories ground their approach in a particular political philosophy, moral theory, social practice or set of legal decisions. When difficult cases come before a court, normativists say it is sources like these where judges should look for their guidance.

As might be anticipated, the differences in the ways each of these theorists derive the substantive rights which distinguish their understanding of law are enormous. At one extreme there are those of an essentially libertarian frame of mind who come closest to thinking of rights as a natural expression of the human condition.[11] Against this view some argue the substantive normative criteria of law are to be found in the prevailing moral, social, political etc arrangements of the community and not in any pre-legal, natural environment.[12] Others including Ronald Dworkin, one of the leading exponents of a rights based approach, contend that whether a rule or regulation satisfies the criteria of legal validity depends on whether it is consistent with the moral values - the rights - which have been expressed in the legal and political decisions a community has made in the past.[13] Still others argue that the normative element which is characteristic of law is implicit in the nature of legal rules.[14] Rather than being embedded in the idea of rights, on this view the 'inner morality of law' requires rules and regulations to be open, not secret; prospective not retroactive; general and not aimed at one particular person etc

---

11 R. Nozick *Anarchy, State and Utopia*, Basic Books, 1974, New York.

12 F. Michaelman "Laws Republic" 97 Yale L.J. 1493 (1988); D. Richards *Foundations of American Constitutionalism* 1989, Oxford University, N.Y.; M. Perry *Morality, Politics and Law*, *supra* note 8

13 See R. Dworkin *Taking Rights Seriously* 1977 Harvard University Press, *A Matter of Principle* 1985 Harvard University Press, *Law's Empire*, *supra* note 8

14 See Lon L. Fuller *The Principles of Social Order*, 1981, Duke University Press, "Positivism and Fidelity to Law - A Reply to Professor Hart" (1958) 77 Harvard L. Rev. 630

- or it just is not law. In the result, not only do those who assume that the ultimate test of what constitutes law lies in some moral or ethical standard disagree with the analytical, procedural approach the positivists recommend, they can not even agree among themselves which values distinguish law from other social and cultural phenomena.

FORMALISTS

In addition to the classic dispute between those who think about law in empirical and moral terms, there is still another group of theorists who believe that the positivists and the normativists are both wrong. Known as the "formalists",[15] they think positivists make the mistake of focusing all their attention on the formal or procedural characteristics of law and of ignoring its substantive, moral dimension. Conversely, they say that while normativists recognise that law has a special ethical character, they fail to pay enough attention to the fact that law does have a distinctive form as well. Formalists criticize normativists for failing to keep law and politics apart.

For formalists, it is imperative that law be defined in its own terms rather than in terms of something (moral values, social practices etc) outside of itself. Otherwise, they say, law would have no autonomy, no independent identity of its own. It would always be parasitic and could be reduced to something else. For formalists the morality of law is something internal to itself. It is a concept or an idea which relates the content of any law to the form in which it is expressed and which exists completely independent of the political world. Formalists say that for a substantive rule or principle to qualify as a valid expression of law it must be cast in a form which is appropriate to the relationship it governs. Where normativists talk about the 'inner morality' of law, formalists believe judges should always seek to clarify and enforce the 'inner logic' of law.

---

[15] Ernie Weinrib, "Legal Formalism: On the Immanent Rationality of Law" (1988) 97 Yale L.J. 949

All of this is pretty abstract and it will be necessary to elaborate on each of these different approaches or understandings about what law is. Enough however has been said to convey the sense of fluidity and controversy which surrounds the idea of law at least among those who worry most about its legitimacy. Even from this brief description of the rival theories that are currently in vogue, it is apparent that the controversy about the integrity of law is much wider and more profound than simply a dispute between those who are sceptical about and those who are believers in law. Even among those in the legal community who are most likely to be committed to the values of constitutionalism and the rule of law, there are fundamental differences about what law is and what it can legitimately and effectively do. Indeed as we have seen, even among those who employ a common, normative definition of law, there can be sharp disagreement on the most basic questions about the proper conception or approach to law. The fact is that within the legal community itself there is nothing close to a single understanding about what the rule of law really implies. Even those theorists most committed to the integrity of law have radically different ideas about what method of reasoning or analysis the judges should employ when they are deciding whether some law regulating abortion, elections, strikes, advertising etc is constitutional or not.

The Paradox: How to Reconcile Law and Politics

It is the persistent failure of those most expert in the law to come to a common understanding about what law is that makes the public's continued endorsement of written bills of rights and the rule of law so perplexing. For those in the legal community, if there is no consensus on the most basic issues concerning the meaning and legitimacy of law, the thought that written bills of rights might provide an objective and meaningful check on the possibility of state power being used arbitrarily seems inexcusably naive. In the face of so many profoundly different conceptions about the nature of law, it seems unavoidable that judges will enjoy a considerable amount of personal discretion in how they decide many of the most difficult and controversial cases they will hear. When the very idea of law and legal analysis is so open and contested it seems to be a serious act of self deception to think that, in close or difficult cases, like those in which the validity of laws about abortion, pornography, capital punishment etc. are at stake, it will be the law rather than a judge's personal views or legal philosophy which will determine the outcome. Each legal theory supports a different understanding about the rule of law and the way the courts and judges should analyze the cases they are asked to hear. Giving judges the power to decide the ultimate shape and substance a community will have, (and especially at those moments when the people are able to reclaim their sovereignty and enjoy the authority of democratic rule), seems quite incongruous if not down right self-defeating.

How then can we explain why so many different groups of people, at the moment of their liberation choose to authorize a very exclusive and privileged legal elite to provide answers to the most controversial and complicated questions of our times (such as abortion or capital punishment or affirmative action) instead of settling them by themselves? Why is it that, at the moment when societies are finally able to enjoy the freedom of democratic rule, the public and their elected representatives insist on putting their faith in a legal instrument, like a written bill of rights, even though those who are most expert in law are warning that this may increase the possibility of arbitrary rule by an unrepresentative and an unaccountable legal elite?[16]

Broadly speaking only two explanations are possible. Either the public is simply unaware of how the law really works, or the controversy that exists in the legal community is somehow mistaken and misconceived. The people and the professionals can't both be right.

---

[16] Perhaps the most notorious period of judicial obstruction was the so called "Lochner era" when the U.S. Supreme Court struck down numerous pieces of progressive social policy. For a discussion of those decisions see L. Tribe *American Constitutional Law*, Foundation Press, 1989, Mineola, N.Y.

Instinctively, I suspect, many will be inclined to pursue the first possibility and to hold up the public's perception about the integrity of law to a closer and more critical scrutiny. One might, for example, tell an unflattering story of simple ignorance. Alternatively, one could recount a more menacing tale of covert manipulation. On the more benign explanation the people and the politicians would simply be ill informed about how objective the law really is. On the more sinister version, one would argue that the public generally has very little choice in the adoption of a constitutional bill of rights, and that historically they have been imposed externally by a foreign authority or from above by a political and/or economic elite.

Although these are stories which those who are most radically sceptical about the legitimacy of all political structures might want to tell, they are not the sort which will be developed here. Such explanations require a knowledge of the public's mind that seems difficult to substantiate empirically, and they entail a very unflattering assessment of the ability of ordinary people to resist institutions which will effectively disempower and subordinate them. In this volume we shall explore the other possibility and inquire whether the faith the public continues to place in written bills of rights to organize the powers of the state can be reconciled with how those with the most intimate knowledge of law understand constitutional and international guarantees of basic human rights.

The Solution: A Principled Approach to Judicial Review

In general terms I want to suggest that the way to make most sense of the apparent contradiction between the professional and public belief in the rule of law is to re-examine what the legal community thinks the constitutional protection of basic human rights really entails. The idea is that when written bills of rights are understood in a slightly different way from how they are conventionally described, there really is no incongruity in the public putting its faith in constitutionalism and judicial review even as those most knowledgable about law continue to dispute its meaning and legitimacy. The paradox, it turns out, is more apparent than real.

The ambition of this essay is to show that if, instead of thinking of bills of rights as guaranteeing individuals will be able to act in certain ways and have specific interests recognized by the state, we see them as entrenching basic principles of rationality and proportionality – of necessity and consistency – into the framework of government, the differences among legal theorists which have threatened the objectivity and determinacy of law will for the most part disappear. Reconceiving constitutional bills of rights in terms of a set of duties or rules lawmakers are required to meet should allow legal theorists to see that the rule of law is capable of providing an objective measure of protection for human freedom and enhancing the quality of justice in the communities which embrace them and that it can do so in a way which is sensitive not only to the concerns of sceptics and critics for the democratic character of our systems of government, but also to the different understandings of those who continue to believe in the integrity of law. In this essay I want to suggest that regardless of what format or text drafters may have employed, all conventional written bills of rights have within them a set of precepts and principles which are quite congenial to all of the major ways law has come to be understood and to our tradition of democratic rule. However intractable the basic philosophical differences which divide legal theorists turn out to be, in the area of constitutional law, the uncertainty and division is not as pervasive as the paradox seems to suggest.

Traditionally written bills of rights have been understood as catalogues of very important interests and activities over which individuals rather than the state has been given final control. Both within and outside the legal community the conventional thinking has been that constitutional guarantees of freedom of conscience, expression, association, of equality, and of life, liberty and security of the person etc. create islands of sovereignty for the individual. Rights and other constitutional guarantees are seen as fencing off very discrete interests and activities over which the individual has absolute sovereignty to do and think as he or she pleases. Within these spheres of interest, individuals are entitled to insist that everyone else in the community must "mind their own business" and respect each person's right to control their own lives as much as they possibly can. On these matters, it is thought, the State has little or no authority to interfere.

On this traditional understanding of what written bills of rights are all about, courts are cast in the role of readers of constitutional texts. Their primary job is to specify exactly what entitlements a constitution guarantees. According to the conventional wisdom (which only adds to the critic's and sceptic's doubts)[17] the courts' primary responsibility is to interpret the constitution in order to identify the precise boundaries that define and separate the legitimate interests and activities of the individual and the State. In performing the function of constitutional review, the expectation is that a court's basic job is an interpretive one and its main focus is on the constitutional document itself.

This characterization of bills of rights, as protecting a series of very particular and specific claims which individuals can make against the state, is not wrong so much as it is incomplete. It only tells part of the story of what bills of rights contain and the way courts decide whether a law or some action by a state official is constitutional or not. It obscures the fact that in law rights give rise and are attached to duties[18] and for the courts it is these duties and obligations which lawmakers owe to those who claim their rights have been ignored which are really critical to the outcome of a case.

Broadly speaking, in every case in which the constitutionality of a law or the act of some state official is put in issue the

---

17 On the indeterminacy of interpretation, see S. Levinson and S. Mailloux (eds) *Interpreting Law and Literature*, Northwestern University Press, Evanston Ill. 1988; Stanley Fish, *Is There a Text in This Class*, Harvard Press 1980

18 See Richard Flathman *The Practice of Rights*, Cambridge University Press 1976

reasoning process followed by the court is essentially the same. There are two stages or phases in the analysis. Initially the judges focus their attention on the constitution (or international instrument) in which the human rights are entrenched. Here the role of the judges is to act as a reader or an interpreter in order to identify which interests and activities fall within the rights and freedoms which are recognized in the text and what limits must be respected by those who have been entrusted with the powers of the state. In the second stage of the process, after the constitutional boundaries are fixed, the court's attention shifts to the law or bureaucratic ruling that it has been asked to review. Here the court looks at the most important features of the challenged law in order to see whether it conforms to the limits and restrictions which the constitutions contain. They make sure that the politicians and their officials have lived up to the duties and allegation which are inherent in the concept of rights.

As a practical matter, the process of review is even simpler than that. In reality, the second stage of the review process is much more important than the first. Over time the meaning of the large and sweeping phrases which distinguish all constitutional texts and international proclamations of human rights get settled. The rules of constitutional law get worked out. Each judicial decision, each precedent provides more detail about what the constitution means and for the most part courts everywhere have been inclined to interpret the basic rights and freedoms in a very expansive and all encompassing way. In the vast majority of cases, individual claimants have little difficulty establishing that one of the rights and freedoms which the constitution (or convention) guarantees covers the interest or activity which is being restricted by the law whose validity they attack.

As time goes by, in most cases, the focus of the courts is centred less and less on the constitution and more and more on the law whose constitutionality they have been asked to review. The principles and boundaries of review that are embedded in the constitution are taken as a given and the only issue is how they should be applied in a particular case. Practically all of the action takes place in the second stage of the review process. Constitutional law becomes like many other areas or bodies of law in which the role of the court is to apply broad principles like unconscionability or negligence to the facts of each case. Like cases in contract and tort, in most disputes about the constitutionality of a law there is not much disagreement about what the governing principles are, only a question about how they should be applied to the facts of a particular case. Principles of rationality (necessity) and proportionality (consistency), not a catalogue of interests and activities, it turns out, are what constitutional bills of rights are mostly about.

Essentially, there are two basic principles which are common to all constitutions which guarantee basic human rights and which collectively prohibit Governments from enacting into law policies which restrict people's freedom either (i) gratuitously (whether carelessly or intentionally) or (ii) more deeply and pervasively than how Governments have treated others with similar interests elsewhere and in the past. Rather than differentiating a set of discrete interests and activities as being beyond the bounds of governmental regulation, on this understanding of constitutional bills of rights, the elected branches of government are pretty much free to pursue whatever social agenda they care to draw up so long as they do so in ways which respect these two principles of equality or distributive justice.

Both principles insist on a measure of proportionality - of moderation - in the policies Governments want to enact into law, although the focus of each is quite different. One principle concentrates on the ends or objectives a Government wants to pursue and insists that the balance that is struck between the social well-being the law promotes and the freedom of those it adversely affects is reasonable or fair. The principle guarantees a basic equality in how individuals are treated by their Governments over time and across different communities by requiring the latter to establish that the social benefits they point to, to justify a law to those whose liberty is adversely affected by it, are similar in weight and significance to the kinds of interests which have supported similar constraints of other people's freedom in the past. One could call this a principle of "reasonableness"[19] or "fairness" or "consistency".

The other principle focuses on the means Governments use to pursue their objectives and it guarantees Governments will respect a basic equality in the interest and capacity of all people to organize their own lives in a different way. It insists Governments respect a basic equality in the freedom of every individual to control their own destiny by not acting irrationally or arbitrarily, viz for irrelevant or malicious reasons. Functionally, it prohibits law makers from drafting laws which are either over or under inclusive. It ensures that Governments cannot pass laws which limit peoples' freedom more than is necessary to accomplish their objectives. They cannot pass laws which are overly broad or especially heavy handed. Nor can they limit the benefits of a legislative scheme to a particular group of individuals unless there is some good reason to do so. Laws of both kinds fail a basic measure of proportionality in the means they employ and in so doing deny those they affect (or leave out) the equality which is implicit in the concept of constitutional rights. Every restriction Governments impose on the freedom of those whose lives they control must be relevant to - in the sense of furthering - the social objectives which have motivated them "to act".

On this understanding of what constitutional bills of rights are really about, the purposes to which the powers of the state can be put are virtually unlimited. Effectively, there are only two constraints on the kind of objectives laws can validly pursue. On the one hand the principle of rationality or necessity implicitly rules unconstitutional any law motivated by an ambition to limit an individual's or group's freedom to act for no other reason than to restrict their freedom. On the other hand, the ends oriented principle of proportionality or consistency rules out of order laws promoting interests which, when they are compared to the grounds

---

[19] See e.g. G. Marshall, "Notes on the Rule of Equal Law" in R. Pennock and Chapman (eds) *Equality* 1967, Atherton Press, New York (Nomos 9)

on which other people's freedom has been limited in the past, can be said to be relatively unimportant. Contrary to the traditional view, constitutional bills of rights do not remove whole areas of individual activity from social control. Even in the United States where the constitution says Congress can make no law which abridges people's freedom of religion and expression, neither of these interests is completely immune from social regulation. So long as the means that are chosen are necessary to the ends being pursued, and the constraint that is imposed is roughly proportional to those that have been pursued elsewhere and in the past, the sovereignty of the people to act as they please remains virtually unlimited.

When constitutional bills of rights are understood in this way, the role of the courts will come to be seen in a quite different light. Rather than being primarily an interpreter of a constitutional text, the judicial function becomes one of evaluating the particular policy chosen by the lawmakers to accomplish their objectives and asking whether it could have been formulated in a more sensitive, less discriminatory way. The focus of the court is centred on the particular law that it has been asked to review rather than the constitution itself. Issues of justification not interpretation are what judges struggle to resolve. Insisting that Governments meet basic standards of relevance and consistency, of rationality and reasonableness, in the policies they intend to infuse with the authority of law is what constitutional review is all about.

For many who have been schooled in the traditional understanding of what constitutional bills of rights are all about, there is likely going to be an instinctive reluctance to talk about constitutional entitlements in these terms. Thinking about rights as duties flies in the face of the common understanding that rights are very special and distinctive interests and activities which warrant extra protection in law. It seems to ignore or at least pay scant attention to the long list of rights and freedoms which account for the largest part of any constitutional text. Notwithstanding all of the energy expended in designing and drafting constitutions all over the world, it seems to suggest that the way in which such basic freedoms like religion, expression, association etc., or rights to life, liberty and equality are described is really quite unimportant.

It is in recognition of the fact that old habits die hard that the rest of this book is organized. The chapters that follow describe the way Courts around the world go about protecting people's rights and they are meant to illustrate how important and pervasive these principles have become in the jurisprudence that surrounds all of the most important constitutional and international bills of rights. In this introductory essay my purpose is simply to suggest (to those in the legal community as well as to the public at large) that, even in conceptual terms, rethinking rights as duties which lawmakers must respect rather than specific entitlements which individuals can claim is not nearly as radical as it might first appear.

As far as the public is concerned, thinking about constitutional bills of rights in this way will not in any way compromise its belief in the capacity of the "rule of law" to limit the possibility of Governments using their powers in arbitrary and abusive ways. In fact, it should have precisely the opposite effect. On the traditional approach, the civilizing effect of bills of rights is limited to laws which impinge on those special interests and activities which are identified as falling within the domain of one or other of the rights and freedoms which a constitution may guarantee. If a law unfairly burdens an individual or a group in the pursuit of an interest or activity which falls outside the constitutional text, on the conventional understanding of what bills of rights are all about, a Government would be free to legislate as it saw fit. The Constitution would be understood to have no effect.

By contrast, thinking about constitutional review in terms of courts evaluating the justifications Governments give for the laws they adopt would make bills of rights and the powers of the Courts co-extensive with the mandate of Governments and legislative assemblies.[20] Whatever the substance of a Government's law, the expectation would be that it would be subject to judicial review. Any law that burdened or withheld a benefit from an individual or group must meet the standards of justice which the principles of rationality and proportionality imply. On this view, the protection which a constitutional bill of rights can provide against the temptation to abuse the powers of the state is as comprehensive and inclusive as it can possibly be. Understood as guaranteeing all Government activity will conform to these two basic principles of justice and equality, bills of rights give the fullest possible expression to the ethical ideal implicit in the popular preference for Governments to be subordinate to law and not men.

Thinking about bills of rights as introducing broad, egalitarian principles of justice into the framework of government not only enhances the ideal with which ordinary people usually associate the rule of law more than the traditional approach, it is also one which, on reflection, should be congenial to virtually all legal scholars no matter which particular theory they may espouse. However intractable their larger philosophical differences may be, everyone in the legal community should see in this definition of what constitutional rights are really all about a good deal of common ground. Not only does the idea that all bills of rights can be reduced to a set of principles which evaluate the methods and means of social policies against their ends or goals conform to what the major theorists think that law really is, it also captures what most of them say law can and does do best.

Positivism and Judicial Review

To see how this is so we must consider how each of the major theories of law would respond to the idea that bills of rights constrain the power of the state by broad principles of equality - of rationality (necessity) and proportionality (consistency) - and

---

20 M. Walzer "Philosophy and Democracy" *supra* note, 4 p. 391 also recognizes that thinking about human rights in this way involves "a deeper penetration" into the legislative domain.

how it would fit with their general understanding of what law really is all about. For positivists and others (e.g. pragmatists) who think about law in empirical terms, reconceiving bills of rights in this way should not be a particularly jarring thing to do. Both theoretically and practically, thinking of bills of rights as insisting that Governments must act in accordance with broad principles of justice conforms very closely with the way these theorists understand what distinguishes valid from invalid law.

We have already noticed that one of the distinguishing characteristics of positivism (and pragmatism) is that when theorists of these schools reflect on the meaning of law, they insist on a clear separation between law and morality. For positivists and pragmatists what law is, and what it should be, are two radically different things. For them, a clear lesson of history is that laws are no less laws just because they may be egregiously unfair.

In addition to drawing a sharp boundary between the domains of law and morality, those who embrace a positivist conception of law also think it is important to distinguish law from the crude use of force. Positivists believe the coercive power of the legislator is not the same as that of the robber whose only authority flows from the barrel of a gun. For positivists, the legitimacy of the coercive power inherent in law lies in the fact that it issues from institutions and people who are licensed to exercise the authority of the State. Acts of Parliament and rulings by judges have a legitimacy, which orders of a gunman lack, precisely because they have been carried out in ways which are recognized by everyone in the society as infusing otherwise coercive behaviour with the force (and legitimacy) of law.

Thinking about law in this way has meant for most positivists that in all but the simplest legal regimes it is necessary to distinguish between two kinds of law. On the one hand there are primary directives, like the orders of a gunman, which impose obligations directly on the individual. Thou shalt not: kill other humans, foetuses, even animals etc.; or behave 'indecently'; or try to 'buy' votes; would be laws of this kind. On the other hand, there are secondary rules like the procedures of Parliament, or the conventional modes of judicial reasoning, which contain the criteria and standards which determine whether a primary order will be recognized as valid law. Labelled by some theorists as "rules of recognition"[21] it is these secondary rules which for many positivists constitute the supreme or ultimate principles of any mature legal regime. For the positivist, it is the union of primary and secondary rules which constitutes the essence of law.

Within this general account of what law is and how it comes into being, it is easy to see how bills of rights, understood as a set of principles which will ensure Governments do not act arbitrarily or unfairly, would fit. Imposing duties, and instructing lawmakers on how they must exercise the powers they possess, these principles of justice would be regarded as paradigmatic "rules of recognition". By their terms, policies which were proposed to be enacted into law would have to satisfy two basic measures of rationality and proportionality between the objectives they pursue and the methods they employ. Policies which imposed heavier burdens on more members of the public than was necessary to accomplish their objectives, or than had been imposed in the past, or which arbitrarily denied advantages to individuals who would otherwise benefit from their receipt, could not satisfy those basic measures of justice and equality and so would not be recognized as instruments of valid law.

Not only do the rationality and proportionality principles conform to the positivists' idea of secondary rules or basic norms, they themselves have a pedigree and are the product of a legal (judicial) process which should guarantee their legitimacy even for the most demanding theorists of a positivist persuasion. Although some adherents of positivism[22] take the position that it is a mistake to question the validity of the basic norms or rules of recognition in any legal system, - that they simply exist and are accepted as criteria of legitimacy, - in the case of the principles of

---

21 H.L.A. Hart *The Concept of Law*, *supra* note 9 pp. 97 and ff

22 H.L.A. Hart, *The Concept of Law*, *supra* note 9, p.105

rationality and proportionality it is possible to ground their validity even more securely by examining the process through which they have come into being.

As we shall see in the essays that follow, when one compares how the courts with the most extensive experience in the practice of judicial review have enforced bills of rights it is striking how central the principles of rationality and reasonableness are to their analysis and reasoning process. As the product of the judicial process, operating in ways which courts are expected to work, these two principles can be grounded in the positivists' account of law empirically as well as theoretically. Not only do they fit naturally within the positivists' two-tiered structure of legal regimes, they also can trace their own legitimacy to a valid source of law. Although these principles are applied in different ways and to different degrees by judges around the world, the fact remains that they lie at the core of the jurisprudence that has been authored by the highest national and international courts.

It is easiest to see the central role that the principles of rationality and proportionality have played in the enforcement of written bills of rights in the jurisprudence that has been developed by the Constitutional Courts in Germany and Italy, the Supreme Courts of India, Japan and Canada and by the European Court of Human Rights. Usually referred to as principles of reasonableness or proportionality by all of these courts, the principles are, in the vast majority of cases, determinative of whether a challenge to the validity of a primary law will end in success or defeat. In these courts the judges acknowledge quite openly and quite consistently that one or other of these principles of justice and equality settles the outcome of the case.

In the United States the centrality of these principles is not so open and explicit. Here, as we shall see in chapter 2, constitutional discourse is still carried on in much more traditional terms. On its face, most of American constitutional law is cast in the traditional, interpretive, rights based mode. The focus is on identifying specific entitlements from the language of the constitutional text. Even in the United States, however, there are a set of rules which provide for different levels or degrees of review by the Court, which are crucial to whether the American Supreme Court will find a law or other Government activity constitutional or not. On close examination, one can see that the standards or "levels" of review that have been fashioned by the American Supreme Court are simply the principles of rationality and proportionality by other names. They measure exactly the same relation between the ends and means of a challenged law as the rationality and proportionality principles do. Levels of scrutiny are just one way (and an inherently restrictive way it turns out) for these principles of necessity and consistency to be applied.

For positivists, however, to qualify as a valid source of law it is not enough that a rule or order emanate from a source, like a court, which everyone recognizes as an institution which has been entrusted with certain powers of the State. Positivists also insist that their coercive authority be exercised in a manner which conforms with the general expectations of how such institutions should do their work. Thus, in the absence of some extraordinary circumstance, positivists generally would not be inclined to characterize as valid, a law which a Government had adopted secretly, or passed through only one reading of one chamber of a bicameral legislature, or that went through the required number of readings in both houses but only after the life of the legislature had come to an end.

As we have already noticed, the general expectation about the proper approach courts should take in cases in which someone's constitutional rights are at stake is that it is, broadly speaking, interpretative in nature. On the conventional understanding of how courts decide whether a law is constitutional or not, each judge is expected to justify his or her decision on a reading of the constitutional (or international) text. Although it is widely recognized that interpretation has a creative and discretionary component to it, especially with texts like constitutional bills of rights, which have been drafted with very large and open words (and several generations in the past), still the expectation is the words of the document and the context in which they are enveloped will exercise some constraining influence over how the judicial power will be exercised.[23]

Within this broad consensus of what the power of judicial review is all about, there are, not surprisingly, often a diversity of conflicting views as to how the interpretative task should be performed. Some think that the words of any legal document, including a constitutional bill of rights, should be given their plain or literal meaning. One of America's most distinguished judges - Oliver Wendell Holmes - was an exponent of one version of this approach.[24] Others, such as Robert Bork, the American legal scholar and jurist whose nomination to the Supreme Court was turned back by the Senate, argue in favour of construing a bill of rights according to the intention of those who originally wrote it.[25] Still others say one should give a text the meaning which will best serve the overall purposes that constitutional bills of rights are meant to accomplish.[26]

Although all of these interpretative methods can be applied and developed in ways which call their legitimacy into question, it is also recognized that in the appropriate circumstances each of them provides legitimate ways for judges to ascribe meaning to the provisions of a constitutional text. In some circumstances each of these methods will be able to illuminate how a constitutional guarantee should be defined.

Within this pluralistic framework of how a constitutional document like a bill of rights may be approached, positivists should have no difficulty endorsing the validity of the proportionality principles as straightforward derivations of a

---

23 See Stanley Fish, *Is There a Text in This Class*, *supra* note 17

24 Holmes, "The Theory of Legal Interpretation", 12 Harv. L. Rev 417 (1899)

25 R. Bork, *The Tempting of America*, *supra* note 8

26 R. Dworkin, *Law's Empire*, *supra* note 8 p. 77; see R. Posner, *The Problems of Jurisprudence*, *supra* note 8

purposeful method of interpretation. The jurisprudence of the German Constitutional Court, the Canadian Supreme Court and the European Court of Human Rights provide especially clear illustrations of how a logical or deductive approach to reading a constitution works. All of these courts have ruled that principles of rationality and proportionality are implicit in the constitutional framework of any society which claims to be "democratic and free" and which professes respect for the "inherent dignity" of its people. As we have seen, the principles of rationality and consistency guarantee a measure of equal autonomy for every person by insisting that no one's freedom can be restricted gratuitously or in a way which differs sharply from how others have been treated elsewhere and/or in the past.

The designation of some basic guarantee of equal autonomy or personal self government, as the overarching and overriding objective that bills of rights have traditionally advanced, can also be defended as the product of reading the individual entitlements traditionally specified in modern constitutional texts in a holistic and purposive way. As one reads through of all the major national and international human rights documents, one can see that two different techniques are conventionally employed by their drafters to realize this overriding constitutional objective. First, a certain degree of physical and intellectual independence, which is taken to be a precondition for an individual to be autonomous and in control of his or her own development, is guaranteed. A space is recognized in each person's life free from the intrusions of others, in which the individual may determine the most basic aspects of his or her separate existence. Thus, in their guarantee of the integrity of our physical persons against unreasonable search and seizure, arbitrary arrest and detention, cruel and unusual treatment and the associated legal rights to counsel, and against self-incrimination, etc. we see bills of rights protecting the aspects of human freedom which have the deepest roots in our legal system. Simultaneously, guaranteeing the fundamental freedoms of conscience and religion, of thought, belief, opinion, and expression, of assembly and of association, protects the corresponding intellectual independence which is equally essential and a precondition of individual autonomy and self-control. Together these rights, to our physical and spiritual independence, mark off an area of privacy and personal responsibility in which each of us is entitled to be equally (but not absolutely) free from the interference of others.

The commitment in constitutional bills of rights to the political ideal of equality of liberty is not, however, a concept which is exclusively negative or anti-social in character. It has a positive, social dimension to it as well. In addition to requiring legislators to respect a "private" sphere within which people may govern and choose for themselves, free from the interference of others, traditionally bills of rights extend their commitment to equality to the public arena as well. Thus democratic rights (to vote, stand for election etc) and equality rights together guarantee that each person has a right to participate as an equal in, and be treated as an equal by, the political processes when the community collectively settles the rules which will govern its affairs. Where conditions of conflict and scarcity prevail, where our ambitions as individuals collide and must therefore be reconciled by rules jointly and publicly determined, guaranteeing our democratic rights and equality rights ensures that each person can participate to some minimum (and therefore equal) degree in the formulation of those rules and will benefit from and be protected by their equal application. It guarantees the integrity of the democratic process itself.

In short, some conception of equal liberty, guaranteed in the collective expression of the rights and freedoms, can be characterized as a kind of universal, first principle of justice which inheres in the concept of rights. "Ordered liberty," as it is sometimes described, is in a sense the most basic rule of political life in countries which have chosen to incorporate a bill of rights into the constitutional framework of their governments. With respect to those conditions which are recognized as essential to being able to choose a lifestyle for oneself, each individual is guaranteed equal protection against all forms of legal coercion.

And, in the processes and institutions which settle the rules of social cooperation to which everyone's life plans must conform, the principle insists on a further dimension of the equality that derives from membership in a common community. Together the political, civil, legal, and equality rights traditionally entrenched in bills of rights commit legislatures to, and constrain them by, what Ronald Dworkin has called a "general requirement of justice."

So, on reflection, it is unlikely that positivists should have much difficulty thinking about constitutional bills of rights in terms of broad principles of equality and justice rather than as claims for protection for a series of very discrete and particular interests and activities. Principles of this kind fit naturally into the two-tiered structure by which positivists analyze the law and they can, if required, be grounded in a source which positivists would accept as having the authority to identify such principles as valid expressions of law. As the product of a straightforward deductive analysis of what constitutional and international bills of rights traditionally contain, the principles of rationality and proportionality should meet the positivists' ultimate test for what constitutes valid law.

Formalism and Judicial Review

As well as fitting comfortably within the positivists' conception of the rule of law, thinking about constitutional bills of rights in terms of principles of justice and equality also squares with the very conceptual framework that formalists use to distinguish law from other instruments of social control. Formalism is perhaps the most abstract definition of law among the major theories that contest its meaning. For formalists, law is an idea and understanding it is an act of cognition rather than an empirical fact, like a pronouncement by a judge who is licensed to issue orders of this kind, as positivists believe. Formalists think of law as a particular way of reasoning about how interpersonal relations should be organized.

Although the formalists' approach to law is not as popular among legal scholars today as it has been in the past, it has pedigree going back to ancient Greece, and there are respected legal scholars who still insist that formalism provides the only coherent and intelligible understanding of law that we have. In their eyes, formalism is the only theory which preserves both a moral value and an independent identity for the concept of law. Formalists claim that only they have defined law in a way which distinguishes it from political rule.

As we noted earlier, formalists find all other theories of law to be wanting either because they define law in "extra legal" terms or in terms which make no reference to substantive moral values, like justice, with which most lay people associate the law. Formalists criticize positivists, as we saw, on both grounds. They say positivists define law in terms that are purely instrumental and have no moral integrity. Law is given no independent existence of its own. The essence of law is seen to be a political act or procedure which transforms something (a rule or policy) which is not law into something that is.

The approach formalists employ to understanding anything - whether a physical object or an abstract concept - is to focus on the relationship that exists between the form and content of whatever is being examined. Formalists say things like "form is content" or "a thing's content reveals its form." Form and content are said to be correlative, congruent, interpenetrating. Again, this is true whether what is being examined is a physical object, such as a table, or a more abstract idea like the law. In either case, form and content are inextricably bound. A table is a table precisely because all of its essential formal characteristics, - its elevation, flatness, hardness, etc. - mark it off as a table and not something else.

The same is true for law where formalists believe its essential meaning, (its intelligibility), lies in recognizing how its content relates to its form. In contrast with other theorists who concentrate their attention exclusively on either the content (like the normativists) or on the form (like the positivists) of the law, formalists believe that it is the relationship between the two which defines and illuminates what law really is. For formalists, it is essential that the content of law (its substantive principles, rules etc.) must conform (be suitable) to its appropriate form.

Formalists believe that all law can, indeed must, be cast in one of two forms. Following Aristotle, they label these forms corrective justice and distributive justice. The two forms of justice are said to reflect different aspects of equality and to operate in different domains. Corrective justice is the form of law that is appropriate for those rules and principles which are used to regulate the interpersonal relations between people which are immediate and direct. The central feature of these relationships is that one person has done something to harm another. Corrective justice is the form appropriate to relationships characterized by the wrongful doing and suffering of harm. Distributive justice, by contrast, is the form of law that constrains the rules, statutes, regulations etc. which govern the relations of individuals which are impersonal and indirect. Here, the relation between the parties is not defined by one person doing something to another, but rather by a common benefit or burden which they share or endure.

The difference between the two forms of justice corresponds to the two different ways humans interact. Each form of justice expresses a different measure or standard of equality which is appropriate to the two modes of human relations. Corrective justice focuses on the direct, unmediated interaction between two individuals and endeavours to restore the equality that existed before their lives intersected. The rules of contract and tort, which govern consensual and non consensual interaction between people, are classic examples of laws which fit this form. In the eyes of the formalist, the principles of contract and tort - indeed of all 'private' law - should conform to the corrective form. For them, an award of damages in contract or tort simultaneously quantifies the wrong suffered by the victim and the wrongfulness inflicted by the perpetrator. By ordering the wrongdoer to compensate the innocent party (roughly) in the amount of the latter's loss, the law restores the initial equality that existed between them before their paths crossed.

Distributive justice focuses on the relations of people who are related, not as doer and sufferer, but rather as persons who are subject to a common benefit or burden. Minimum wage laws and no fault compensation schemes, which group together people who share some common characteristic, are paradigmatic examples of laws which fit this form. Here the law's task is not to restore the equality that existed between people before they met, but rather to ensure that everyone who shares the characteristic or meets the criteria that such laws contain are treated equally. The concern of distributive justice is to ensure that there is an appropriate "tightness of fit" between the persons, the things and the criteria of distribution that are characteristic of laws of this kind. Distributive justice enforces a geometric rather than (as in the case of corrective justice) an arithmetic measure of equality between people by insisting that whatever criterion of distribution is chosen by the lawmaker is made to apply equally to all who fall under its justifactory force, without underinclusion or overinclusion. On this standard of justice, everyone who falls within the purpose of a legislative regime, like minimum wages or accident compensation, is entitled to claim an equal standing in the distribution.

Described in this way, the proportionality principles should fit easily within a formalist's understanding of law. For a formalist, the principles of rationality and proportionality are the most generalized, inclusive account of juridical relationships which are based on "human rights". By providing the widest possible form for the concept of rights, they offer the most basic explanation of these kinds of legal relations. Just as these principles can be viewed by positivists as paradigmatic rules of recognition, formalists can see them as rules designed to guarantee the distributive justice of the positive law which connects people impersonally and indirectly. Both principles, - of necessity and consistency, - reflect standard measures or forms of distributive justice. They are, by their terms, about distributions or proportions. They require that the content - the substance - of laws meet our most basic conceptions of what we think is distributively fair. Each insists on a basic coherence in how laws relate the benefits or burdens that they are distributing to people according to the criteria that they contain. Together they give effect to the central idea of distributive justice by securing a measure of equal autonomy for everyone. They insist Governments' distribution of benefits and burdens must respect a basic equality in the interest and capacity of all people to control as much of their own lives as they possibly can.

As we have seen, the first principle of rationality or necessity guarantees that no one's freedom will be limited gratuitously. By invalidating enactments which are arbitrarily under or over inclusive, it ensures that when some one is not relevant to a Government's projects he or she will be left alone. Some political philosophers have referred to variants of this distributive criterion as the 'maximization' principle.[27] By ruling constraints on peoples' freedom, which are not necessary for a Government to realize its purposes, as unconstitutional, it maximizes the amount of freedom and personal autonomy a community will enjoy. Put positively, it ensures that the burdens or benefits contained in any law will be distributed equally to all who fall within its purposes or objects.

The distributive fairness that is promoted by the second principle of proportionality or consistency relates to how Governments have treated people in similar circumstances in other societies and over the course of time. It insists Governments respect the autonomy of people roughly to the same degree that they and neighbouring societies have treated others with similar interest. It rules invalid laws which restrict people's freedom more than the policies adopted by other Governments which have regulated similar interests in the past. Like the first principle, it

---

27 G. Vlastos, "Social Justice", in R.B. Brandt *Social Justice*, Prentice Hall, Englewood Cliffs; J. Rawls, *A Theory of Justice*, 1971 Harvard University Press

guarantees a basic measure of equality in the extent to which everyone in a society is entitled to be free.

In addition, in their application, the principles of rationality and proportionality give effect to a distinction formalists draw between the purposes or criteria of a distribution on the one hand, and the things being distributed and the persons to whom they are allocated on the other. On the formalists' account, the purpose of the distribution is "not immediate to the relationship of person to person but is brought to bear from outside".[28] The purpose of any distributive scheme is extrinsic to the relation of persons as such. On the formalist's account, the choosing of any particular purpose or distribution lies outside the concern of law. Whether a Government chooses to pursue a fault based system of accident compensation, with the objective of deterring accidents and compensating victims who suffer wrongdoing by another, or whether it pursues a system which emphasizes rehabilitation through a universal, no fault, accident scheme is for the legislator to decide. Justice, on the formalist's account is limited to testing the "inner coherence" of either distribution not the choice of one purpose over another. Its focus is to ensure there is "an internal harmony" between the elements of distribution [the criteria, things and persons identified in the rule] by rectifying underinclusion and overinclusion.[29] It is the proportion - the relationship between the people, the things and the criteria involved in the distribution - not the purpose of the law as such - which is the law's domain.

This division in the formalist's account of what elements of a distributive regime fall within the sphere of politics and which fall under the authority of law, corresponds with the emphasis which the principles of rationality and proportionality place on testing the means, rather than ends, of any law whose validity is

---

[28] E. Weinrib, "Legal Formalism", *supra* note 15 cp. 988

[29] E. Weinrib, "The Intelligibility of the Rule of Law", in A. Hutchinson and P. Monahan *The Rule of Law: Ideal or Ideology*, Carswell, Toronto, 1987 p. 76

under review. The first principle we saw was exclusively about means; about the way in which a Government went about its purposes and social agenda. In applying this principle, the purposes themselves are taken as a given and the focus of the review is whether the law can be condemned as incoherent on grounds of under or over inclusion. The analysis is aimed entirely at the tightness of the fit between the ends and the means and not on the ends as such.

Similarly, when the second principle of consistency comes into play, there is no attempt to evaluate the merits of the Government's objectives or programme on their own. As the concept of a "European standard" which the European Court of Human Rights has developed makes especially clear,[30] the assessment of how a particular law balances the social welfare it promotes against the freedom it restricts is limited to a comparison of how other Governments have weighed similar interests elsewhere and in the past. It is the requirement that Governments be consistent in how they go about reconciling the competing interests affected by a law, and not the validity of the programmes a Government is pursuing, which is what the second principle is designed to guarantee.

So, it turns out that thinking about constitutional bills of rights in terms of broad principles of justice and fairness, which constrain how Governments translate their policies and programmes into law, should prove to be as congenial to those who, like formalists, think about law in the most abstract, conceptual terms as it is to those who, like positivists understand law as a brute, empirical fact. It remains to consider how easy it will be for those who, like members of the public, put certain moral values or ideas of justice at the centre of their definition of law, to focus on principles of necessity and consistency - of

---

30 See R. St.J. Macdonald "The Margin of Appreciation" in Macdonald, Matscher and Petzold (eds.) *The European System of the Protection of Human Rights*, Martinus Nijhoff, Dordrecht, 1993

rationality and proportionality, - rather than discrete constitutional entitlements when they come to think about bills of rights.

Normativism and Judicial Review

Broadly speaking theorists who approach the concept of law from a normative framework can be divided into two groups which roughly correspond to the two values which are most commonly associated with the rule of law. First, there are those who emphasize the moral value of an individual's autonomy, - the right of personal self government, - and who think of law as promoting that ideal by protecting people from the arbitrary and abusive exercise of state power. Traditionally it has been those who have belonged to the natural law and Kantian traditions who have made the ideal of the individual, freely choosing how he or she will go about living his or her life, as the distinguishing characteristic of law. Today it is theorists like Ronald Dworkin, David Richards or Michael Perry whose approach to law is grounded in the concept of rights, who have stressed the individual as a rational, responsible moral agent as the ultimate value which the law is designed to protect.

Although it has been theorists in the natural law and natural rights tradition who have generally pressed the individual and the idea of personal autonomy forward more emphatically than anyone else, it is not the case that other theorists have completely ignored the relationship between law and personal freedom. Advocates of the sparsest legal theories - even positivists - recognize the value of law in enhancing the capacity of everyone to maintain a measure of control over how they live out their lives.[31] If nothing else than by establishing a set of fixed rules as to how society expects its members to behave, positivists emphasize how law makes it possible for each individual to organize their lives within the framework it establishes. So long as people live within the

---

[31] See e.g. H.L.A. Hart, *The Concept of Law*, *supra* note 9 (esp p. 153-163) and J. Raz *The Authority of Law*, *supra* note 9

limits of the law, they can assume the coercive powers of the state will leave them and their projects alone.

There are, however, some theorists who are unwilling to assume that personal autonomy is the only or even the most important moral value which lies at the root of the concept of law. For them, the virtue of law lies just as much in helping a community organize itself into the kind of society it wants to be. Law is conceived as serving the very practical, utilitarian goal of making society a better place in which to live. Instead of the individual being the critical value in the definition of law, society and its needs (however they may be defined) becomes the central, motivating idea. Defended in the past by philosophical pragmatists and legal realists the utilitarian method continues to be championed by distinguished scholars around the world.[32]

In evaluating how these two groups of theorists are likely to respond to the idea of reconceptualizing bills of rights in terms general duties which lawmakers are required to respect, instead of specific entitlements which individuals can claim, it makes sense to consider each of them separately. In addition to the different emphasis they place on the moral values that are stake, the two approaches tend to use quite different sets of conceptual apparatus to study the structure and the method of law. For those who say that law's moral centre of gravity lies in guaranteeing every individual as much freedom as possible, the concept of rights plays a central role in their understanding of law. The specific rights and freedoms which we traditionally associate with bills of rights and the rule of law are the legal instruments by which a measure of personal autonomy can be achieved. By contrast, those who take a more pragmatic, utilitarian approach are likely to eschew such conceptual apparatus as obfuscating or "reifying" the essence of law. Theorists who emphasize the well-being of the community as a whole are generally only interested in knowing the way law

---

32 See e.g. R. Summers, *Instrumentalism and American Legal Theory*, *supra* note 5; R. Posner *The Problems of Jurisprudence*, *supra* note 8; J. Raz, "The Politics of the Rule of Law" (1990) 3 Ratio Juris. 331

actually works. For positivists and pragmatists law is simply a method of social engineering and ought to be studied as such without enveloping it with a legal jargon and conceptual apparatus which can only obscure that fact.

Of the two normative frameworks by which law has been analyzed, it might seem, at first blush, that those in the first group, who insist that the essential moral criteria of law are best captured in the concept of rights, would have the most difficulty reorienting their thinking. For "rights" theorists it might seem to be abandoning the central concept in their approach to law to subordinate all of the fundamental human rights to an analytical framework organized around a set of abstract principles of justice and equality. With a moments reflection however, it can be seen that nothing could be further from the truth. In fact, rights theorists should be as open to reorienting their understanding of constitutional bills of rights as formalists and positivists. Indeed, the leading advocates of defining law in terms of the rights people have, have already made the connection.

Among liberal political theorists, the relationship between rights and principles of justice has been widely recognized for some time. What is just, in traditional, liberal political philosophy, is a function of the rights people have.[33] Conventionally, political philosophers who work within the framework of liberal values would regard Government action as just, only if it respected the rights of those who were affected by its laws and administrative rulings. Generally they would say rights establish the criteria on how the powers of the State can be used. Rights define the circumstances in which it is just for one group in society to coerce another to do (or to refrain from doing) something which they otherwise would prefer to abstain from doing (or to do).

As well as making human rights the centre of their definition of what makes a society just, liberal political theorists also emphasize how, at bottom, it is principles of justice which shape

---

[33] G. Vlastos "Social Justice" p. 55; A. Gewirth "Political Justice", 123 in R. Brandt *Social Justice*, *supra* note 27

and explain the rights people have. The relationship between rights and justice is understood as a reciprocal or symbiotic one. Justice is defined in terms of respect for basic human rights and rights in turn are identified with and derived from the principles of justice they help define.

In determining what rights an individual can legitimately assert, liberal theory has traditionally turned to principles of justice which, explicitly or implicitly, were predicated on and gave expression to the idea that at some basic level of human existence, all individuals are of equal worth. Principles of justice reflect the Kantian ideal that characterizes all individuals as ends in themselves, of equal value as rational, autonomous persons entitled to receive equal concern and respect from the societies in which they live.

Within this overarching ambition of promoting a measure of freedom for all individuals, equal to that enjoyed by everyone else, the practical function of principles of justice in a liberal theory of law is to identify the particular rights and duties that will be recognized in any society.[34] As we saw earlier, all of the most basic rights we traditionally associate with constitutional bills of rights can be derived from principles of justice which are committed to respecting some basic equality of liberty for all individuals. Freedom of speech, freedom of religion and association etc can all be seen as very specific and particular ways this basic equality can be recognized and guaranteed. The principles act as the ultimate moral values which prescribe what rights and freedoms people will enjoy. Each principle of justice acts as a kind of criterion or benchmark against which the rights of individuals can be identified and equalized.

The way in which political philosophers have defined and explained the nature of rights and principles of justice in terms of each other has not been lost on legal philosophers. Ronald Dworkin, one of the leading rights theorists, has taken up the

---

[34] J. Rawls, "A Kantian Conception of Equality" (1975) Cambridge Review 94

connection between rights and principles of justice and pressed it further than anyone else. For Dworkin, law is synonymous with rights, but for him rights are, in the end, nothing more than the logical derivatives of arguments about principles which endeavour to ensure that the desire and capacity of all rational people to organize their own lives is respected as much as possible.[35]

For Dworkin, like most legal theorists, the central task any legal theory must be able to perform is to distinguish those circumstances in which state power can legitimately require the citizens of a society to act contrary to their own expressed interests from those in which it cannot. At one level, for theorists like Dworkin, the way to distinguish these two sets of affairs lies in the concept of rights. It would, therefore, be characteristic for someone like Dworkin to say that law is a scheme of rights and responsibilities which define when force can be legitimately be used. To act in accordance with the rule of law (viz constitutionally) a Government must respect the rights which past political and legal decisions have recognized individual citizens to have.

At a deeper level however, it is clear that Dworkin and others, like Robert Alexy,[36] think that law and legal rights (whether constitutional or otherwise) are best understood as a specific way of reasoning; as a unique method of argument. Law (and rights) are about arguments of a particular kind. Specifically, in Dworkin's view, law (and rights) are built on and derived from arguments of principle which aim at protecting the freedom and integrity of individuals. It is the fact that it is based on arguments of principle, about respecting the equal dignity of every human being and ensuring a basic measure of freedom of choice, which gives law its distinctive character. Being limited to arguments of

---

[35] See Dworkin *supra* note 13

[36] Robert Alexy, *A Theory of Legal Argumentation*, Clarendon Press, Oxford, 1989, "Rights, Legal Reasoning & Rational Discourse" (1992) 5 Ratio Juris 143

principle, aimed at promoting personal independence and freedom of choice, is what separates law from other forms of social organization, like politics, where the method of argument is less restrictive and where, for example, arguments about policy, based on what will make society as a whole better off, - can also be in play and indeed often may carry the day. In the end, on this view, rights are simply the product of arguments about principles whose focus is on respecting some basic equality in the capacity of all individuals to freely choose and define for themselves the lives they want to live.

Certainly when rights are described in this way, there would be little reason to expect rights theorists to be anything other than very sympathetic to analysing the substantive guarantees provided by constitutional bills of rights from the perspective of broad principles of justice and equality. In fact, some political philosophers have already observed that the means oriented principle of rationality or necessity is a logical imperative for any theory of law which is committed to the equality of human beings as masters of their own destinies.[37] Their argument is that where lawmakers have a choice between two different policies to accomplish their agenda, one of which can provide more opportunities for freedom of choice than the other, a system of government built on the ethic of autonomy and personal self government is bound to choose the policy which will maximize human freedom overall.

The principles of rationality and proportionality operate exactly the way theorists like Dworkin think about rights. They give expression to the basic value of human freedom on which the concept of rights is based. Collectively the two principles provide a very broad definition of when one group in a community can make use of the powers of the State to coerce others to behave in ways they would not otherwise choose. They insist Governments and other lawmakers respect a basic equality in the freedom of all

---

[37] G. Vlastos, "Social Justice" *supra* note 27 56-62; Rawls *A Theory of Justice*, *supra* note 27

people to choose how they will live, consistent with recognizing a similar entitlement for everyone else. On the one hand the rationality principle eliminates laws which needlessly and gratuitously restrict people's freedom to act. On the other, the requirement of proportionality renders unconstitutional laws which compromise freedom in a way and to a degree which is out of line with how the balance between individual freedom and the community's well-being has been drawn in the past. Together the two principles insist Governments and their officials must be vigilant in respecting a basic equality in the autonomy of all individuals every time they invoke the power of the state. By the first principle, any distinction or classification a Government wishes to draw in a policy it proposes to enact into law must be relevant to the larger purposes which the policy is designed to achieve. By the second, the imposition of burdens or the denial of benefits must be reasonable in the sense of respecting the same kinds of freedom and autonomy societies have recognized in the past.

As principled arguments, based on respecting a basic equality between all individuals in having a measure of choice and control over the direction of their lives, the rationality and proportionality principles fit the method and structure of legal argument which theorists like Dworkin present as the distinguishing characteristic of law. The criteria of necessity and consistency ensure that both the recognition of rights and the limits that can legitimately be placed on their reach, derive from the same values of personal autonomy, moral responsibility and freedom of choice. Laws which respect the equality of freedom which the principles of rationality and proportionality secure, even though they limited the freedom of some people to do as they pleased, would be recognized as valid exercises of the State's authority to act.

For rights theorists principles of rationality and proportionality operate in a manner which parallels the way rules of recognition function for those, like positivists, who understand law in more empirical and institutional terms. In both instances they serve to distinguish instances of lawmaking which are valid from those which are not. Whether they are characterized as rules of recognition or as abstract, "background rights", the principles operate as a kind of second order reason or justification from which the primary rights and duties of individuals are derived. The principles of rationality and proportionality provide the arguments from which individual rights and freedoms will be recognized. A person's constitutional entitlements come into being and will be defined by the way these two principles are applied. When national or international courts recognize that someone's constitutional rights have been infringed, it is almost always the case that the offending law does not satisfy one of these foundational principles. Either the law has gratuitously restricted the claimants' rights or it has done so in a way or to a degree which is out of all proportion with the way others have weighed similar interests in their own or neighbouring communities.

But enough, I suspect, has been said to make the point that, no less than positivists and formalists, legal theorists who think about law in terms of the rights people have should also be sympathetic to the idea of organizing their analysis of constitutional bills of rights in terms of broad principles of justice controlling the behaviour of Governments rather than thinking of them as guaranteeing the freedom to individuals to act in very specific and particular ways. To complete our survey of how the principles of consistency and rationality are likely to be received in the legal community, we can now turn to the other group of normative theorists who associate law with utilitarian values and with the idea that the ultimate virtue of the rule of law is that it can produce a more effective and efficient social order. As we have observed, this has been the view to which many positivists have been inclined[38] and it was pressed most strongly by the American pragmatists in the first half of the century. When we have considered how those who concentrate on the practical and social dimension of law are likely to respond to the idea of

---

[38] One notable exception would be F.A. Hayek, *Road to Serfdom* Chap. 6, London: George Routledge, 1944.

reconceptualizing the notion of human rights we will have covered all of the major theories which debate which characteristics and features define the essential meaning of law.

For theorists who think about law in pragmatic terms, legal concepts and rules are like tools which are available to those with the authority to exercise the powers of the state to accomplish their purposes. Rather than insisting law must reflect some essential intrinsic value, law is understood in purely instrumental terms. The value of law lies in promoting and making more effective the social order and community well-being regardless of the moral character of the latter. Law is, in the end, just a way lawmakers can ensure the policies they espouse will be as effective as they possibly can be. This is a definition of the rule of law which contemplates government by rules to achieve Governments' ends, whatever the worth of those ends might be.

The attribute of law which is linked most closely with its pragmatic or utilitarian character is, of course, its power and authority to coerce. It is because legal rules and regulations are backed by powerful sanctions and rewards that law works in a way which other forms of social regulation cannot. Policies backed with the force of law are usually able to motivate people to conform to the lawmaker's ambitions in a way which rules which are grounded only in custom or convention often cannot.

We have already noticed however, that many legal theorists who define law in such functional terms are at pains to distinguish the circumstances in which the rule of law prevails from those (like an armed robbery) which are nothing more than the brute assertion of illegitimate force. Thus, in addition to its coercive character, those who are inclined to think about law in very practical, utilitarian terms frequently make reference to a list of other attributes such as generality, clarity, accessibility, stability, consistency, non retroactivity etc. which rules must possess if they are to merit the authority of law. In the famous phrase of the distinguished American pragmatist, Lon Fuller, these and related characteristics are what constitute the "inner morality" of law. A law which is not accessible, clear, consistent, prospective etc.

cannot meet the essential normative condition of being a law. It would be thought of as being a contradiction in terms. As we noticed before, for those who think about law in this way, laws passed in secret or retroactively do not generally warrant the title of law.

It is not difficult to see how those characteristics which positivists and pragmatists think define and distinguish law from other acts of coercion are very supportive of - indeed are essential to - its effectiveness as an instrument of social order. If laws were unclear, retroactive, inconsistent, frequently changed etc. they would be incapable of guiding peoples' behaviour in the way lawmakers intended and would be ineffective in realizing the social welfare that prompted their enactment. Those whose lives were affected by such laws would be incapable of acting in the way the lawmakers desired.

Within this utilitarian understanding of the essential attributes of law the principles of rationality and consistency fit right in. Like the conditions of generality, clarity, accessibility etc., insisting on a measure of rationality and proportionality between the ends and means of policies and programmes Governments intend to inject with the power of law would support the efficiency and effectiveness of any social order. The principle of rationality or alternative means promotes the central idea of the utilitarian creed of maximizing the satisfaction of society's preferences. An analogue to what economists call the "Pareto principle", the requirement of rationality guarantees that whatever purposes underlie a policy they will be realized in a way which respects the interests of those who may be adversely affected as much as it is possible to do. Satisfying the principle of alternative means guarantees there is no other policy available which would either treat people in the same way or make them better off. As a matter of administrative regulation it will mean Governments and their agents must draft and design their laws as carefully as they can. Any distinction or classification which a Government wants to incorporate into a law must meet a strict standard of being relevant to the larger purposes the law is designed to serve.

Similarly, the ends oriented principle of consistency fits comfortably within the normative framework utilitarian theorists think captures the essential character of law. Comparing how a challenged law weighs the freedom of those whose lives it constrains against the social welfare of the community which it promotes, with how other Governments and policy makers have balanced similar interests in the past, reflects the same concern with values of stability, certainty, and consistency which positivists and pragmatists have always emphasized. Insisting that Governments respect roughly the same degree of individual autonomy and freedom of choice in their pursuit of whatever they believe is in the best interests of their community enhances the "inner morality" of stability, certainty, generality etc. which for these theorists distinguish law from other forms of social order. It promotes the efficacy of the legal order by guaranteeing a measure of consistency and uniformity in how Governments go about their business of lawmaking and of reconciling the interests of those who favour and those who oppose the social agenda and political programmes they are intent on pursuing as a matter of law.[39]

The Paradox Resolved

With this description of why those who think about law in very practical and utilitarian terms should find the idea that principles of rationality and proportionality lie at the core of all constitutional bills of rights very congenial, we are now in a position to return to and resolve the paradox with which this essay began. It should now be clear why the paradox is more apparent than real. We have now considered the major theories about what law is and how it is best understood and we have found that notwithstanding the fact legal theorists employ quite different concepts to understand and define the law, in the area of constitutional review there is the possibility of substantial

---

39 J. Raz, "The Politics of the Rule of Law" *supra* note 32 calls this "democratic continuity"

agreement about what bills of rights are all about and what role the courts can and should perform.

With a common understanding of what constitutional bills of rights are all about, the jurisprudence of "human rights" should be much less vulnerable to the charge of subjectivity and indeterminacy which has been so corrosive of the integrity of law. By guiding and constraining the courts in how they must exercise their powers of review, the principles of rationality and proportionality should be seen as securing a measure of objectivity and determinacy which goes a long way in guaranteeing its legitimacy and distinguishing it from unfettered, personal rule-making by the judges. Regardless of which theory of law a judge thought the two principles best fit, the function of judicial review and the task of the court is the same. Whether one thinks about law empirically, conceptually, or in normative terms, each judge engages in a very simple form of syllogistic or practical reasoning. Using the principles of rationality and proportionality as the major premises from which the review process proceeds, each judge evaluates a claim that someone's human rights had been violated by measuring the challenged law against alternative policies available to a Government to accomplish its objectives and against the way earlier and other societies had weighed similar interests in the past.

With this unity of understanding about the meaning and method of judicial review, constitutional bills of rights acquire a degree of objectivity and legitimacy which explains and makes entirely appropriate the public's strong instinct in favour of entrenching their community's most basic precepts of law in a constitutional bill of rights. When judges of all legal persuasions embrace a common framework for analysing and applying bills of rights, the fear that judges will have an unfettered discretion in deciding whether particular laws regulating abortion, pornography, capital punishment, the conduct of elections etc. violate basic human rights loses much of its force. In these circumstances constitutional law has roughly the same degree of objectivity we accept in other areas of law and indeed in the scientific community.[40]

Even for those who are most sceptical about the integrity of law, there should be considerable appeal in thinking about human rights and constitutional review in this way. For one thing, it respects a very basic separation of powers between the different branches of government which should be attractive to anyone who is dubious about law, whatever their political stripe. Moreover, it separates the domains of politics and law by assigning the courts a role which is very sympathetic to the principle of democratic rule. It integrates Dicey's two great principles of the liberal democratic form of government - the rule of law and the sovereignty of the popular will - in a way which maximizes the opportunity of the people to define the kind of community and social order within which they want to live.

Emphasizing the centrality of the principles of rationality and consistency in the process of constitutional review assigns judges the task of worrying most about questions of the methods and means by which state power is exercised rather than about questions of the ends to which the legal authority of the state can be put. Legislative goals and social objectives are, for the most part, left for the people to decide. In reviewing the proportionality between the social benefits promoted by a challenged law and the restrictions on human freedom which it entails, the courts' primary function is to ensure a degree of even handedness with the treatment of others who are in similar situations and of continuity with the past. The only constraint on the power of the people to create the community of their dreams is that no one's freedom to organize their lives should be compromised in a way and to a degree that differs sharply with the way others with similar interests have been treated elsewhere and in the past.

Sceptics, and indeed anyone concerned about what role the third branch of government should play in the organization and supervision of the legal powers of the state, should also be

---

40 R. Posner, *The Problems of Jurisprudence*, *supra* note 8 p.7

attracted by the very practical, fact oriented, non conceptual character which the process of constitutional review takes on when it is thought of as the judicial enforcement of a measure of moderation and balance between the ends and means of Government policy. Rather than concern itself with trying to identify the linguistic core of some very general and ill-defined word or phrase that appears in a constitution or convention, the judicial role is focused on a set of factual questions concerning the aptness of the particular means a Government has chosen to pursue its social agenda. It frees the courts from the highly contentious task of trying to establish that, as a matter of textual exegesis or psychological intent (of the framers of the constitution), very vague and general words like 'liberty,' 'expression', 'association' etc. have fixed and very particular meanings which are determinative of whether someone's constitutional rights have been violated. Seeing the court's task as essentially the factual one of judging how a challenged law compares with other policies or states of affairs, should avoid what many critics have thought to be the most problematic and discredited part of the review process. Transforming what have traditionally been thought to be issues of interpretation and moral values into questions of fact, will, to paraphrase Holmes again, force judges to think about 'things' instead of about 'words'. Making the constitutional inquiry of whether a law is valid or not essentially a factual one avoids the protracted debate that has separated positivists and normativists concerning the moral quality of law.

Oriented in this very pragmatic way, the function of the third branch of government is effectively limited to making comparative judgements about two different sets of facts or states of affairs. With the means oriented principle, judges focus on how competing policies compare in promoting a given objective. The court assesses how rationally the policy chosen by a Government to pursue its objectives is in terms of the degree of coercion it exerts. Alternative policies are evaluated to see whether there are other options available to the lawmakers to realize their programmes which might have interfered with some people's freedom less.

Essentially, the role of the court is to identify and invalidate laws which were drafted carelessly and which were over or under inclusive in the number of people they burdened or failed to benefit.

Similarly, with the second, ends oriented principle of balance and consistency, courts are concerned with comparing two different states of affairs. Here the focus is on measuring how different sets of laws trade off the social benefits they are expected to achieve against the coercion which they inflict. The balance struck by the challenged law is assessed against the equilibrium which previous and neighbouring Governments and policy makers have accepted in the past. Like the evaluation of whether the means of a particular policy are proportional to its ends, the assessment of the balance between the costs and benefits of a law is a very simple, direct, non "polycentric" comparison of two relatively concrete states of affairs. Like its function in a typical piece of accident or tort litigation, a court compares the behaviour of those exercising the powers of the state against the way similar powers have been exercised in the past and asks whether their judgment and/or behaviour was reasonable. Like defendants who are found to have acted unconscionably or negligently, a Government which ignore standards that have been widely accepted by other lawmakers who have fashioned similar policies will find it very difficult to establish that the benefits of the law justify the particular policy it adopted.

When the process of constitutional review is understood as being primarily one of comparing different policies available to lawmakers, even the most sceptical students of law should be able to see a major comparative advantage which courts and judges enjoy over politicians and the elected branches of government. Judges have an independence and distance from the issues that are raised when someone argues that a law violates his or her constitutional rights, which Governments and their agents can not, by definition, claim. Because they have an obvious, direct interest in the question of whether a law is constitutional or not, the political branches of government can not bring the same measure of impartiality and disinterested judgment as the courts. To assign the task of evaluating how a challenged law or regulation compares with other policies, to any branch of government except the court, would be to allow one of the parties in a constitutional case to be the judge of its own cause.

Recognizing that the court's primary role is to evaluate the way other policies have attempted to reconcile interests which are similar to those affected by whatever law is under review should be as helpful to those who press forward and defend claims of constitutional rights as to the judges who have the duty to decide. From the perspective of the litigants, the idea that the essential task of the Court is to evaluate the strengths and weaknesses of competing policies and social programmes against fixed principles of fairness and justice would allow them to participate in the process of review in precisely the way many legal theorists think the process of adjudication works best. Rid of legal jargon and abstract definitions of legal concepts, persons who are not trained in the law would not be prejudiced or alienated in any way. Litigants would be directed to adducing proofs and reasoned argument comparing definable states of affairs. Alternative policies and past decisions would be examined for the social benefits they would be expected to accomplish and the restrictions on human freedom they would entail. Claimants who adduced cogent evidence, about alternative policy options available to a Government or about how similar interests had been reconciled in the past, would be entitled to succeed. In the way the parties to a constitutional challenge would be called on to address the courts, judicial review would mirror exactly the way in which adjudication - as a form of social ordering - works best.[41]

In anticipating that those who traditionally have taken a very critical view of the role of law and the courts should find the idea of thinking about constitutional review in terms of evaluating laws against broad principles of proportionality or distributive justice

---

[41] Fuller, "The Forms and Limits of Adjudication", (1979) 92 Harv. L. Rev. 353

more attractive than the traditional emphasis on interpretation and the identification of a set of very specific constitutional rights, one must avoid the mistake of going too far the other way. Disagreements about whether a law violates a person's constitutional rights will not become a thing of the past. Testing the legality of how Governments and other lawmakers exercise the powers of the State against broad principles of distributive justice is not a formula for mechanical jurisprudence. The principles of rationality and proportionality only serve as guidelines or as a framework for analysis, as intermediate premises or "indexing devices", to borrow another phrase from Holmes. It is to be expected that the evaluation of alternative policies, or how particular freedoms have been balanced against the community's welfare in the past, will continue to be the subject of legitimate debate. As long as theorists continue to discuss the most basic empirical, conceptual and normative questions of law, judges can be expected to disagree about which resources they can rely on - what comparisons are most relevant - in evaluating the reasonableness of a challenged law. In the result, as with the larger theories of law to which they can be allied, there is room for pluralism in the exercise of the powers of judicial review both within the membership of a specific court and between different courts around the world. That, after all, is what makes "practical reasoning" different from "strictly logical" modes of analysis.

It is, in fact, on the premise that between both individual judges and whole legal cultures there are likely to be significant differences in how the rules of constitutional law will be applied that the greater part of the rest of this book is organized. In the chapters that follow, I have prevailed on seven jurists, who currently sit on their countries highest courts or as a member of the European Court of Human Rights, to describe how they and their colleagues decide whether laws which are alleged to infringe someone's basic human rights are valid or not. Although ideas about the rational and the reasonable form the core of the jurisprudence written by all the major courts given the responsibility of protecting people's most basic human rights, there is in fact considerable variation in how these ideas are applied. In the same way that some judges acquire reputations as strong advocates of constitutional guarantees, while others become known as being more solicitous of the choices lawmakers have made, it should not be surprising that national and international courts can be spread out along a spectrum in the way in which they use these principles to protect human rights. By analysing and comparing how these principles have figured in the leading decisions handed down by the highest courts in Japan, India, Germany, Italy, the United States, Canada and Europe, we should be able to identify the major features which characterize and distinguish the jurisprudential mindsets of each of these courts.

With this general picture of the record of human rights protection which the principles of rationality (necessity) and proportionality (consistency) have been able to provide in the countries with the most extensive experience with constitutional review, we will be in a position, in the last essay in this book, to speculate a little on where we should go from here. Having a clearer fix on how important ideas of rationality and reasonableness are in determining whether a law is constitutional or not, we will be in a better position to think about the future of human rights. Are there other principles these courts might employ in reviewing the constitutionality of a law or, rather, is it time to add new rights and freedoms - second or third generation entitlements - to the guarantees found in the traditional bills of rights? What are the lessons for those countries particularly in eastern Europe, the former Soviet Union and the third world who are just emerging from or embarking on a process of constitutional reform?

The final chapter of the book will reflect on the future development of constitutional and international bills of rights by speculating on the idea of entrenching special "social and economic" guarantees and so-called "group rights" alongside the more traditional political and civil rights. We will review how the courts have used the principles of rationality and proportionality to answer claims for various group rights and basic entitlements in the social and economic field and reflect on the implications of asking them to do more. Through an analysis of the ways in which and the extent to which social and economic entitlements can be guaranteed in a written bill of rights, we will be able to get a better idea of whether the protection that law can provide for personal freedom has gone about as far as it can or whether there is more to the rule of law than broad principles of fairness and moderation which can develop our humanity even further.

FEDERAL CONSTITUTIONAL GUARANTEES OF INDIVIDUAL RIGHTS IN THE UNITED STATES OF AMERICA

Antonin Scalia*

I Scope

This essay is directed to the guarantees of individual liberty contained in the United States Constitution. Since the United States is a federal republic, guarantees beyond those contained in the United States Constitution can be accorded (as against the *state* governments, which exercise the vast majority of governmental powers) by the constitutions of the various States. As a practical matter, these additional state-created guarantees are not significant — but they will in any event be excluded from our consideration here. Only *federal* guarantees will be discussed.

A second limitation upon this study is that it is directed only to *constitutional* guarantees. Many significant individual rights against federal and state officials are secured by federal *statute* rather than constitutional provision. One statute, for example, sets forth detailed restrictions upon the use of electronic surveillance, well beyond what the Constitution alone would impose.[1] Another requires detailed procedures of notice and hearing to be followed

---

*Antonin Scalia is an Associate Justice of the Supreme Court of the United States. He has engaged in the private practice of law, has been a Professor of Law at the University of Virginia and the University of Chicago, and has served in various positions in the Federal government, including Assistant Attorney General for the Office of Legal Counsel at the Department of Justice. He was appointed to the United States Court of Appeals for the District of Columbia Circuit in 1982 and to the Supreme Court in 1986.

[1] See Omnibus Crime Control and Safe Streets Act of 1968, codified as amended at 18 U.S.C. ss.2510–2521.

D.M. Beatty (ed.), Human Rights and Judicial Review, 57-91.

in all administrative proceedings.[2] And yet another severely restricts the use that government agencies may make of files containing personal information about individuals.[3] In the aggregate, these federal statutory guarantees against various forms of state and federal government action are enormously significant — and some of them are, as a practical matter, almost as unlikely of amendment as is the Constitution itself. But they will form no part of our consideration here.

Finally, by limiting ourselves to federal constitutional guarantees, we automatically limit ourselves to guarantees of individual rights *against the government*. Many aspects of what are loosely called "civil rights" — for example, the right not to be discriminated against by private employers, or by private hotels and restaurants, on the basis of race — consist of restrictions not upon the *government*, but upon private individuals. The United States Constitution, which addresses individual rights only *vis-à-vis* the government, does not include these civil rights, though they are liberally guaranteed by federal statutory law. Very often, therefore, the first question that a court must answer in determining whether there has been a constitutional violation is whether there has been any "state action" — that is, whether the actor was acting for, or on behalf of, or with the active assistance of, the government, or rather was acting in purely private capacity. A person, for example, who without permission enters and rummages through another person's house, will undoubtedly be guilty of violating a state law against trespass; but unless he has the requisite connection with state or federal government, he will not be violating the provision of the Constitution that prohibits "unreasonable searches and seizures."

---

[2] Administrative Procedure Act, codified as amended at scattered sections of 5 U.S.C., including ss. 551–559.

[3] Privacy Act of 1974, codified as amended at 5 U.S.C. s. 552a.

II Judicial Review

It was not a foregone conclusion under the United States Constitution that courts would have authority to determine its proper application, rather than being bound to accept whatever application was adopted by Congress. Nothing in the text of the Constitution explicitly gives courts the power to declare federal legislation unconstitutional. To appreciate how significant that power is, one must understand how difficult it is to override a judicial determination by amending the Constitution. Amendments can be proposed only by a vote of two-thirds of both Houses of Congress, or by a Constitutional Convention requested by the legislatures of two-thirds of the States.[4] Those proposals must then be adopted ("ratified") by the legislatures of (or State conventions in) three-fourths of the States. Given current population figures, and assuming that a bare majority of a state legislature or convention would correspond to a bare majority of the State's population, opposition by as little as 2% of the nation's population can theoretically prevent a proposed amendment from being adopted. And even reaching the proposal stage requires a massive and coordinated political effort. It is unsurprising that only sixteen Amendments have been adopted in over two centuries (*i.e.*, since the adoption of the Bill of Rights in 1791).

In the famous 1803 case of *Marbury* v. *Madison*,[5] the Supreme Court held that it must decline to give effect to legislation which in its view violates the Constitution; the Court's own assessment of constitutionality, and not the legislature's, must determine the judgment. There is now general, if not universal, agreement that when the Supreme Court has decided a case on the basis that a particular statute (or particular executive action) is unconstitutional, the *judgment* in that case is binding not only on the States but on the other two federal branches. The President

[4] See U.S. Constitution, Article V.

[5] 5 U.S. (1 Cranch) 137 (1803).

would risk impeachment, for example, if he should ignore a Court order to cease certain action because he disagrees with the Court's assessment that it is unconstitutional. Beyond that conclusive effect in the case at hand, however, the Supreme Court's constitutional construction is sometimes spoken of as having a universal legal effect — as being, like the text of the Constitution itself, see Art. VI, "the supreme Law of the Land." That is technically, perhaps, an exaggeration: the strictly *legal* effect of any judicial judgment extends only to the rights of the particular litigants before the court. Since, however, under the doctrine of *stare decisis* the Court normally adheres to the reasoning of its prior opinions,[6] the principle of constitutional interpretation the Court applied in yesterday's lawsuit can be assumed to be the principle it will apply in today's lawsuit as well. As a practical matter, therefore, it is the course of civic responsibility and prudence for citizens and officials to conform their actions to the Supreme Court's most recently expressed constitutional views.

Although the Supreme Court has the last word on constitutional interpretation, it does not have the *only* word. The theory of *Marbury* v. *Madison* is that the Constitution is a super-law, which judges must apply, where there is a conflict, in preference to ordinary legislation. That reasoning applies, of course, to *all* judges — so that not only the Supreme Court of the United States, but also the lower federal courts, and the supreme courts and lower courts of all of the States, have the authority, indeed the obligation, to pass upon the constitutionality of the official actions (state or federal, executive or legislative) that come before them. Their decisions on that point are, of course, subject to review by the Supreme Court.

---

[6] Although adherence to past precedent is the normal course, it is not the invariable one. See Justice Brandeis' discussion in *Burnet* v. *Coronado Oil & Gas Co.*, 285 U.S. 393, 405–13 (1932) (Brandeis, J., dissenting).

III Text of Constitutional Guarantees

The original United States Constitution, ratified by the people in 1787, contained no separate Bill of Rights. A very few guarantees of individual liberty were contained in the midst of the structural provisions:

> "The Privilege of the Writ of Habeas Corpus [*i.e.*, the power of the courts to direct the release of a person detained without proper authority] shall not be suspended, unless when in Cases of Rebellion or Invasion the public Safety may require it." Article I, §9, clause 2.
>
> "No Bill of Attainder [*i.e.*, legislation aimed at punishing a particular individual] or ex post facto Law shall be passed." Article I, §9, clause 3.
>
> "No State shall ... pass any Bill of Attainder, ex post facto Law, or Law impairing the Obligation of Contracts ...." Article I, §10, clause 1.
>
> "The Trial of all Crimes, except in Cases of Impeachment, shall be by Jury; and such Trial shall be held in the State where the said Crimes shall have been committed ...." Article III, §2, clause 3.
>
> ".... No Person shall be convicted of Treason unless on the Testimony of two Witnesses to the same overt Act, or on Confession in open Court.... [N]o Attainder of Treason shall work Corruption of Blood, or Forfeiture except during the Life of the Person attainted." Article III, §3, clause 1, 2.
>
> ".... [N]o religious Test shall ever be required as a Qualification to any Office or public Trust under the United States." Article VI, clause 3.

The Framers of the Constitution did not think that a separate Bill of Rights was necessary, believing that the surest protection of the people's liberties lay in the proper division and equilibration of government powers, so that no institution would have unchecked power.[7] During the ratification debates, however, it became clear

---

[7] See The Federalist Nos. 47, 51 (Madison).

that many Americans wanted a Bill of Rights — and the ratification of several States was conditioned upon the understanding that a Bill of Rights would shortly be adopted.

Accordingly, a constitutional amendment embodying a Bill of Rights was proposed by the very first Congress, in 1789, and was ratified by the requisite number of States in 1791.[8] This is the source of most constitutional protection of individual rights. It is short enough to be set forth verbatim:

AMENDMENT I

Congress shall make no law respecting an establishment of religion, or prohibiting the free exercise thereof; or abridging the freedom of speech, or of the press; or the right of the people peaceably to assemble, and to petition the Government for a redress of grievances.

AMENDMENT II

A well regulated Militia, being necessary to the security of a free State, the right of the people to keep and bear Arms, shall not be infringed.

AMENDMENT III

No Soldier shall, in time of peace be quartered in any house, without the consent of the Owner, nor in time of war, but in a manner to be prescribed by law.

AMENDMENT IV

The right of the people to be secure in their persons, houses, papers, and effects, against unreasonable searches and seizures,

---

[8] For historical material surrounding the drafting and adoption of the Bill of Rights, see B. Schwartz, THE BILL OF RIGHTS: A DOCUMENTARY HISTORY (1971).

shall not be violated, and no Warrants shall issue, but upon probable cause, supported by Oath or affirmation, and particularly describing the place to be searched, and the persons or things to be seized.

AMENDMENT V

No person shall be held to answer for a capital, or otherwise infamous crime, unless on a presentment or indictment of a Grand Jury, except in cases arising in the land or naval forces, or in the Militia, when in actual service in time of War or public danger; nor shall any person be subject for the same offence to be twice put in jeopardy of life or limb; nor shall be compelled in any criminal case to be a witness against himself, nor be deprived of life, liberty, or property, without due process of law; nor shall private property be taken for public use, without just compensation.

AMENDMENT VI

In all criminal prosecutions, the accused shall enjoy the right to a speedy and public trial, by an impartial jury of the State and district wherein the crime shall have been committed, which district shall have been previously ascertained by law, and to be informed of the nature and cause of the accusation; to be confronted with the witnesses against him; to have compulsory process for obtaining witnesses in his favor, and to have the Assistance of Counsel for his defence.

AMENDMENT VII

In Suits at common law, where the value in controversy shall exceed twenty dollars, the right of trial by jury shall be preserved, and no fact tried by a jury, shall be otherwise re-examined in any Court of the United States, than according to the rules of the common law.

AMENDMENT VIII

Excessive bail shall not be required, nor excessive fines imposed, nor cruel and unusual punishments inflicted.

AMENDMENT IX

The enumeration in the Constitution, of certain rights, shall not be construed to deny or disparage others retained by the people.

AMENDMENT X

The powers not delegated to the United States by the Constitution, nor prohibited by it to the States, are reserved to the States respectively, or to the people.

Three post-Civil War Amendments also bear significantly upon individual rights. The Thirteenth Amendment, adopted in 1865, prohibits laws permitting slavery, and the Fifteenth, ratified in 1870, provides that "[t]he right of citizens of the United States to vote shall not be denied or abridged by the United States or by any State on account of race, color, or previous condition of servitude." And most important of all, the Fourteenth Amendment, adopted in 1868, contains the following provision:

> "No State shall make or enforce any law which shall abridge the privileges or immunities of citizens of the United States; nor shall any State deprive any person of life, liberty, or property, without due process of law; nor deny to any person within its jurisdiction the equal protection of the laws."

As we shall see, this has been made the means of extending the prohibitions of the Bill of Rights (which originally restricted only the *federal* government) to the States.

Finally, the Nineteenth Amendment, adopted in 1920, provides that "[t]he right of citizens of the United States to vote shall not be denied or abridged by the United States or any State on account of sex."

IV Basic Structure of Constitutional Jurisprudence

The entire body of United States constitutional protection for individuals against government action — and it is an extensive body of protection indeed — has been elaborated from the few textual provisions set forth above. It is impossible to describe for the reader the interpretive technique by which this elaboration has occurred, because over the years various and sometimes contradictory techniques have been employed, often simultaneously. Some opinions, for example, seek to determine, through scholarly inquiry, the original meaning of the governing constitutional text, as it was understood at the time of its adoption.[9] Others rely upon longstanding practice as validating or invalidating particular government action — even though the practice is of more recent vintage than the governing text, and so cannot represent evidence of original meaning.[10] Still others ignore both original meaning and traditional practice, asserting a judicial authority to announce "evolving standards" of conduct that the Constitution from age to age requires.[11] And others focus neither on constitutional text nor on longstanding practice nor on desirable normative standards, but rely upon (and reason from) statements and holdings in earlier Supreme Court decisions, as though they, rather than the Constitution itself, were the ultimate criteria.[12] All of these approaches — and especially the "original meaning" and "evolving standards" approaches — have their ardent proponents and harsh critics.

---

[9] See, *e.g.*, *Marsh* v. *Chambers*, 463 U.S.783 (1983).

[10] See, *e.g.*, *Lockett* v. *Ohio*, 438 U.S. 586, 602–05 (1978) (plurality opinion).

[11] See, *e.g.*, *Trop* v. *Dulles*, 356 U.S. 86, 99–103 (1958) (plurality opinion); *Woodson* v. *North Carolina*, 428 U.S. 280, 289–95 (1976) (plurality opinion); *Shaffer* v. *Heitner*, 433 U. S. 186, 211–12 (1977).

[12] See, *e.g.*, *County of Riverside* v. *McLaughlin*, 111 S.Ct. 1661 (1991); *Estelle* v. *Gamble*, 429 U.S. 97, 102–03 (1976).

Whatever interpretive technique is used, however, it is common ground that every constitutional decision must ultimately rest, at least formally, upon a particular constitutional text. Some of those texts are clear and straightforward — in the subjects that they deal with, if not in the details of what they prescribe. The First Amendment, for example, deals with freedom of religion and freedom of expression; the Fourth with freedom from unreasonable searches and seizures; the Fifth and Sixth with procedures in criminal prosecutions; the Seventh with the right to jury in civil cases. But there are several provisions of the text whose import (as it has come to be interpreted) is not readily apparent. Two of these are of such preeminent structural importance to United States constitutional law that they require separate discussion.

I refer to the dual "Due Process Clauses," which appear in the Fifth Amendment ("No person shall ... be deprived of life, liberty, or property, without due process of law") and in the Fourteenth Amendment ("nor shall any State deprive any person of life, liberty, or property, without due process of law"). One would suppose that a guarantee of proper *process* does not guarantee any particular *substantive* right. That is to say, it would appear from the text and structure of the Constitution that other provisions guarantee certain substantive rights against abridgment (*e.g.*, freedom of speech and religion), and that the Due Process Clause simply assures that, even as to those rights that can be abridged, the abridgement must be accomplished through proper procedure (*i.e.*, a properly enacted law or a lawfully conducted judicial proceeding). In fact, however, "due process" has been interpreted to include the categorical guarantee of certain rights. During the first quarter of this century, for example, the Supreme Court held that it guaranteed certain economic freedoms, such as (in a case invalidating social legislation limiting the work-week) the right to work as many hours a week as one wished.[13] The use of the Due Process Clause to protect unenumerated economic liberties has been abandoned (the above described case was effectively

[13] See *Lochner* v. *New York*, 198 U.S. 45 (1905).

overruled in the 1930's),[14] but its use to protect other unenumerated liberties has continued. It was, for example, one of the provisions relied upon in *Roe* v. *Wade* to establish the constitutional right to an abortion.[15] Such use of the Due Process Clause, which bears the oxymoronic name "substantive due process," remains a source of some controversy in American jurisprudence.

One of the substantive uses of the Due Process Clause of the *Fourteenth* Amendment (and no longer, it is fair to say, a controversial use) has been to apply against the States some of the guarantees in the Bill of Rights. The 1791 Bill of Rights contained guarantees only against the *federal* government. The First Amendment, for example, provides that "*Congress* shall make no law" abridging freedom of speech or prohibiting the free exercise of religion, and it is clear that the next nine Amendments were also directed only against *federal* power. Once it had been held, however, that the Fourteenth Amendment's guarantee of "due process" against the States had some substantive content — that it included, as some Supreme Court cases put it, those freedoms that are "implicit in the concept of ordered liberty"[16] — it was natural to conclude that rights important enough to be included in the federal Bill of Rights were also implicit in the Due Process Clause. But were *all* of them implicit — even, for example, the right to a jury trial in all common-law civil cases involving more than $20 (Amendment VII)? And as to those liberties mentioned in the Bill of Rights that *were* implicit in the Due Process Clause (for example, freedom of speech), did the application to the States have to be precisely the same as the application to the Federal Government? Was it possible to say that every jot and tittle of the

---

[14] See, *e.g.*, *West Coast Hotel Co.* v. *Parrish*, 300 U.S. 379 (1937); *Nebbia* v. *New York*, 291 U.S. 502 (1934).

[15] 410 U.S. 113, 152–53 (1973).

[16] *Palko* v. *Connecticut*, 302 U.S. 319, 325 (1937).

Supreme Court's First Amendment jurisprudence — even holdings on points so close that they were decided by a 5–4 vote — was "implicit in the concept of ordered liberty"? This dispute, which enlivened Supreme Court opinions particularly during the late 1940s and 1950s,[17] has never been entirely resolved, but at this point the principal provisions of the Bill of Rights, including all of the First and Fourth Amendments, all of the Fifth except the Grand Jury guarantee, all of the Sixth except the venue provision, and all of the Eighth, have been fully "incorporated" into the Fourteenth Amendment, so that whatever the Supreme Court holds these provisions require of the federal government they require of the States as well.[18]

Before proceeding to describe the concrete application of the Constitution's individual-right guarantees, I must make a disclaimer: Not all judicially pronounced applications of the constitutional text can be assumed to have the same permanence as the text itself. The Supreme Court has often said, and often demonstrated, that the doctrine of *stare decisis* is not applied rigidly in the field of constitutional law — a prudent course, given the difficulty of correcting by constitutional amendment whatever mistakes the Court might make. Constitutional holdings have frequently been overruled,[19] and the lawbooks are full of derelict theories (such as economic substantive due process) that survive

---

[17] See, *e.g.*, *Adamson* v. *California*, 332 U.S. 46 (1947), a case whose holding (subsequently overruled, see *Malloy* v. *Hogan*, 378 U.S. 1 (1964)) was that the Fourteenth Amendment does not incorporate the Fifth Amendment privilege against self-incrimination. In dissent, Justice Black argued for total incorporation of the Bill of Rights, and in a concurring opinion Justice Frankfurter attacked that proposal.

[18] See *Duncan* v. *Louisiana*, 391 U.S. 145, 158–159 n.30 (1968).

[19] See, *e.g.*, *Garcia* v. *San Antonio Metropolitan Transit Authority*, 469 U.S. 528 (1985) (overruling a case decided nine years earlier); *United States* v. *Dixon*, No. 91–1231 (June 28, 1993) 61 L.W. 4835 (overruling a case decided three years earlier).

only as historical curiosities whereas they were once the clearest of constitutional law. In its details, at least, and even in some of its significant aspects, United States constitutional law is in a state of constant motion.

V Freedom of Religion

Pride of place in the Bill of Rights is accorded to freedom of religion. The first provision of the First Amendment states that "Congress shall make no law respecting an establishment of religion, or prohibiting the free exercise thereof." The two parts of this provision, which are referred to in American jurisprudential parlance as the Establishment Clause and the Free Exercise Clause, respectively, have quite different and sometimes conflicting effects.

The Establishment Clause, in its original application — that is, in its application to the federal government alone, before its "incorporation" into the Fourteenth Amendment — not only forbade the federal government to *create* an established church, but also forbade it *undo* any State-created establishment. Several of the States possessed established churches when the First Amendment was adopted,[20] and the language of the Establishment Clause ("Congress shall pass no law *respecting* an establishment of religion") plainly prohibited interference with these. By the mid-nineteenth century, however, established churches had been eliminated throughout the United States, so that when, in 1947, the Supreme Court first held that the Establishment Clause applied to the States,[21] the effect was simply to prevent an establishment of religion.

There are two major analytic issues involved in application of the Establishment Clause, neither of which has been fully resolved

---

[20] See R. Cord, SEPARATION OF CHURCH AND STATE 4 (1982).

[21] *Everson* v. *Board of Education*, 330 U.S. 1 (1947).

in United States jurisprudence. The first is the degree of government favoritism or assistance that suffices to constitute an "establishment." Some have argued that no "establishment of religion" has occurred unless the favoritism and assistance have reached the degree that there is an established church, that is, an official state religion supported by public tax funds. That narrowest of views has long (and conclusively) been rejected.[22] It remains unclear, however, just how much or what sort of assistance to religion will constitute a prohibited "establishment" for First Amendment purposes. The Supreme Court has approved, for example, laws exempting church property from real estate taxes,[23] but has invalidated laws exempting religious publications from sales taxes.[24] It has approved State payment of bus transportation to carry students to sectarian schools,[25] but has disapproved State payment of bus transportation to carry students on sectarian-school outings.[26] It has approved State provision of textbooks to sectarian schools, but has disapproved State provision of other instructional materials (such as maps and globes of the world).[27] It would be an understatement to say that the unifying principle which reconciles these decisions is not readily apparent; the cases reflect an instability that characterizes not only the

---

[22] See, *e.g.*, *Everson*, *supra*, at 15–16.

[23] *Walz* v. *Tax Comm'n of New York City*, 397 U.S. 664 (1970).

[24] *Texas Monthly, Inc.* v. *Bullock*, 489 U.S. 1 (1989).

[25] See, *e.g.*, *Everson*, *supra*.

[26] *Wolman* v. *Walter*, 433 U.S. 229, 252–55 (1977).

[27] *Meek* v. *Pittenger*, 421 U.S. 349 (1975).

Court's treatment of this particular issue, but the Court's Establishment Clause jurisprudence in general.[28]

Once it has been decided that "establishment" does not mean only an official State church, the second analytic issue presented is whether it includes favoritism or assistance for *religion in general*, or only preference for a particular sect of religion (*e.g.*, Christianity). As late as 1952, the Supreme Court held that officially favoring religion in general over irreligion did not violate the Establishment Clause. ("We are a religious people, whose institutions presuppose a Supreme Being. . . . When the state encourages religious instruction or cooperates with religious authorities . . . it follows the best of our traditions. For it then respects the religious nature of our people and accommodates the public service to their spiritual needs."[29]) Just over thirty years later, the Court seemed to reverse course, and said that the Establishment Clause requires the State to adopt a stance of "neutrality," not merely between religious sects, but between religion and irreligion. ("The solution . . . adopted by the Framers and consistently recognized by this Court is jealously to guard the right of every individual to worship according to the dictates of conscience while requiring the government to maintain a course of neutrality among religions, and between religion and nonreligion."[30])

That position has not been formally repudiated, but there are later decisions inconsistent with it — for example, a decision approving exemption of religious organizations from the Civil

---

[28] In his dissent in *Wallace* v. *Jaffree*, 472 U.S. 38, 107 n° 6 (1985), Justice Rehnquist noted that many Establishment Clause cases decided over the past few decades have produced only plurality or bare majority opinions. That pattern has continued. See, *e.g.*, *Lee* v. *Weisman*, 112 S. Ct. 2649 (1992) (5-to-4 decision); *Zobrest* v. *Catalina Foothills School Dist.*, No. 92–94 (June 19, 1993) 61 L.W. 4641 (same).

[29] *Zorach* v. *Clauson*, 343 U.S. 306, 313–14 (1952).

[30] *School Dist. of City of Grand Rapids* v. *Ball*, 473 U.S. 373, 382 (1985).

Rights Act's prohibition of religious discrimination in employment,[31] and a decision approving nondenominational prayer to open the sessions of State legislatures.[32] On the other hand, the Court has forbidden the use of even nondenominational voluntary prayer in public schools (compulsory prayer would of course violate the Free Exercise Clause) — not only in the classroom[33] but even as an invocation at graduation.[34] Perhaps the current state of the law can best be described by saying that State favoring of particular religious sects is always forbidden, and that State favoring of religion in general is ordinarily permitted, though never in a context where school-age children would be affected.

One reason it would be quite impossible to forbid all government favoritism for religion in general is the Free Exercise Clause. In stating that "Congress shall make no law ... prohibiting the free exercise [of religion]," the First Amendment *requires* the government to give religious belief and practice a privilege it need not accord to other activities. The more broadly the Establishment Clause is interpreted, the more it comes into conflict with the Free Exercise Clause. The converse is also true: the more broadly the Free Exercise Clause is interpreted, the more it comes into conflict with the Establishment Clause. If, for example, the free exercise of religion were held to include the right of religiously minded public-school students to open their class day with a voluntary prayer, it would overturn the prohibition of such prayer under the Establishment Clause. One of the enduring difficulties of First Amendment jurisprudence is reconciling the two religion clauses.

Although the Free Exercise Clause speaks of "prohibiting the free exercise" of religion, the Supreme Court has long interpreted

---

[31] *Corporation of Presiding Bishop of the Church of Jesus Christ of Latter-Day Saints* v. *Amos*, 483 U.S. 327 (1987).

[32] *Marsh* v. *Chambers*, *supra*.

[33] *Engel* v. *Vitale*, 370 U.S. 421 (1962).

[34] *Lee* v. *Weisman*, *supra*.

it to embrace not only absolute prohibition, but also any government action designed to penalize, deter, or burden religious practice. It would invalidate, for example, a statute imposing a special tax upon attendance at Mass. The question arises, what about government action that is not *designed* to burden religious practice, but incidentally has that effect — *i.e.*, a general law prohibiting action which some people engage in as a matter of religious practice? Is such a law invalid as to those individuals? In the late nineteenth century, Mormons claimed such a defense to the application against them of a federal law criminalizing bigamy. The Supreme Court held, categorically, that religious belief provided no basis for a constitutional exemption from such a general law.[35] The Court seemingly altered its view in 1963, striking down a State's denial of unemployment compensation to persons who refused to accept available work, when the reason for the refusal was a religious one (*viz.*, that the job required work on Saturday, the employee's Sabbath).[36] Only a "compelling state interest," the Court said, could justify applying a general law against religious objection. This was thought to be the law until 1990 — though some question whether it was forthrightly applied as announced.[37] In 1990, in a case involving a claim by two members of the Native American Church that they were constitutionally entitled to use legally proscribed psychotropic drugs in their traditional religious ceremonies, the Court reverted to its earlier formulation, holding that religious practice or belief is no basis for an exemption from a State law of general

---

35 *Reynolds* v. *United States*, 98 U.S. 145 (1878).

36 *Sherbert* v. *Verner*, 374 U.S. 398 (1963).

37 See, *e.g.*, *Goldman* v. *Weinberger*, 475 U.S. 503 (1986) (holding that there *was* a "compelling state interest" in forbidding Jewish soldiers to wear yarmulkes).

application, *i.e.*, one that is not directed at religion.[38] That decision remains controversial, and Congress has under consideration legislation that would seek to establish by statute a "compelling state interest" test.

This last issue suggests one final significant point regarding the Free Exercise Clause. Creating a "religious practice" exception to every law would be a much simpler matter if the concept of "religion" were limited to well known, traditional, organized faiths (Christianity, Judaism, Islam, etc.). In fact, however, for purposes of the First Amendment it includes not only minor and novel sects,[39] but even, it seems clear, entirely idiosyncratic personal religious belief.

VI Freedom of Speech

If freedom of religion occupies the first place in the Bill of Rights, because of its moral preeminence, freedom of speech occupies the second, because of its political importance. The First Amendment provides that "Congress shall make no law ... abridging the freedom of speech, or of the press." As Supreme Court opinions have suggested, in a properly functioning democracy freedom of speech is not only a human right but a prerequisite of successful government.[40] The people cannot govern themselves intelligently if the people are not open to be persuaded.

---

[38] *Employment Division, Dept. of Human Resources of Oregon* v. *Smith*, 494 U.S. 872, 876–82 (1990).

[39] See, *e.g.*, *Church of the Lukumi Babalu Aye* v. *City of Hialeah*, No. 91–948 (June 11, 1993), 61 L.W. 4587 (sect of Santeria, believing in animal sacrifice); *Employment Division*, *supra* (Native American Church, believing in sacramental ingestion of the psychotropic drug peyote).

[40] See, *e.g.*, *New York Times Co.* v. *Sullivan*, 376 U.S. 254, 269–72 (1964); *Whitney* v. *California*, 274 U.S. 357, 375–77 (1927) (Brandeis, J., concurring).

It is not only political speech that the First Amendment protects, however, but speech on art, science, philosophy, baseball — all speech. And not merely the individual's personal expression is protected, but also his right to amplify his voice by means that money can buy, such as space in newspapers and time on television. Thus, the Supreme Court held unconstitutional a feature of federal campaign-financing legislation that limited the amount of money that individuals could personally spend to further particular candidacies.[41] Moreover, not only oral and written speech, but other means of conveying ideas are protected — for example, the burning of the United States flag as a symbol of protest against the government and its policies.[42] Several cases hold that even expressive conduct that conveys no ideas but merely emotion is protected — for example, dancing and music.[43]

To say that all expressive activity is protected by the First Amendment is not to say that all expressive activity is protected equally. There are varying degrees of protection, which render First Amendment jurisprudence more complex than might appear at first glance. The highest degree of protection, accorded to what might be termed "verbal speech," invalidates prohibition of that conventional means of conveying ideas (with certain exceptions that will be discussed later), unless the prohibition can be justified by a compelling state interest.[44] Thus, for example, a prohibition of open-air public speeches would be unconstitutional except, perhaps, in a riot situation where such speeches would be likely to provoke or attract violence. This highest degree of protection is not accorded acts that constitute nonverbal means of communication. Those acts may be proscribed without any

---

[41] *Buckley* v. *Valeo*, 424 U.S. 1, 39–59 (1976) (*per curiam*).

[42] See *Texas* v. *Johnson*, 491 U.S. 397 (1989).

[43] See, *e.g.*, *Schad* v. *Borough of Mt. Ephraim*, 452 U.S. 61 (1981) (nude dancing); *Ward* v. *Rock Against Racism*, 491 U.S. 781 (1989) (music).

[44] See, *e.g.*, *Terminiello* v. *Chicago*, 337 U.S. 1 (1949).

heightened justification, so long as the proscription is not specifically directed at the communicative nature of the acts.[45] For example, a municipal ordinance prohibiting the burning of materials in the public streets can constitutionally be applied against the burning of a flag as a form of political protest; such an ordinance is to be contrasted with a law prohibiting only the public burning of flags, which is obviously directed against the communicative nature of that activity.

"The freedom of speech" preserved by the First Amendment has traditionally not included freedom to use speech for certain purposes: to convey obscenity, to propagate libel, and to hurl personal insult provocative of violence.[46] These three categories, obscenity, ordinary libel, and so-called "fighting words," are sometimes referred to in the Supreme Court's jurisprudence as "nonspeech." That shorthand is not entirely accurate, neither as a matter of fact (they obviously *are* speech) nor as a matter of law. Some First Amendment protections continue to apply to these communications — notably, the rudimentary First Amendment principle that *all* regulation of speech must be content-neutral, *i.e.*, that prohibitions cannot be based upon the *content* of the speech, except to the extent that the content is itself proscribable. Thus, although "fighting words" are proscribable, it is unconstitutional to prohibit only those "fighting words" that express certain disfavored ideas.[47]

Besides these three categories of "unprotected" speech, there are several categories of speech that have been accorded limited

---

[45] See, *e.g.*, *Clark* v. *Community for Creative Non-Violence*, 468 U.S. 288 (1984) (sleeping in public parks may be prohibited, even when that activity is engaged in for the communicative purpose of demonstrating the plight of the homeless).

[46] See *Roth* v. *United States*, 354 U.S. 476 (1957) (obscenity); *Beauharnais* v. *Illinois*, 343 U.S. 250 (1952) (libel); *Chaplinsky* v. *New Hampshire*, 315 U.S. 568 (1942) (fighting words).

[47] See *R. A. V.* v. *City of St. Paul*, 112 S. Ct. 2538 (1992).

protection. The first is so-called "commercial speech," which consists of speech proposing a commercial transaction, such as advertising and sales offers. "The freedom of speech" referred to in the First Amendment did not include freedom from control over this sort of communication, which is a particularly hardy sort of speech, and one that bears special risks of fraud and deception.[48] The Supreme Court has held, however, that commercial speech is entitled to this limited protection: any regulation of it must directly advance a substantial government interest, and be no more extensive than necessary to serve that interest.[49] A second category of speech that receives reduced protection is a relatively new beneficiary of First Amendment concern. In the 1964 case of *New York Times Co.* v. *Sullivan*,[50] the Supreme Court held that certain libel — libel against "public figures" — cannot be proscribed or made the subject of civil liability unless it is willful, *i.e.*, knowingly or recklessly false. Subsequent cases have held, moreover, that the determination of willfulness cannot be left entirely to the jury, but must be independently assessed by the courts.[51] It bears emphasis that this special protection is applicable only to libel of "public figures." That category includes such persons as politicians, writers, and movie stars, who have thrust themselves into public attention; it is not yet clear to what extent it includes other persons (for example, the victims of highly publicized crimes) who involuntarily become the subject of widespread public interest. Some cases suggest that a third

---

[48] See *Valentine* v. *Chrestensen*, 316 U.S. 52 (1942) (upholding an ordinance forbidding distribution in the streets of handbills bearing commercial advertisements).

[49] See *Central Hudson Gas & Electric Corp.* v. *Public Service Comm'n of New York*, 447 U.S. 557, 564-566 (1980).

[50] 376 U.S. 254 (1964).

[51] See, *e.g.*, *Bose Corp.* v. *Consumers Union of United States, Inc.*, 466 U.S. 485 (1984).

category of speech is to be accorded only reduced constitutional protection: speech that is pornographic or indecent, though not proscribable as obscene.[52] This new category must be understood in light of the extremely high test the Court has applied in recent years to define obscenity. It is not enough that the material contain sexual portrayals patently offensive to community standards; in addition, the dominant theme of the material, taken as a whole, must appeal to a "prurient interest in sex," and the material must lack "serious literary, artistic, political, or scientific value."[53]

The First Amendment restricts not only what the government may decree as ruler with regard to speech, but also what the government may do as property owner and employer. Absent compelling emergency, speech cannot be banned in those publicly owned areas that are "traditional public fora" — notably, public streets, sidewalks, and parks.[54] The government may create, by usage, new public fora, to which the same speech rights would attach.[55] (A recent Supreme Court decision holds that airports are not public fora, so that charitable solicitors may be banned.[56]) On government property where this "public forum" doctrine does not apply, the government may restrict speech — always provided, of course, that the restriction does not discriminate on the basis of content, except to the extent that particular content is incompatible

---

[52] See, *e.g.*, *Young* v. *American Mini Theatres*, 427 U.S. 50 (1976) (upholding a municipal zoning ordinance restricting locations of theaters showing pornographic films).

[53] See *Miller* v. *California*, 413 U.S. 15, 23–25 (1973).

[54] See, *e.g.*, *Hague* v. *Committee for Industrial Organization*, 307 U.S. 496 (1939) (plurality opinion); *Schneider* v. *State*, 308 U.S. 147 (1939).

[55] See *Widmar* v. *Vincent*, 454 U.S. 263 (1981) (a state university could not exclude student religious groups from use of facilities generally made available to other student groups).

[56] *International Society for Krishna Consciousness, Inc.* v. *Lee*, 112 S. Ct. 2701 (1992).

with the use of the property. Thus, it is permissible to prohibit all political speech on army bases,[57] and all charitable solicitation in post offices;[58] those are not public fora, and the speech proscribed is particularly disruptive to the government use.

In the employment field, the government cannot, as a condition of hiring, impose speech restrictions that are unrelated to job performance. In one case, for example, the Supreme Court set aside the dismissal of a secretary for a municipal police department who had expressed satisfaction at the shooting of President Reagan.[59] This principle has been held not to prevent, however, restrictions upon government employees' engaging in partisan political activities such as election campaigns.[60]

Even that speech which enjoys the highest degree of protection can be subjected to reasonable "time, place and manner" regulation. On the public streets, for example, soundtrucks can be prohibited during the nighttime, and their volume regulated during the day.[61] Parades and marches may be conditioned on first obtaining a permit, so that conflicts can be avoided and adequate crowd control assured.[62]

---

[57] See *Greer* v. *Spock*, 424 U.S. 828 (1976).

[58] See *United States* v. *Kokinda*, 497 U.S. 720 (1990).

[59] *Rankin* v. *McPherson*, 483 U.S. 378 (1987).

[60] *U.S. Civil Service Comm'n* v. *National Assn. of Letter Carriers*, 413 U.S. 548 (1973).

[61] See, *e.g.*, *Kovacs* v. *Cooper*, 336 U.S. 77 (1949).

[62] See, *e.g.*, *Cox* v. *New Hampshire*, 312 U.S. 569 (1941) (upholding a statute that required permits for parades on public streets); *Grayned* v. *Rockford*, 408 U.S. 104 (1972) (upholding an ordinance that prohibited conduct likely to disturb the order of nearby schools); *Frisby* v. *Schultz*, 487 U.S. 474 (1988) (upholding an ordinance that prohibited certain residential picketing).

VII Restrictions of Police and Penal Authorities

As described earlier, the Fourth Amendment provides that the people shall "be secure in their persons, houses, papers, and effects, against unreasonable searches and seizures," and sets forth evidentiary and particularity requirements for the obtaining of warrants. This is the only provision of the Constitution that explicitly sets forth "reasonableness" as the criterion of legality. In practice (though not without dissenting views), the Court has determined reasonableness on the basis of contemporary notions, rather than according to the standards that prevailed when the governing provisions were enacted.

Although the Fourth Amendment's principal application is to investigative searches and seizures conducted by law enforcement authorities, it also applies to searches conducted by the government as regulator or even as employer. Recent cases, for example, have considered and upheld the power of the government to require operating personnel of (company-owned) railroad trains to submit to urinalysis drug-tests after a train wreck,[63] and to require its own law-enforcement personnel who carry firearms to submit to such tests on a random basis.[64] The case-law has also expanded the Amendment beyond its textual limitation to "persons, houses, papers, and effects." Business premises, for example, have been held to be covered,[65] and public telephone booths.[66]

In determining what constitutes a "seizure" (to which the constitutional test of reasonableness is applicable) the Supreme Court case-law has hewn fairly closely to common-law tradition: Seizure of property occurs when physical possession is taken,

---

[63] *Skinner* v. *Railway Labor Executives' Ass'n*, 489 U.S. 602 (1989).

[64] *Nat'l Treasury Employees Union* v. *Von Raab*, 489 U.S. 656 (1989).

[65] *Mancusi* v. *DeForte*, 392 U.S. 364 (1968).

[66] *Katz* v. *United States*, 389 U.S. 347 (1967).

whether or not that taking involves an intrusion upon privacy;[67] seizure of the person requires restriction of physical freedom, either by force or by show of authority that would cause a reasonable person to believe he was not free to leave.[68] In determining what constitutes a "search," however, the case-law has departed from the originally governing common-law concepts of trespass upon property rights, and assault upon the person. The criterion has been said to be whether the government action, whether or not it constitutes a trespass on property or an assault upon the person, violates an expectation of privacy that society recognizes as reasonable.[69] Thus, the interception of telephonic communications, or the use of electronic devices to eavesdrop upon conversations held in private locations, has been held to constitute a search even though no trespassory invasion of property occurs.

In most Fourth Amendment litigation, however, the existence of a search or seizure is unquestionable, and the contested issue is whether it was "reasonable." In the late 1940's, the Supreme Court set forth the general rule that to be reasonable a search or seizure must be conducted pursuant to a warrant issued by an impartial magistrate.[70] Over the years, however, that rule has been made subject to many exceptions, including (in addition to the long established exception for searches incident to arrest[71]) exceptions

---

[67] See, *e.g.*, *Soldal* v. *Cook County*, 113 S.Ct. 538 (1992).

[68] See, *e.g.*, *Terry* v. *Ohio*, 392 U.S. 1, 16–20 (1968); *INS* v. *Delgado*, 466 U.S. 210, 216–217 (1984).

[69] See, *e.g.*, *Katz*, *supra*.

[70] See *Johnson* v. *United States*, 333 U.S. 10, 13–14 (1948).

[71] See *Weeks* v. *United States*, 232 U.S. 383, 392 (1914).

for "administrative" searches by regulatory authorities,[72] searches of automotive vehicles,[73] brief "stop and frisk" searches of pedestrians[74], and (most expansive of all) searches under "exigent circumstances," which includes any circumstance in which taking the time to obtain a warrant would risk imminent destruction of evidence, prevention of a felon's escape, or danger to police or the community.[75] Even where the warrant requirement does not exist, however, the search or seizure must be otherwise reasonable, which means (in the case of investigative searches or seizures of property) that the officer must have "probable cause" — that is, reason to believe that he is seizing, or that his search will disclose, a criminal, contraband, or evidence of criminal activity.[76]

The other constitutional provision most relevant to police investigative activities is the Fifth Amendment's guarantee that no person shall be compelled to give evidence against himself. This has been interpreted very expansively, to include psychological as well as physical compulsion. In *Miranda* v. *Arizona*,[77] the Supreme Court held that police interrogation of a suspect who is in custody is so inherently coercive that any confession elicited in those circumstances will be deemed to have been compelled, unless its eliciting is preceded by what has come to be known as a "*Miranda*" warning, informing the suspect of his right to remain

---

[72] See, *e.g.*, *Donovan* v. *Dewey*, 452 U.S. 594 (1981) (upholding warrantless inspections of mines under the Federal Mine Safety and Health Act); *New York* v. *Burger*, 482 U.S. 691 (1987) (upholding warrantless inspections of automobile junkyards pursuant to a state statute).

[73] See, *e.g.*, *Chambers* v. *Maroney*, 399 U.S. 42 (1970).

[74] See *Terry*, *supra*.

[75] See, *e.g.*, *Schmerber* v. *California*, 384 U.S. 757, 770–771 (1966). See also *Minnesota* v. *Olson*, 495 U.S. 91, 100–01 (1990).

[76] See, *e.g.*, *Illinois* v. *Gates*, 462 U.S. 213, 232–39 (1983).

[77] 384 U.S. 436 (1966).

silent, to consult with counsel, and to have counsel appointed if he is indigent. If, moreover, the suspect in custody says, upon the initial attempt to interrogate him, that he wants to consult counsel, the police are not thereafter allowed to initiate any interrogation — even to ask him whether he wants to change his mind about speaking; and any confession resulting from such police-initiated interrogation will be deemed coerced, *even if* preceded by a *Miranda* warning *and* accompanied by an express, written waiver of Fifth Amendment rights.[78] The Court has said that *Miranda* and the elaborations upon *Miranda* are not constitutionally required, but are prophylactic rules to assure compliance with the Fifth Amendment.[79] (It is difficult, however, to identify the Court's authority to impose these rules if they are not constitutionally required.)

Coerced confessions can of course not be received in evidence at criminal trials, since that would violate the Fifth Amendment's proscription of compelled self-incriminating testimony. In addition, however, the Supreme Court has imposed in relatively recent times an "exclusionary rule" barring all courts from receiving in evidence confessions obtained in violation of the Supreme Court's *Miranda* jurisprudence,[80] and evidence obtained (immediately or derivatively) from a search or seizure that violates the Fourth Amendment.[81] This means that confessions uncoerced in the ordinary sense, and the most plainly incriminating physical evidence, must sometimes be excluded, and that convictions obtained after improper admission of such evidence must sometimes be overturned. The exclusionary rule remains somewhat

---

[78] *Edwards* v. *Arizona*, 451 U.S. 477 (1981).

[79] See, *e.g.*, *Michigan* v. *Tucker*, 417 U.S. 433, 443–446 (1974).

[80] See, *e.g.*, *Edwards*, *supra*.

[81] See, *e.g.*, *Mapp* v. *Ohio*, 367 U.S. 643 (1961).

controversial, because the source of the Court's authority to impose it upon state courts is less than clear.[82]

A further constitutional restriction upon law enforcement authorities worthy of mention here is the Eighth Amendment's prohibition of "cruel and unusual punishments." The Supreme Court has held that this bans not only those punishments that were considered "cruel and unusual" in 1791, when the Eighth Amendment was adopted, or in 1868, when it was applied to the States through the Fourteenth Amendment, but in addition those punishments that have later come to be regarded as "cruel and unusual," according to "the evolving standards of decency that mark the progress of a maturing society."[83] In other respects, also, the Eighth Amendment has seemingly been expanded: The provision was formerly understood to address only the cruelty and unusualness of the *type* of punishment (*e.g.*, scourging, maiming), and not the cruelty and unusualness of its imposition for the particular offense (*e.g.*, ten years' imprisonment for petty theft). In recent years, however, the Supreme Court has held that it covers extreme *disproportionality* of punishment as well.[84] The Court has recently held that the Eighth Amendment applies not merely to the formal sentence but also to the *de facto* conditions of incarceration — so that prison authorities' harsh treatment of

---

[82] See *Wolf* v. *Colorado*, 338 U.S. 25 (1949) (illegal seizure not grounds for objection to admissibility in state proceedings). *Mapp*, *supra*, essentially overruled this case.

[83] *Trop* v. *Dulles*, 356 U.S. 86, 101 (1958) (plurality opinion).

[84] See, *e.g.*, *Solem* v. *Helm*, 463 U.S. 277 (1983) (invalidating a life sentence without parole for a seventh nonviolent felony).

inmates can violate the Constitution.[85] This has involved the federal courts in overseeing state and federal prison conditions.[86]

Capital punishment is mentioned in the very text of the Constitution: the Fifth Amendment requires grand jury indictment for prosecution of capital crimes, and forbids the deprivation of "life, liberty or property" without due process of law. Nonetheless, in 1972 the Supreme Court came close to deciding that the death penalty was proscribed by the "Cruel and Unusual Punishments" Clause.[87] Though avoiding that step, the Court has declared that the Eighth Amendment imposes certain substantive and procedural limitations upon imposition of the death penalty — for example, that a capital sentence can be decreed only for the willful taking of a life, and not for lesser offenses;[88] that it cannot (at least without age-specifying legislation) be imposed upon persons younger than 16 at the time of the offense;[89] that the law defining the capital crime must narrow the class eligible for death, so that the

---

[85] See *Estelle* v. *Gamble*, 429 U.S. 97 (1976) (holding that deliberate indifference to an inmate's serious medical needs violates the Eighth Amendment).

[86] See *Wilson* v. *Seiter*, 111 S.Ct. 2321 (1991) (addressing an Eighth Amendment claim based on, *inter alia*, overcrowding, excessive noise, inadequate heating and cooling, unclean restrooms, and housing with physically and mentally ill inmates); *Helling* v. *McKinney*, No. 91–1958 (decided June 18, 1993) (holding that housing a prisoner in a cell with a heavy cigarette smoker may violate the Eighth Amendment).

[87] See *Furman* v. *Georgia*, 408 U.S. 238 (1972).

[88] See *Enmund* v. *Florida*, 458 U.S. 782 (1982) (the death penalty may not be imposed solely on the basis that the defendant participated in a robbery, during the course of which a codefendant committed murder).

[89] See *Thompson* v. *Oklahoma*, 487 U.S. 815 (1988) (setting aside death sentence of a defendant who was 15 at the time of the murder).

sentencer's decision to impose that penalty will not be random;[90] and that the sentencer must be permitted to consider all relevant mitigating factors in determining whether to impose the sentence.[91]

In this far-from-complete list of constitutional restrictions upon police and penal authorities, the last I shall mention is the Eighth Amendment's provision that "[e]xcessive bail shall not be required." An accused person cannot be held in custody pending trial unless there is reason to believe he will flee, or unless his prior convictions demonstrate a high risk of continuing criminal activity pending trial.[92] The bail set must be no higher than is reasonably necessary to assure appearance for trial, rather than a figure designed to assure that the accused cannot afford to secure his release.[93]

VIII Restrictions Upon Discrimination

The Fourteenth Amendment provides that "[n]o State shall ... deny to any person within its jurisdiction the equal protection of the laws." While the principal purpose of this provision, adopted shortly after the Civil War, was to prevent discrimination by the former Confederate States against newly freed slaves, the guarantee it contains goes further than that, and requires the States to provide equal protection, that is to say equal treatment, to *all* persons. By a process similar to that by which the Due Process

---

[90] See *Zant* v. *Stephens*, 462 U.S. 862 (1983).

[91] See *Lockett* v. *Ohio*, 438 U.S. 586, 604 (1978) (plurality opinion); *Eddings* v. *Oklahoma*, 455 U.S. 104 (1982).

[92] See *United States* v. *Salerno*, 481 U.S. 739 (1987) (upholding the constitutionality of the Federal Bail Reform Act of 1984, which allows for pretrial detention under certain circumstances).

[93] See *Stack* v. *Boyle*, 342 U.S. 1 (1951).

Clause of the Fourteenth Amendment has been held to extend the Bill of Rights (which is addressed to the Federal Government) to the States, the Due Process Clause of the Fifth Amendment has been held to extend the later-enacted Equal Protection Clause of the Fourteenth Amendment (which is addressed to the States) to the Federal Government.[94] Of course, equal treatment need not be accorded when there is good reason for making a distinction: government employees performing different jobs may be given different salaries. But if it were up to the courts to determine in each case whether the reason for different treatment was a *good enough* reason, judges would become the ultimate arbiters of vast numbers of social policies. Is it proper, for example, to grant social security retirement benefits only to persons over 65, or should 60–year-olds, or maybe even 55–year-olds, also qualify? To avoid the obvious impropriety of being drawn into such questions, the Supreme Court has held that, as a general matter, the Equal Protection Clause is satisfied so long as there is a "rational basis" for the disparate treatment. This is such a lenient test that in most fields the Equal Protection Clause provides no significant limitation upon government action.[95]

There are exceptions to this general rule, however, and the exceptions are enormously important. If the law involves disparate treatment based on race, mere "rational basis" will not suffice; a compelling justification is required.[96] One can conceive of some rare cases that may pass this test — for example, a government-funded inoculation program that is available only to blacks because only blacks are affected by the disease in question. Generally

---

[94] *Bolling* v. *Sharpe*, 347 U.S. 497 (1954).

[95] See, *e.g.*, *Williamson* v. *Lee Optical of Oklahoma, Inc.*, 348 U.S. 483 (1955) (upholding a state law that banned advertising of eyeglasses, but made an exception for advertising by sellers of ready-to-wear eyeglasses).

[96] See, *e.g.*, *City of Richmond* v. *J.A. Croson Co.*, 488 U.S. 469, 498–506 (1989).

speaking, however, the "strict scrutiny" accorded to race-based laws will result in their invalidation.

Singling out racial discrimination for this special Equal-Protection-Clause treatment is understandable, since the Fourteenth Amendment was intended primarily to eliminate racial injustice. Legal scholars, however, and some dicta in Supreme Court opinions, have suggested that disparate treatment accorded to any "historically disfavored" group must be subjected to similar "strict scrutiny."[97] That has not become the law, although the Court has subjected discrimination on the basis of sex to what it terms "intermediate scrutiny" — not as strict as that applied to race, but not as permissive as the "rational basis" test applied elsewhere.[98]

A second broad category of cases in which the Supreme Court has applied "strict scrutiny" under the Equal Protection Clause is that in which the disparate treatment is based upon, or affects, the exercise of "fundamental rights." Thus, a one-year residency requirement to obtain state welfare benefits was held unconstitutional because (although it had a rational basis) there was

---

[97] See *United States* v. *Carolene Products Co.*, 304 U.S. 144, 152–53 n.4 (1938) (stating that the Court did not in that case have to decide "whether prejudice against discrete and insular minorities may be a special condition, which tends seriously to curtail the operation of those political processes ordinarily to be relied upon to protect minorities, and which may call for a correspondingly more searching judicial inquiry").

[98] See, *e.g.*, *Reed* v. *Reed*, 404 U.S. 71 (1971) (holding unconstitutional a statute establishing an order of priority for persons to be appointed as administrators of intestate estates, preferring male relatives over female relatives of the same degree of relationship); *Weinberger* v. *Wiesenfeld*, 420 U.S. 636 (1975) (holding unconstitutional a Social Security Act provision granting a widowed mother, but not a widowed father, benefits based on the earnings of a deceased spouse); *Geduldig* v. *Aiello*, 417 U.S. 484 (1974) (holding constitutional a State disability insurance program that excluded pregnancy-related disabilities).

no compelling state interest, as there had to be in order to justify this burden upon the federal right to interstate travel.[99]

IX Nature and Importance of Constitutional Guarantees

The foregoing describes the current state of United States law regarding the most significant constitutional guarantees of individual rights. I conclude with some rather more subjective observations regarding the nature and importance of constitutionally guaranteed rights.

The significance of a constitutional Bill of Rights should not be exaggerated. Some of the worst tyrannies in the world (*e.g.*, the former Union of Soviet Socialist Republics) have had marvelous Bills of Rights; and some of the freest democracies (*e.g.*, the United Kingdom) have had none at all. If the organs of government (legislature, executive and judiciary) can readily disregard the Bill of Rights, it is nothing but a paper guarantee — at best the expression of an aspiration, and at worst a false certificate of liberalism. Several conditions are necessary to avoid that consequence. First, and I think most important, the power of government must not rest entirely within the control of a single person or a single assembly. I am speaking here not merely about the need for an "independent" judiciary. If an independent Supreme Court were given full and unchecked governmental power, I have no doubt that it would soon bend the Bill of Rights to its own ends, just as any unchecked power will inevitably aggrandize itself. The separation and equilibration of power among the three branches of government has been an essential element of the preservation of individual rights in the United States. Indeed, if one were faced with the stark choice between structural checks and balances, on the one hand, and a Bill of Rights, on the other hand, he would be foolish to choose the latter.

---

[99] See *Shapiro* v. *Thompson*, 394 U.S. 618 (1969).

The second condition for an effective Bill of Rights is clarity of content. Its formidable purpose — which, in a democracy, is to prevent The People from doing what they wish — cannot be achieved by judges who lack, for any significant proportion of their decisions, the support of a clear text or tradition to justify their flouting of the popular will. On this point, one should not be misled by the modern American experience. The United States Supreme Court has, particularly since the 1960's, successfully used general provisions of the Bill of Rights (notably, the Due Process Clause) to create new entitlements, such as a right to abortion[100] and a right to die,[101] that have no clear justification in text and no clear antecedent in tradition. But such decisions are accepted only because of a popular respect for the Court developed by 200 years of much less imaginative jurisprudence. The rights originally guaranteed by the Bill of Rights, and originally enforced by the federal courts, were not the vague abstractions of the 18th-century philosophes, but the down-to-earth "rights of Englishmen" set forth explicitly in such provisions as the jury-trial guarantee, or alluded to by such provisions as the Due Process Clause. The vast bulk of United States constitutional jurisprudence is firmly based in text and tradition, and it is that solid and well-accepted base which has given the Supreme Court the ability to branch out, now and then, into constitutional innovation. It is also noteworthy that the innovation has, by and large, *not* protected minority rights, except to the extent that the majority has *wished* to protect minority rights. That is to say, it has generally created as a *federal* constitutional right what a majority of voters nationwide would desire, even though the voters in some States might disagree. The Court's record of protecting "new" constitutional rights (i.e., rights based upon neither explicit text nor clear tradition) against *national* majority sentiment is not a strong one. When, for example, public opinion during the era of Franklin Roosevelt's

---

[100] See *Roe* v. *Wade*, 410 U.S. 113 (1973).

[101] See *Cruzan* v. *Director, Missouri Dept. of Health*, 497 U.S. 261 (1990).

"New Deal" would not support the restrictions on economic regulation that the Court had found to be a part of "substantive due process," the Court changed its jurisprudence and ran before the wind.[102] And more recently, when national majority sentiment would not support the right to unrestricted abortion-on-demand enunciated in *Roe* v. *Wade*, the Court adjusted the right so as to preclude only "undue" restrictions on abortion.[103] In other words, constitutional decisionmaking unsupported by clear text and tradition has been more effective in extending federal majoritarian rule over dissenting States than in preserving minority rights from national majorities.

The last condition for an effective Bill of Rights is a genuine, underlying attachment of the people to the liberties it expresses. In a well-functioning democracy, a Bill of Rights can serve as a remedy for the society's temporary forgetfulness of its better self. It can, for example, enable judicial invalidation of a particular piece of illiberal legislation adopted in the heat of passion or under the stress of a supposed emergency. But in the nature of things a Bill of Rights cannot — assuming a well-functioning democracy — permanently prevent the people from doing what they continuously and earnestly desire to do. A long-term, fundamental misalignment between a society's beliefs and its Bill of Rights must produce either an amendment of the constitution to permit what the people wish, or the appointment of judges who will disregard or distort the Bill of Rights. Hence the need for a democratic society constantly to renew its dedication to the principles of liberty set forth in its constitution. When their importance is forgotten among the people, no paper text can preserve them.

---

[102] See, *e.g.*, *Nebbia* v. *New York*, 291 U.S. 502 (1934).

[103] See *Planned Parenthood of Southeastern Pennsylvania* v. *Casey*, 112 S.Ct. 2791 (1992).

JUDICIAL REVIEW BY THE SUPREME COURT OF CANADA UNDER THE CANADIAN CHARTER OF RIGHTS AND FREEDOMS: THE FIRST TEN YEARS[1]

Frank Iacobucci*

Introduction

In this commentary, I will attempt to provide an overview of the process of judicial review in the ten years since the constitutional entrenchment of rights and freedoms in Canada. The last decade has been a time of fundamental change in the role assigned to the courts of Canada, particularly the Supreme Court of Canada. Before turning to a discussion of the general approach which has been adopted by the Supreme Court towards the enforcement of the *Canadian Charter of Rights and Freedoms*, I will briefly examine the process leading to the entrenchment of the *Charter*, and some of the features of the *Charter* which are unique to Canada. I will then consider the question of to whom the *Charter* applies, and finally proceed to discuss judicial interpretation of the *Charter* in its first decade, ending with some comments on the tension between collective interests and individual rights. Understandably, my comments are brief and general, and readers should seek other sources for more detailed analysis and

*Professor of Law at the University of Toronto from 1971 to 1985, Dean, Faculty of Law, 1979-1983, Vice-President and Provost of the University of Toronto from November 1983 to September 1985, Deputy Minister of Justice and Deputy Attorney General of Canada 1985-1988, Chief Justice of the Federal Court of Canada 1988-91, and Judge of the Supreme Court of Canada 1991. Justice Iacobucci is also the author of numerous articles and books in the area of corporate and securities law.

[1] I should like to acknowledge the invaluable assistance I have received from my law clerk, Penney Lewis, in the preparation of this commentary.

D.M. Beatty (ed.), Human Rights and Judicial Review, 93-133.

criticism.[2]

The Process Leading to Entrenchment

Prior to the entrenchment of the *Canadian Charter of Rights and Freedoms*, judicial review in Canada was confined to division of powers questions under the *British North America Act, 1867*. Courts had the power to review legislative enactments and to determine which level of government - federal or provincial - was empowered to legislate on the matter at issue. This limited role of judicial review embraced the parliamentary supremacy theory that is a part of the United Kingdom system of governance. Under that theory, the sole question was to ascertain where legislative competence lay; once this was found, the appropriate legislature was basically free to do as it chose without fear of a court invalidating the legislation. This changed with the advent of the *Charter* which was passed by the Parliament of Canada and legislatures of the provinces of Canada, save for Quebec. Courts are now directed to declare legislation invalid to the extent it conflicts with provisions of the *Charter*.

The reasons which inspired the *Charter* have been the subject of much discussion. Perhaps foremost in the mind of the Prime Minister of the day, Pierre Trudeau, the *Charter* (together with the new constitutional amending formula) was seen as a means of national unity, a way of formally binding French and English Canada into a single political entity by such means as making

---

[2] See, for example, M. Mandel, *The Charter of Rights and the Legalization of Politics in Canada* (Toronto: Wall & Thompson, 1989); A.C. Hutchinson, "Waiting for Coraf (Or the Beatification of the Charter)" (1991) 41 U.T.L.J. 332 at 340; D.M. Beatty, *Talking Heads and the Supremes: The Canadian Production of Constitutional Review* (Toronto: Carswell, 1990); R.J. Sharpe, "A Comment on David Beatty's 'A Conservative's Court: The Politicization of Law'" (1991) 41 U.T.L.J. 469 at 477; J. Fudge, "The Public/Private Distinction: The Possibilities of and the Limits to the Use of Charter Litigation to Further Feminist Struggles" (1987) 25 Osgoode Hall L.J. 485; L. Clark, "Liberalism and the Living-Tree: Women, Equality , and the Charter" (1990) 28 Alta. L. Rev. 384.

English and French language rights uniform across the country.[3] The inclusion of mobility rights in the *Charter* was an additional attempt to avoid the "balkanization" of Canada and advance national unity by affording individuals the right to live and work in the province of their choosing "without discrimination based on the previous province of residence."[4] Further, the symbolic value of the *Charter* in promoting national unity was considered important by its proponents:

> A clear statement in the Constitution of the fundamental values all Canadians share would . . . have an important unifying effect. It would inculcate in all citizens, young and old, a consciousness of the importance of civil liberties and an authoritative expression of the particular rights and liberties our society considers fundamental.[5]

The Content of the Charter

1. INTRODUCTION: HEREIN FUNDAMENTAL RIGHTS AND FREEDOMS

Clearly, another motivation for the passage of the *Charter* was the promise of protection of legal and social rights. In some

---

[3] P.E. Trudeau, "Quebec and the Constitutional Problem", in P.E. Trudeau, *Federalism and the French Canadians* (1968) at 54. See also, P.H. Russell, "The Political Purposes of the Canadian Charter of Rights and Freedoms" [1983] 61 Cdn Bar Rev. 30 at 34. The relevant *Charter* sections are ss. 16-20 which focus on the language of government, and s. 23 concerning the language of education.

[4] The Hon. Jean Chretien, House of Commons Debates, Oct. 6th, 1980 at 3286. Cited in Russell, *id.* at 38. The importance of the unifying function of the language and mobility rights provisions is emphasized by the fact that the s. 33 override provision does not apply to either language or mobility rights.

[5] Canadian Bar Association Committee on the Constitution, *Towards a New Canada* (1978) at 15.

respects, the *Charter* is similar to the constitutional guarantees of individual rights found in other countries such as the American *Bill of Rights*, the *International Covenant on Civil and Political Rights*, and the *European Covenant for the Protection of Human Rights and Fundamental Freedoms*. For instance, the *Charter* contains broad guarantees of civil liberties including freedom of religion and conscience, expression, the press, assembly, association, life, liberty and security of the person, and equality.[6] The *Charter* also enumerates basic legal rights such as the right not to be unreasonably searched or arbitrarily detained or imprisoned, the right to a fair trial, the right to counsel and the right to be presumed innocent until proven guilty. In addition, the *Charter* contains various democratic rights such as the right to vote and be a candidate for democratic office. An interesting feature of the *Charter* is the presence of provisions regulating the terms and sittings of the legislative assemblies of both levels of government.

This mix of Parliamentary and human rights provisions is one of the unique features of the *Charter*, of which there are many. I will now discuss some of these unique features in greater detail before proceeding to an examination of the process of judicial interpretation which has evolved under the *Charter* in response to these features.

2. GROUP AND MINORITY RIGHTS

(a) Introduction

What is perhaps most distinctive about the Canadian *Charter* is the emphasis on the rights of minorities and groups. Many of the rights in the *Charter* are guaranteed to individuals as members of groups, rather than to groups themselves.[7] In addition to the general freedom of association found in s. 2(d) of the *Charter*,

---

[6] See *Charter*, ss. 2, 7, 15.

[7] *Reference re Alberta Public Service Employee Relations Act*, [1987] 1 S.C.R. 313.

such rights are defined linguistically, culturally, historically, and by gender. This emphasis on group rights reflects the Canadian commitment to respecting the many cultural differences found in Canadian society.

(b) S. 27 — Multiculturalism

This concern of the *Charter* with group rights is illustrated in many of its provisions. One such provision of importance is s. 27 which reads,

> This *Charter* shall be interpreted in a manner consistent with the preservation and enhancement of the multicultural heritage of Canadians.

The judicial interpretation of s. 27 is still in its infancy. Those cases which have interpreted s. 27 have seen it as, to use the words of former Chief Justice Dickson, "a strong commitment to the values of equality and multiculturalism".[8] In another case,[9] s. 27 was described as "a mandate for the preservation of the pluralistic society." S. 27 represents the overarching commitment in our *Charter* to the preservation and enhancement of a society made up of many groups with as many different histories, languages and cultures. Equally clear is that the characteristics of these groups are not only to be preserved within our constitutional framework, but that their contributions to the fabric of Canadian society are also to be recognized and valued. S. 27 "supports the protection of the collective rights, the cultural integrity and the dignity of Canada's ethnic groups. In doing so it enhances the dignity and sense of self worth of every individual member of

---

[8] *R. v. Keegstra*, [1990] 3 S.C.R. 697 at 755.

[9] *R. v. Fatt*, [1986] N.W.T.R. 388 at 398, Marshall J.

those groups and thereby enhances society as a whole."[10]

(c) Language Rights, S. 16-23

The collective interests aspect of the *Charter* is nowhere more evident than in the language and educational rights found in ss. 16 through 23. Ss. 16 through 22 of the *Charter* entrench English and French as the two official languages of Canada. Specifically, these sections of the *Charter* guarantee that English and French can be used in any federal Court, in the federal Parliament, and in dealings with the federal government. The provisions reflect our constitutional commitment to the linguistic rights of the two founding language groups in Canada.

Perhaps even more distinctive than language rights are the educational rights in ss. 23 and 29 of the *Charter*. S. 23, entitled "Minority Language Education Rights" guarantees children the right to be educated in the first language of their parents, whether English or French, even where the speakers of that language are in the minority. Former Chief Justice Dickson stated that the purpose of s. 23 "is to preserve and promote the two official languages of Canada, and their respective cultures, by ensuring that each language flourishes, as far as possible, in provinces where it is not spoken by the majority of the population."[11] The Supreme Court has not been hesitant to require legislative action to uphold minority language education rights: in *Mahe*, the Court directed the province of Alberta to enact legislation to ensure that the s. 23 rights of French speakers in Edmonton were respected.

(d) Denominational, Separate, and Dissentient Schools — S. 29

S. 29 of the *Charter* protects existing rights in respect of denominational, separate or dissentient schools. S. 29 reads,

---

[10] *R. v. Zundel* [1992] 2 S.C.R. 731, 817; 95 D.L.R. (4th) 202, Cory and Iacobucci JJ., dissenting.

[11] *Mahe v. Alberta*, [1990] 1 S.C.R. 342 at 362.

> Nothing in this *Charter* abrogates or derogates from any rights or privileges guaranteed by or under the Constitution of Canada in respect of denominational, separate or dissentient schools.

These rights referred to in s. 29 of the *Charter* are guaranteed by other sections of the original *Constitution Act, 1867.* S. 93(1) of that Act constitutionalizes all rights and privileges with respect to denominational schools which may have existed at the time of Confederation. As a result, the right to religious education is to some extent constitutionally protected.

S. 29 was included in the *Charter* to deal with the problems posed by the interaction between the guarantee of freedom of religion found in s. 2(a), and s. 93 of the *Constitution Act, 1867*, which guarantees the rights of Protestants and Roman Catholics to separate schools at the time of Confederation.[12] In *Reference Re: Bill 30, An Act to Amend the Education Act to provide full funding for Roman Catholic Separate High Schools*, the Court held that

---

[12] Section 93 reads in part:

> 93. In and for each Province the Legislature may exclusively make Laws in relation to Education, subject and according to the following provisions:--
>
> > (1) Nothing in any such Law shall prejudicially affect any Right or Privilege with respect to Denominational Schools which any Class of Persons have by Law in the Province at the Union;
> >
> > ...
> >
> > (3) Where in any Province a System of Separate or Dissentient Schools exists by Law at the Union or is thereafter established by the Legislature of the Province, an Appeal shall lie to the Governor General in Council from any Act or Decision of any Provincial Authority affecting any right or Privilege of the Protestant or Roman Catholic Minority of the Queen's Subjects in relation to Education;
> >
> > ...

religious education funding statutes passed under a province's plenary power in relation to education under the opening words of s. 93 of the *Constitution Act, 1867* were protected from *Charter* review.[13]

(e) Equality Rights — Affirmative Action

Equally important in the *Charter* landscape are the equality rights contained in s. 15, which is the Canadian equivalent of the Equal Protection Clause of the XIVth amendment of the American Constitution. S. 15 is in two parts: the first part guarantees equality before and under the law, and the equal protection and benefit of the law, without discrimination to every individual; the second part specifies that the first part does not preclude affirmative action programs the purpose of which is to ameliorate the condition of disadvantaged individuals or groups.

It is the explicit protection of affirmative action programs from constitutional attack on equality grounds that is distinctive. S. 15(2) specifies that the guarantee of equality outlined in s. 15(1)

> ... does not preclude any law, program or activity that has as its object the amelioration of conditions of disadvantaged individuals or groups including those that are disadvantaged because of race, national or ethnic origin, colour, religion, sex, age or mental or physical disability.

A comparison with the American Constitutional position is illustrative of the very different course taken by the drafters of the *Charter*. The U.S. Supreme Court has ruled that only those affirmative action programs which are essential and carefully restricted will be found to pass constitutional muster.[14] Since affirmative action programs breach the anti-discrimination principle

---

[13] [1987] 1 S.C.R. 1148 at 1198.

[14] *University of California Regents v. Bakke*, 438 U.S. 265 (1977).

embodied in the XIVth Amendment, they must be justified by the party seeking to support them. The approach used by the U.S. Supreme Court is to scrutinize both the objective of the affirmative action program and the means employed to achieve that objective. The type of governmental or judicial body involved and the classification used are relevant to the determination of the appropriate level of scrutiny to be applied.[15]

Judicial interpretation of s. 15(2) in Canada remains in relative infancy but it appears clear that s. 15(2) operates to excuse discrimination in some circumstances. It is the determination of these circumstances which will have to await further judgments. In the words of Huddart L.J.S.C., "S. 15(2) excuses discrimination ... if the persons in favour of whom the distinction is made are disadvantaged and the object of the discrimination is the amelioration of that disadvantage".[16] Huddart L.J.S.C. also concluded that s. 15(2) was included in the *Charter* precisely to silence the debate that often rages over the legitimacy of affirmative action. In the result, Canadian courts may well take a considerably different approach to affirmative action from that of American courts.

(f) Gender Equality: S.s 28 and 15

Another important section of the *Charter* is s. 28, which guarantees sexual equality in the application of the *Charter*. In itself, s. 28 creates no new rights; it is an interpretive clause affecting the application of the rights and freedoms guaranteed elsewhere in the *Charter*. S. 28 reads,

Notwithstanding anything in this *Charter*, the rights and

---

[15] See, for example, *City of Richmond v. J.A. Croson Co.*, 488 U.S. 469 (1989); *Metro Broadcasting, Inc. v. F.C.C.*, 111 L.Ed. 2d 445 (1990).

[16] *Re MacVicar and Superintendent of Family and Child Services*, 34 D.L.R. (4th) 488 at 502 (B.C.S.C.), cited with approval by McLachlin J. in *R. v. Hess and Nguyen*, [1990] 2 S.C.R. 906 at 945.

> freedoms referred to in it are guaranteed equally to male and female persons.

In combination with the equality provisions in s. 15(1) of the *Charter*, s. 28 has resulted in significant changes in judicial decisions dealing with statutes that do not explicitly discriminate on the basis of sex.

Before the advent of the *Charter*, a case involving discrimination on the basis of pregnancy was decided by the Supreme Court of Canada. Under a government unemployment insurance scheme, women who were unable to work because they were pregnant were disentitled to benefits which were available to all other claimants.[17] The Supreme Court of Canada held that the scheme was a valid one under the statutory human rights legislation then in force, because it satisfied the Aristotelian requirement of formal equality: "things that are alike should be treated alike, while things that are unalike should be treated unalike in proportion to their unalikeness."[18]

The formal equality approach has been firmly rejected by the Supreme Court of Canada under the *Charter*. Instead, "[c]onsideration must be given to the content of the law, to its purpose, and its impact upon those to whom it applies, and also upon those whom it excludes from its application."[19] Under the *Charter*, the Court must inquire into the effect of a law or scheme which is on its face neutral. The Supreme Court has since declared expressly that discrimination against pregnant women *is* sex

---

[17] *Bliss v. A.G. Canada*, [1979] 1 S.C.R. 183.

[18] *Ethica Nicomacea*, quoted in *Andrews v. Law Society of British Columbia*, [1989] 1 S.C.R. 143 at 166, McIntyre J. (dissenting on other grounds).

[19] *Andrews*, *id.* at 168.

discrimination.[20] In expressly overruling the earlier decision of the Court, former Chief Justice Dickson said, in part,

> ... I am prepared to say that [the earlier case] was wrongly decided, or, in any event that [it] would not be decided now as it was decided then. Combining paid work with motherhood and accommodating the childbearing needs of working women are ever-increasing imperatives. That those who bear children and benefit society as a whole thereby should not be economically or socially disadvantaged seems to bespeak the obvious. It is only women who bear children; no man can become pregnant ... it is unfair to impose all of the costs of pregnancy upon one half of the population. It is difficult to conceive that distinctions or discriminations based upon pregnancy could ever be regarded as other than discrimination based upon sex, or that restrictive statutory conditions applicable only to pregnant women did not discriminate against them as women ... Distinctions based on pregnancy can be none other than distinctions based on sex ...[21]

3. ABSENCE OF PROPERTY RIGHT PROTECTION

The *Charter* does not contain provisions protecting property rights of individuals.
S. 7 reads:

---

[20] *Brooks v. Canada Safeway*, [1989] 1 S.C.R. 1219, 59 D.L.R. (4th) 321. *Brooks* is not a *Charter* case; it is concerned with the application of a human rights statute. Nonetheless, its finding that discrimination on the basis of pregnancy is sex discrimination is equivalent in effect to a finding that discrimination on the basis of pregnancy is a violation of s. 15(1) of the *Charter*.

[21] *Id.* at 1243-44.

> Everyone has the right to life, liberty and security of the person and the right not to be deprived thereof except in accordance with the principles of fundamental justice.

S. 7 of the Canadian *Charter* corresponds to the Vth and XIVth Amendments of the American *Bill of Rights*, colloquially known as the Due Process Clause. Unlike its American counterpart, the Canadian Due Process Clause contains no explicit reference to property. The Supreme Court has held that this intentional choice of wording requires the drawing of an inference that property rights do not fall within the parameters of s. 7.[22]

4. S. 1

S. 1 of the *Charter* reads:

> The *Canadian Charter of Rights and Freedoms* guarantees the rights and freedoms set out in it subject only to such reasonable limits prescribed by law as can be demonstrably justified in a free and democratic society.

It may be somewhat trite to observe that rights may and often do, conflict with one another. The tension between individual and collective rights is inherent in any developed society. S. 1 attempts to provide a balance to resolve that tension. Because we are concerned with constitutional and *legal* rights, it falls to the courts to find the appropriate balance.[23]

---

[22] *Irwin Toy Ltd. v. Quebec (A.G.)*, [1989] 1 S.C.R. 927 at 1003.

[23] The judicial role in attempting to resolve this tension was recognized in the very first *Charter* decision, *Law Society of Upper Canada v. Skapinker*, [1984] 1 S.C.R. 357 at 367:

> With the *Constitution Act, 1982* comes a new dimension, a new yardstick of reconciliation between the individual and the

S. 1 of the *Charter* not only establishes criteria to facilitate the reconciliation of conflicting rights; it is also a means of recognizing that no one right is absolute and that all rights are subject to certain limitations. The s. provides a test to determine whether limits placed on rights are consistent with the values which must be protected in order to preserve a free and democratic society. The content of this test will be discussed below in the section on judicial interpretation. The s. 1 inquiry is to be conducted "in light of a commitment to uphold the rights and freedoms set out in the other sections of the *Charter*."[24]

Early in the interpretation of the *Charter*, the Supreme Court discussed the meaning of the words "free and democratic" contained in s. 1 which provide the basis for the judicial test developed by the Court:

> The Court must be guided by the values and principles essential to a free and democratic society which I believe embody, to name but a few, respect for the inherent dignity of the human person, commitment to social justice and equality, accommodation of a wide variety of beliefs, respect for cultural and group identity, and faith in social and political institutions which enhance the participation of individuals and groups in society.[25]

The advantage of this unique provision is that it allows for an expansive interpretation of the rights enumerated in the *Charter*, without requiring the substantial internal limitations of those rights which have been judicially created in countries whose constitutions

---

> community and their respective rights, a dimension which, like the balance of the Constitution, remains to be interpreted and applied by the court.

[24] *Singh v. Minister of Employment and Immigration*, [1985] 1 S.C.R. 177 at 218, Wilson J.

[25] *R. v. Oakes*, [1986] 1 S.C.R. 103 at 136, Dickson J.

do not contain such a provision.[26]

5. S. 33 — THE "NOTWITHSTANDING CLAUSE"

A discussion of the unique features of the Canadian *Charter* would be incomplete without making reference to s. 33, otherwise known as the "notwithstanding clause". The section reads, in part:

> 33. (1) Parliament or the legislature of a province may expressly declare in an Act of Parliament or of the legislature, as the case may be, that the Act or a provision thereof shall operate notwithstanding a provision included in s. 2 or ss. 7 to 15 of this *Charter*.

In effect, s. 33 allows Parliament or a provincial legislature to restrict the applicability of certain sections of the *Charter*, specifically those sections dealing with such fundamental freedoms as expression, religion, the press, peaceful assembly and association, or certain legal rights associated with due process and equal protection. The existence of s. 33 is a vivid reminder of Canada's tradition of parliamentary supremacy, that sovereignty resides not in the people, but in Parliament and the provincial legislatures and that parliamentary supremacy is not yet a matter of pure historical interest. S. 33 has been described as the "quintessential Canadian compromise".[27]

These then are the main unique Canadian provisions. There

---

[26] For example, there is no corresponding section in the American *Bill of Rights*. The balancing of conflicting rights in the American context has been accomplished by the judiciary without explicit support from within the four corners of the Constitution itself.

[27] The academic debate surrounding the merits of s.33 has been vigourous. See, for example, L. Weinrib, "Learning to Live With the Override" (1990) 35 McGill L.J. 541; J.D. Whyte, "On Not Standing For Notwithstanding" (1990) 28 Alta. L. Rev. 324; P. Russell, "Standing Up for Notwithstanding" (1991) 29 Alta. L. Rev. 293.

are two other provisions that are also uniquely Canadian: ss. 24 and 52 which deal with constitutional remedies which I will discuss below. Before proceeding to the discussion of judicial interpretation of the *Charter*, the preliminary question of its application should be addressed.

Applicability of the Charter

The question of to whom the *Charter* applies is governed by s. 32(1) which states, in part:

32(1) This *Charter* applies
- (a) to the Parliament and government of Canada in respect of all matters within the authority of Parliament . . .
- (b) to the legislature and government of each province in respect of all matters within the authority of the legislature of each province.

In *R.W.D.S.U. v. Dolphin Delivery*, the Supreme Court held that under s. 32(1), the *Charter* does not apply to private litigation which has no connection with government. McIntyre J. stated that

> the *Charter*, like most written constitutions, was set up to regulate the relationship between the individual and the Government. It was intended to restrain government action and to protect the individual. It was not intended in the absence of some governmental action to be applied in private litigation.[28]

The *Charter* will therefore apply to the common law only when the common law provides the basis for a governmental action which

---

[28] [1986] 2 S.C.R. 573 at 593.

allegedly infringes a guaranteed right or freedom.[29] The Court held in *Dolphin Delivery* that the *Charter* could not be invoked by a private party seeking an injunction to restrain secondary picketing using the common law tort of inducing breach of contract.[30]

In a recent case, a majority of the Court held that statutorily created and publicly funded universities are not subject to the *Charter*. The fact that the universities perform a public service was considered insufficient to bring them within the ambit of the Charter.[31]

The Court has recently held, however, that when interpreting the common law, judges can and should make incremental changes so that the common law develops in accordance with the values enshrined in the Charter.[32] Thus a rule making an accused's spouse an incompetent witness for the prosecution was held not to apply to the case of irreconcilably separated spouses in light of the *Charter* commitment to sexual equality.[33]

Cabinet decisions and action by the executive branch of government fall under s. 32(1)(a) and are therefore subject to the *Charter*.[34] Unlike the American position, in Canada there is as yet

---

[29] *Ibid.*

[30] *Ibid.*

[31] *McKinney v. University of Guelph*, [1990] 3 S.C.R. 229 at 265-66. The fact that some university decisions may be subject to judicial review was also considered insufficient to bring universities under Charter scrutiny. *Id.* at 268.

[32] *R. v. Salituro*, [1991] 3 S.C.R. 654 at 675. Such changes should only be made where to do so would not upset "the proper balance between judicial and legislative action."

[33] *Ibid.*

[34] *Operation Dismantle v. R.*, [1985] 1 S.C.R. 441 at 455, Dickson J.

no express political questions doctrine.[35] In *Operation Dismantle*, the Supreme Court held that the Executive's decision to allow testing of the Cruise Missile in Canada was a decision reviewable under s. 7 of the *Charter*.[36] Wilson, J., in rejecting the appropriateness of the political questions doctrine in the Canadian context, was of the view that as long as the judiciary did not "second guess" the executive as to the wisdom of the policy, and confined itself solely to the issue of whether a particular act violates the rights of citizens, the courts were fulfilling their constitutional duties under the *Charter*.[37] Thus in Canada, any governmental action or legislative provision is potentially reviewable.

Judicial Interpretation

1. IN GENERAL

At the early stages of *Charter* interpretation, then Chief Justice Dickson asserted the purposive nature of the *Charter*. He

---

[35] In the United States, American courts have always held that certain types of issues are non-justiciable. In other words, some issues are of such a political nature that a court by its very institutional nature is incapable of deciding them. Political issues most often cited as being problematic for the courts are questions concerning foreign policy or those that touch on the very nature of the constitutional infra-structure. It should be noted however, that the existence of the political questions doctrine has not stopped the American courts from expressing their opinion on some very "political" issues. For example, *Marbury* v. *Madison*, 5 U.S. (1 Cranch) 137 (1803) deals with the limits of executive authority as does the more recent case of *United States* v. *Nixon*, 418 U.S. 683 (1974). In a similar fashion, the Supreme Court addressed the very sensitive political question of racial segregation in *Brown* v. *Board of Education of Topeka*, 347 U.S. 483 (1954).

[36] *Operation Dismantle*, *supra*, note 34 at 455.

[37] *Id.* at 467-474. Dickson J. (for the majority) expressed his agreement with the analysis of Wilson J. regarding justiciability. *Id.* at 459. See also, *Canada v. Schmidt*, [1987] 1 S.C.R. 500 at 524, La Forest J.

stated that the *Charter*'s purpose is to guarantee and to protect, within the limits of reason, the enjoyment of the rights and freedoms it enshrines . . . [and] to constrain governmental action inconsistent with those rights and freedoms.[38] The *Charter* analysis is broken up into two distinct stages. The first stage concerns the nature of the right and the existence of a violation or infringement of that right, while the analysis in the second stage focuses upon the reasonableness of the limitation of the right under s. 1.[39] This division allows the "different concerns and factors which are, or ought to be, relevant to the two stages of the case [to be] kept separate and distinct."[40]

In order to pursue a purposive approach to the *Charter*, Chief Justice Dickson noted that the necessary first step in the first stage of the process of judicial interpretation is to determine the purpose of the right of which the applicant is alleging infringement. In a later case, the Chief Justice explained that this analysis is to be performed

> by reference to the character and the larger objects of the *Charter* itself, to the language chosen to articulate the specific right or freedom, to the historical origins of the concepts enshrined, and where applicable, to the meaning and purpose of the other specific rights and freedoms with which it is associated within the text of the *Charter*.[41]

The final point in this enumeration of appropriate touchstones

---

38 *Hunter v. Southam Inc.*, [1984] 2 S.C.R. 145 at 156.

39 *Oakes*, *supra*, note 25 at 134.

40 W.F. Pentney, "Interpreting the *Charter*: General Principles" in G.A. Beaudoin & E. Ratushny, eds, *The Canadian Charter of Rights and Freedoms*, 2d ed. (Toronto: Carswell, 1989) 21 at 29.

41 *R. v. Big M Drug Mart, Ltd.*, [1985] 1 S.C.R. 295 at 344.

of analysis requires some elaboration. The Court has emphasized the necessity of viewing the *Charter* as a whole in order to respect its purposive nature.[42] In *Reference Re S. 94(2) of the Motor Vehicles Act (B.C.)*, Lamer J., as he then was, held that ss. 8-14 of the *Charter* "address specific deprivations of the 'right' to life, liberty and security of the person in breach of the principles of fundamental justice" contained in s. 7 and "are designed to protect, in a specific manner and setting" the broad right set out in s. 7.[43] For that reason, Lamer J. concluded that ss. 8-14 provide both an indication that s. 7 must be expansively interpreted, and a guide to the meaning of "principles of fundamental justice."[44]

After the purpose of the right or freedom has been ascertained, the court will then proceed to examine whether the activity or conduct of the applicant falls within the scope of the purposively defined right or freedom. In some cases this determination will be relatively straightforward. For example, in a criminal case, the guarantees found in ss. 8-14 of the *Charter* will always be applicable.[45] However, in cases involving the civil rights found in s. 2 of the *Charter*,[46] whether the applicant's

---

[42] *Lyons v. R.*, [1987] 2 S.C.R. 309.

[43] [1985] 2 S.C.R. 486 at 503.

[44] *Id.* at 502-503. For other examples of this kind of interpretive technique, see also *R. v. Therens*, [1985] 1 S.C.R. 613; *Société des Acadiens du Nouveau-Brunswick Inc. v. Assn. of Parents for Fairness in Education, Grand Falls Dist. 50 Branch*, [1986] 1 S.C.R. 549.

[45] These guarantees include the right to be secure against unreasonable search or seizure; the right not to be arbitrarily detained or imprisoned; the right upon arrest or detention to be informed of the reasons therefor, to retain and instruct counsel; and the right to be tried within a reasonable time and to be presumed innocent until proven guilty.

[46] These guarantees include freedom of religion and conscience; freedom of thought, belief, opinion and expression; freedom of assembly; and freedom of association.

activities are worthy of *Charter* protection will be more difficult to determine. For instance, the Supreme Court has held that the right to strike is not an incident of the freedom of association guaranteed by s. 2(d).[47]

In order to understand better the process of articulating the scope of a *Charter* right, I will examine in more detail the Supreme Court's interpretation of the scope of freedom of expression guaranteed under s. 2(b) of the *Charter*. In *Irwin Toy*, the Court held that any expression designed to convey meaning is protected under s. 2(b), provided its form is an acceptable one. That is, violence as a form of expression would not be protected under the *Charter*.[48] These conclusions were based on a discussion of the rationales underlying constitutional guarantees of free expression enumerated by Professor R.J. Sharpe and adopted by the Court in the earlier case of *Ford v. A.G. Quebec*:

> The first is that freedom of expression is essential to intelligent and democratic self-government . . . The second theory is that freedom of expression protects an open exchange of views, thereby creating a competitive marketplace of ideas which will enhance the search for truth . . . The third values expression for its own sake. On this view, expression is seen as an aspect of individual autonomy. Expression is to be protected because it is essential to personal growth and self-

---

[47] This determination was made on the grounds that "the *Charter* does not give, nor was it ever intended to give, constitutional protection to all the acts of an individual which are essential to his or her personal goals or objectives." *Reference Re Alberta Public Service Employee Relations Act*, *supra*, note 7; *Government of Saskatchewan v. R.W.D.S.U.* (1987), 38 D.L.R. (4th) 277; *Public Service Alliance of Canada v. R.* (1987), 38 D.L.R. (4th) 249.

[48] *Irwin Toy*, *supra*, note 22 at 968-71.

realization.[49]

Because commercial expression attempts to convey a meaning and possesses expressive content it was held to fall within the scope of s. 2(b).[50] A similar conclusion was reached with respect to pornographic materials which were held to be covered by s. 2(b) in *R. v. Butler*, where the Court noted that while the subject matter of such materials is physical, they possess expressive content and attempt to convey meaning.[51]

In two recent cases involving criminal prohibitions against hate literature and spreading false news, the Court has held that under the *Irwin Toy* test, all non-violent expressive communications are protected by s. 2(b), irrespective of their content.[52] Although hate propaganda is "invidious and obnoxious", it remains constitutionally protected, and attempts to regulate or prohibit it must be justified under s. 1.[53] The need to protect unpopular statements which the majority considers false or wrong was emphasized in the hate propaganda cases,[54] and *Butler*, dealing with the criminal regulation of pornography.[55]

Once the scope of the right or freedom at issue has been ascertained, the next step to be undertaken is the determination of whether there is a conflict between the governmental action which

---

[49] R.J. Sharpe, "Commercial Expression and the *Charter*" (1987) 37 U. of T. L.J. 229 at 232, cited in *Ford v. A.G. Quebec*, [1988] 2 S.C.R. 712 at 765.

[50] *Ford*, *id.* at 767; and *Irwin Toy*, *supra*, note 22 at 971.

[51] [1992] 1 S.C.R. 452 at 487, Sopinka J.

[52] *Keegstra*, *supra*, note 8, 99 at 730; *Zundel*, *supra*, note 10.

[53] *Keegstra*, *id.* at 730.

[54] *Keegstra*, *id.* at 828, McLachlin J; *Zundel*, *supra*, note 10.

[55] *Butler*, *supra*, note 51 at 488.

is at issue and the right or freedom. In *R. v. Big M Drug Mart Ltd.*, the Supreme Court concluded that both the purpose and the effects of governmental action are to be considered when assessing whether that action interferes with a *Charter* right or freedom. If the governmental purpose is found to be unconstitutional, then there is no need to consider the effects until the s. 1 inquiry is undertaken. If however the governmental purpose passes constitutional muster, unconstitutional effects will also constitute an infringement of a *Charter* right or freedom.[56]

Cases involving legislative retail selling restrictions on Sundays provide illustrations of infringements of rights based on a purpose and effects analysis. In *Big M Drug Mart*, the Supreme Court found that a federal statute purporting to compel observance of the Christian Sabbath violated the *Charter* provision guaranteeing freedom of religion in s. 2(a).[57] In a later case, the Court decided that a similar provincial statute infringed s. 2(a). Although the statute had a secular purpose, namely to provide a uniform day of rest for retail workers and their families, nevertheless, the effects of the statute abridged the religious freedom of certain retail workers.[58]

It must be noted that later cases have refined this broad examination of interference with *Charter* rights. In *R. v. Jones*, the Supreme Court held that governmental action whose effect on the *Charter* right at issue is "trivial or insubstantial" does not constitute a breach of the *Charter*. That is, not every legislative or governmental action which affects an individual's *Charter* rights will offend the *Charter*.[59]

---

[56] *Supra*, note 41 at 331-334, Dickson J.

[57] *Ibid.*

[58] *Edwards Books & Art Ltd. v. R.*, [1986] 2 S.C.R. 713.

[59] [1986] 2 S.C.R. 284 at 313-314, La Forest J.

2. SECTION ONE

Once the existence of a rights infringement has been determined, the focus shifts to the s. 1 inquiry discussed briefly above. The Supreme Court has enunciated a bipartite test to be used when undertaking a s. 1 analysis:

> Two requirements must be satisfied to establish that a limit is reasonable and demonstrably justified in a free and democratic society. First, the legislative objective which the limitation is designed to promote must be of sufficient importance to warrant overriding a constitutional right. It must bear on a pressing and substantial concern." Secondly, the means chosen to attain those objectives must be proportional or appropriate to the ends. The proportionality requirement, in turn, normally has three aspects: the limiting measures must be carefully designed, or rationally connected, to the objective; they must impair the right as little as possible; and their effects must not so severely trench on individual or group rights that the legislative objective, albeit important, is, nevertheless, outweighed by the abridgement of rights.[60]

Although this test is generally applied to all cases in which a rights infringement has been found, different levels of scrutiny have been suggested by the Supreme Court of Canada depending on the circumstances of the case. For instance, in *Ford v. A.G. Quebec*, the Court discussed the "distinction between the negation of a right or freedom and a limit on it."[61] While the negation of

---

[60] *Edwards Books*, *supra*, note 58 at 768, Dickson C.J., expanding on the test known as the *Oakes* test which was originally set out in *Oakes*, *supra*, note 25 at 135-140.

[61] *Supra*, note 49 at 772.

a right or freedom does not necessarily require that such an infringement not be upheld under s. 1, "the distinction between a limit that permits no exercise of a guaranteed right and one that permits a qualified exercise of it may be relevant to the test of proportionality under s. 1."[62] In *Ford*, the Court held that a complete prohibition on the use of languages other than French on commercial signs could not meet the requirements of the proportionality test, particularly the rational connection and minimal impairment branches.[63] In contrast, in a subsequent commercial expression case, the Court upheld substantial content-based restrictions (as opposed to a total ban) on advertising directed at children.[64] A further example of differing levels of scrutiny will be discussed below in the context of the minimal impairment branch of the *Oakes* proportionality test.

The Court has made it clear that the evidentiary burden under s. 1 lies with the party seeking to justify the limitation of a *Charter* right or freedom. "[W]here the basis for its legislation is not obvious, the government must bring forward cogent and persuasive evidence demonstrating that the provisions in issue are justified having regard to the constituent elements of a s. 1 inquiry."[65]

(a) Pressing and Substantial Concern

The first component of the *Oakes* test requires that the governmental objective "relate to concerns which are pressing and substantial in a free and democratic society."[66] Only objectives

---

[62] *Id.* at 773.

[63] *Id.* at 779-80.

[64] *Irwin Toy*, *supra*, note 22.

[65] *Id.* at 984.

[66] *Oakes*, *supra*, note 25 at 138-39.

which are within the powers of the appropriate level of government will be considered under this section of the test. Thus the federal government could not justify a ban on Sunday retail openings on the grounds that the statutory objective was a secular one relating to labour regulation because such labour law comes under provincial authority.[67] While almost all governmentally proposed objectives have passed constitutional muster under this portion of the test, in *Singh v. Minister of Employment and Immigration*, the three judges of the six member panel who dealt with the *Charter* expressed doubts that considerations such as cost or administrative convenience could be considered "pressing and substantial" within the meaning of the first part of the *Oakes* test.[68]

(b) Proportionality Test

(i) Rational Connection

The standard that will be required by the courts when dealing with regulatory legislation was discussed by Dickson C.J. in the second Sunday retail restrictions case noted above, *Edwards Books*:

> in regulating industry or business it is open to the legislature to restrict its legislative reforms to sectors in which there appear to be particularly urgent concerns or to constituencies that seem especially needy. . . . Legislative choices regarding alternative forms of business regulation do not generally impinge on the values and provisions of the *Charter*, and the resultant legislation need not be tuned with great precision in order to withstand judicial scrutiny. Simplicity and administrative convenience are legitimate concerns for

---

[67] *Big M Drug Mart*, *supra*, note 41.

[68] *Supra*, note 24.

> the drafters of such legislation.[69]

Statutory exemptions which are included for political purposes or administrative ease will not necessarily void a rational connection with the government's legislative objective, although on the surface they might appear to undermine the importance of that objective.[70]

In *Downey v. R.*, the Court dealt with the constitutionality of *Criminal Code* provisions regarding the offence of living on the avails of prostitution. Under s. 195(2) of the *Code*, "[e]vidence that a person lives with or is habitually in the company of prostitutes . . . is, in the absence of evidence to the contrary, proof that the person lives on the avails of prostitution." The Court held that this presumption infringes the presumption of innocence under s. 11(d) of the *Charter*, since it would allow for conviction despite the existence of a reasonable doubt in the mind of the trier of fact as to the guilt of the accused.[71] Under the rational connection analysis the majority held that the inference presumed by Parliament was not unreasonable, and upheld the validity of the provisions.[72]

In dissent, McLachlin J., with myself concurring, asserted the need for a presumption to be both externally and internally rational, in order to pass the rational connection test. External rationality requires a rational connection to the legislative purpose, while internal rationality requires a rational connection between the substituted and presumed facts. McLachlin J. noted that following the *Oakes* decision, a very high degree of internal rationality between the substituted and presumed facts would be required.

---

[69] *Edwards Books*, *supra*, note 58 at 772.

[70] See, for example, *ibid.*

[71] [1992] 2 S.C.R. 10; 90 D.L.R. (4th) 449.

[72] *Id.* at 28.

Having reviewed possible tests, McLachlin J. concluded that in order to pass rational connection scrutiny, "at a minimum, proof of the substituted fact must make it *likely* that the presumed fact is true."[73] Finally, McLachlin J. held that this test was not met with respect to the statutory presumption at issue because the presumption was both irrational and unfair.

(ii) Minimal Impairment

As briefly noted above, the application of the minimal impairment test is characterized by varying levels of scrutiny depending on the nature of the competing interests. For instance, where the interests of competing groups are involved, judicial scrutiny will be less stringent than where the state and the individual are the only parties significantly affected.[74] This particular distinction will be discussed further below, in the concluding section of my commentary.

The Supreme Court has also recognized that statutory regulation often requires the drawing of precise lines which constitute a proxy for a more individualized approach to societal regulation. For instance, in the mandatory retirement context, the cut-off age of 65 is a proxy for "the decline in intellectual ability" in older persons.[75] In *Edwards Books*, the Court held that

> [a] "reasonable limit" is one which, having regard to the principles enunciated in *Oakes*, it was reasonable for the legislature to impose. The courts are not called upon to substitute judicial opinions for legislative ones as to the place at which to draw a precise line.[76]

---

[73] *Id.* at 8, McLachlin J.

[74] *Irwin Toy, supra*, note 22 at 993.

[75] *McKinney, supra*, note 31 at 289.

[76] *Edwards Books, supra*, note 58 at 781-82.

A further distinction with respect to the appropriate level of minimal impairment scrutiny was made in *Swain v. R.*. In that case the Court dealt *inter alia* with a challenge to the constitutionality of the common law rule allowing the Crown to raise evidence of insanity despite the contrary wishes of the accused. The Court held that different considerations should be taken into account under the *Oakes* framework when judge-made law is the subject of a *Charter* challenge. Judicial deference will be inappropriate in cases involving judicially created rules, and the *Oakes* test will be strictly applied.[77]

(iii) Proportionality Between Effects and Objective

In *Oakes*, Chief Justice Dickson stated that "[t]he more severe the deleterious effects of a measure, the more important the objective must be if the measure is to be reasonable and demonstrably justified in a free and democratic society."[78] This assessment is often made on the basis of analysis that has already been performed under other elements of the s. 1 test or the determination of the existence of a rights infringement. The importance of the objective will have generally been determined under the "pressing and substantial" governmental objective portion of *Oakes*. The effects of the infringement are considered

---

[77] [1991] 1 S.C.R. 933 at 983. The Court summarized the current position regarding the application of s.1 to statutory provisions as follows:

> this Court has been cognizant of the fact that such provisions are enacted by an elected body which must respond to the competing interests of different groups in society and which must always consider the polycentric aspects of any given course of action. For this reason, this Court has indicated that Parliament need not always choose the absolutely least intrusive means to attain its objectives, but must come within a range of means which impair *Charter* rights as little as is reasonably possible.

Ibid.

[78] *Supra*, note 25 at 140.

both in the context of the existence of an infringement, and in the prior two elements of the proportionality test. For this reason, the analysis under the third element of the proportionality test often consists of a resumé of previous analysis on the basis of which a decision is made regarding the existence of proportionality between the effects and the objective.[79]

Remedies for Charter Infringements

1. INTRODUCTION

Once the existence of an *Charter* violation which cannot be justified by s. 1 has been ascertained, the judicial focus shifts to a determination of the appropriate remedy. The Canadian *Charter* contains explicit remedial provisions. The power to strike down laws inconsistent with the *Charter* comes from a provision of the *Constitution Act, 1982* (which is not in fact part of the *Charter).* S. 52 of the *Constitution Act, 1982* specifies that:

The Constitution of Canada is the supreme law of Canada, and any law that is inconsistent with the provisions of the Constitution is, to the extent of the inconsistency, of no force or effect.

In addition there are remedial powers in the *Charter* itself. The remedial provisions are found in ss. 24(1) and 24(2). S. 24(1) is the general remedial provision which gives a court the power to order a remedy which is "appropriate and just in the circumstances." S. 24(2) is a specific remedial provision which provides for the exclusion of evidence obtained in contravention of the *Charter* in some circumstances.

---

[79] See, for example, *McKinney*, *supra*, note 31 at 289; *Irwin Toy*, *supra*, note 22 at 1000; *Edwards Books*, *supra*, note 58 at 783.

2. S. 52(1): DECLARATIONS OF INVALIDITY

S. 52(1) applies to legislation which has been found to be unconstitutional.[80] There are five different remedies which are available under s. 52(1): striking down the legislation; severing the offending provision; striking down or severance coupled with a temporary suspension of the declaration of invalidity; reading down the offending provision; and, reading in an appropriate provision.[81]

In *Schachter*, the Court determined that a three part analysis must be undertaken when a statute has been held to be unconstitutional. First, the extent of the inconsistency in the legislation with the *Charter* guarantees must be defined. This will depend on the portion of the *Oakes* test which the legislation failed. For instance, if the governmental objective was not sufficiently pressing and substantial, then the entire statute will be inconsistent with the *Charter*. At the other end of the spectrum will be cases where the legislation failed part of the proportionality test, in which case the extent of the inconsistency will generally be limited to some portion of the statute.[82]

In the second part of the *Schachter* analysis, the court must determine whether the inconsistency can be dealt with by severing it from the legislation, or reading in an extension to the offending provision(s) in order that it comply with the strictures of the *Charter*. These options will only be available "in the clearest of cases" where the following three conditions are met:

A. the legislative objective is obvious, or it is revealed through the evidence offered pursuant to the failed s. 1 argument, and

---

80 *Schachter v. Canada*, [1992] 2 S.C.R. 679; 93 D.L.R. (4th) 1, 27.

81 *Ibid.*

82 *Id.* at 40-41.

severance or reading in would further that objective, or constitute a lesser interference with that objective than would striking down;

B. the choice of means used by the legislature to further that objective is not so unequivocal that severance/reading in would constitute an unacceptable intrusion in to the legislative domain; and,

C. severance or reading in would not involve an intrusion into legislative budgetary decisions so substantial as to change the nature of the legislative scheme in question.[83]

The third part of the *Schachter* framework requires that the court decide whether the declaration of invalidity under s. 52(1) should be temporarily suspended in order to give the legislature time to rectify the inconsistency between the statute and the *Charter*. If striking down the legislation would "pose a danger to the public" or "threaten the rule of law" then temporary suspension of the declaration of invalidity will be considered appropriate. In addition, where the legislation provides a benefit to a deserving group but the group has been unconstitutionally limited, temporary suspension will be appropriate since striking down the law will not benefit those individuals who have been unconstitutionally excluded from its application, and will deprive those to whom the law does apply of the benefit of the law.[84]

3. S. 24(2): THE EXCLUSION OF EVIDENCE

Under s. 24(2) of the *Charter*, the inquiry regarding the admissibility of evidence obtained following a *Charter* violation is

---

[83] *Id.* at 41.

[84] *Id.* at 42.

divided into two distinct phases, the second of which is unique to Canada. First, a violation of a constitutional right must be established. Second, the court must ask whether the evidence should be excluded on the grounds that it tends to bring the administration of justice into disrepute? Evidence will be admitted even if there is a violation of a constitutional right if its admission would not bring the administration of justice into disrepute.

S. 24(2) reads as follows:

> Where ... a court concludes that evidence was obtained in a manner that infringed or denied any rights or freedoms guaranteed by this Charter, the evidence shall be excluded if it is established that, having regard to all the circumstances, the admission of it in the proceedings would bring the administration of justice into disrepute.

The determination of whether or not evidence should be excluded is a flexible one. In determining whether to exclude the evidence, Canadian courts look to the effect of the admission of the evidence on the fairness of the trial and to the seriousness of the violation of the *Charter* right. If these considerations would lead to the conclusion that the evidence should be excluded, the court must then consider whether the effect of *the exclusion* would tend to bring the administration of justice into disrepute.[85]

The advantage of such a two-step approach to the

---

[85] These three sets of factors were first set out in *R. v. Collins*, [1987] 1 S.C.R. 265, 33 C.C.C. (3d) 1. For academic commentary on this decision and s.24(2), see A.W. Bryant, M. Gold, H.M. Stevenson, D. Northrup, "Public Attitudes Toward the Exclusion of Evidence: Section 24(2) of the Canadian Charter of Rights and Freedoms" (1990) 69 Can. Bar Rev. 1; D.G. Casswell, "Through the Admissibility of Evidence Maze: An Attempt at a Purposive Structuring" (1991) 29 Alta. L. Rev. 584; R.J. Delisle, "*Collins*: An Unjustified Distinction" (1987) 56 C.R. (3d) 216.

admissibility of the evidence is that it is open to a court to determine that a *Charter* right has been violated but nonetheless to admit the evidence obtained as a result of the violation. To give an example of the process, in one case a woman was strip searched while passing through customs, and five pounds of hashish oil were found strapped around her abdomen in plastic bags. The Supreme Court of Canada found that because the accused had not been informed of her right to retain and instruct counsel prior to the search, her right to counsel under the *Charter* had been violated. The Court also found that the search had been unreasonable, violating the accused's *Charter* right to be secure against unreasonable search and seizure. Nonetheless, the Court held that the evidence of the hashish oil was admissible under s. 24(2) of the *Charter*. The Court emphasized that the evidence was real evidence existing irrespective of the *Charter* violations, and that the customs officers had acted in good faith, and had treated the accused courteously.[86]

4. S. 24(1): THE GENERAL REMEDIAL PROVISION

The more general remedial provision is contained in s. 24(1) which reads as follows:

> Anyone whose rights or freedoms, as guaranteed by [the] Charter, have been infringed or denied may apply to a court of competent jurisdiction to obtain such remedy as the court considers appropriate and just in the circumstances.

In *Schachter*, the Court concluded that where a law has been found to be unconstitutional, and s. 52(1) is therefore engaged, s. 24(1) will generally be of no application.[87] It will be available in cases

---

[86] *R. v. Simmons*, [1988] 2 S.C.R. 495.

[87] *Supra*, note 80 at 44.

where unconstitutional governmental action has been taken against an individual under a law which is itself constitutional.[88] Remedies which have been granted under this section include: the return of property seized in violation of s. 8 of the *Charter*;[89] substantial reduction in sentence when the accused's right to be protected from arbitrary detention under s. 9 had been infringed;[90] and a declaration of immediate eligibility for parole when the accused's rights under s. 7 had been infringed.[91]

Conclusion: The Fundamental Tension Between Collective Interests and Individual Rights

As I discussed at the beginning of this commentary, one of the most distinctive aspects of the *Charter* is its emphasis on the rights of minorities and groups. The explicit protection of group rights and interests discussed above has been reflected in the Supreme Court jurisprudence regarding the interpretation of the various individual rights enshrined in the *Charter*. The principles articulated by the Court regarding the appropriate methodology to be used when assessing *Charter* cases have been used to promote the values and ideas sought to be protected by constitutional provisions such as the s. 28 guarantee of gender equality, the s. 27 protection of our multicultural heritage, and the s. 15 guarantee of equality to disadvantaged groups.

The tension between the rights or interests of an individual and those of a group has appeared many times in cases brought before the Supreme Court of Canada since the entrenchment of the

---

[88] *Ibid.*

[89] *Lagiorgia v. R.*, [1987] 3 F.C. 28 (C.A.).

[90] *R. v. Charles* (1987), 36 C.C.C. (3d) 286 (Sask. C.A.).

[91] *R. v. Gamble*, [1988] 2 S.C.R. 595.

Charter. This tension has been most visible in three different aspects of *Charter* rights adjudication: defining the scope of a given right; assessing whether the objective of an impugned law is pressing and substantial; and determining whether the impugned law impairs the right or freedom at issue as little as possible. I should like to discuss these three aspects briefly.

I will cite two examples of the impact that group interests have had in determining the scope of a right guaranteed to individuals by the *Charter*. In *Reference Re Provincial Electoral Boundaries (Sask.)*, the Court was faced with the question of whether variance in the size of voter populations in some Saskatchewan constituencies infringed the right to vote enshrined in s. 3 of the *Charter*.[92] The Court examined the extent to which the right to vote permits deviation from the "one person - one vote" rule. McLachlin J., writing for the majority, held that the purpose of the right to vote is not absolute equality of voting power, but rather the right to "effective representation." Although relative parity of voting power is required, other factors must also be taken into consideration such as "geography, community history, community interests and minority representation [in order] to ensure that our legislative assemblies effectively represent the diversity of our social mosaic."[93] McLachlin J. concluded that our "free and democratic society" is best served by this definition of the right to vote:

> The concerns which Dickson C.J. in *Oakes* associated with a free and democratic society--respect for the inherent dignity of the human person, commitment to social justice and equality, respect for cultural and group identity, and faith in social and political institutions which enhance the participation of individuals in society--are better met by an electoral system that focuses on

---

92 [1991] 2 S.C.R. 158.

93 *Id.* at 184.

> effective representation than by one that focuses on mathematical parity. Respect for individual dignity and social equality mandate that citizen's votes not be unduly debased or diluted. But the need to recognize cultural and group identity and to enhance the participation of individuals in the electoral process and society requires that other concerns also be accommodated.[94]

A different kind of group interest was recognized in the recent cases involving the right to be tried within a reasonable time guaranteed by s. 11(b) of the *Charter*.[95] In addition to the primary purpose of this right (to protect the individual rights of the accused to security of the person, liberty, and a fair trial), the Court has also identified a secondary purpose, namely, a societal interest in the fair administration of justice and in law enforcement. It is this latter collective interest which will be adverse to the interests of the accused. That is, society as a whole has an interest "in ensuring that those who transgress the law are brought to trial and dealt with according to the law."[96] While the interests of the accused are the primary focus of s. 11(b), the Court has recognized that the interest of society in law enforcement also has a role to play in the s. 11(b) analysis.[97] In the context of s. 1 jurisprudence, group interests have been especially taken into account in regard to the question of whether the impugned law concerns a pressing and substantial objective. The decisions of the Court in the area of the criminal regulation of hate propaganda are informative in this regard. The interest sought to be protected by hate propaganda laws has been ably articulated by Professor Claire Beckton:

---

[94] *Id.* at 188.

[95] *R. v. Morin*, [1992] 1 S.C.R. 771 at 786.

[96] *R. v. Askov*, [1990] 2 S.C.R. 1199 at 1219-20.

[97] *Morin, supra*, note 95 at 786; *R. v. Conway*, [1989] 1 S.C.R. 1659.

> One of the . . . fundamental human values in our society is equality and the right to preservation of our dignity and self-worth, a value that is also recognized in [s. 15 of] the *Charter*. Dignity and self-worth are important not only to individuals but as individuals identified as members of a particular group. Often times it is the individual's group identity which prompts him or her to take action or to be outspoken on an issue. Many persons, in fact, find that identification with a group helps to define their own sense of self. It is this interest that is allegedly protected by the hate propaganda laws.[98]

In *R. v. Keegstra*, the constitutionality of criminal prohibitions against the wilful promotion of hatred were at issue.[99] The provisions were challenged on the grounds that they infringed freedom of expression and the presumption of innocence. The Court determined that the sections did infringe ss. 2(b) and 11(d) of the Charter, but that both infringements were saved under s. 1. Dickson C.J. emphasized the fact that the balancing of the societal interests against the expression should take place within the s. 1 analysis.

In the context of s. 1, the former Chief Justice asserted that the special role played by equality and multiculturalism in the Charter indicated that the American position "that the suppression of hate propaganda is incompatible with the guarantee of free expression" should not be adopted in Canada.[100] Specifically, Dickson C.J. held that the prevention of harm to those persons and groups towards whom hate propaganda is directed was a pressing

---

98 C. Beckton, "Freedom of Expression - Individual vs Collective Rights" (1987) Cambridge Lectures 31 at 35.

99 [1990] 3 S.C.R. 697.

100 *Id.* at 743.

and substantial objective under the test propounded in *Oakes, supra*. The Court examined the harm suffered, and the discord which occurs between different groups in society as a result of hate propaganda: "The threat to the self-dignity of target group members is . . . matched by the possibility that prejudiced messages will gain some credence, with the attendant result of discrimination, and perhaps even violence, against minority groups in Canadian society."[101]

A similar kind of analysis was undertaken in *Butler, supra*, which concerned the criminal regulation of pornography. When assessing the criminal prohibition under the s. 1 test, the Court discussed the avoidance of harm to society, and especially women, which was seen to be the overriding objective of the prohibition. Sopinka J. stated that

> there is a growing concern that the exploitation of women and children, depicted in publications and films, can, in certain circumstances, lead to "abject and servile victimization". . . . [I]f true equality between male and female persons is to be achieved, we cannot ignore the threat to equality resulting from exposure to audiences of certain types of violent and degrading material. Materials portraying women as a class as objects for sexual exploitation and abuse have a negative impact on "the individual's sense of self-worth and acceptance".[102]

The final area of *Charter* analysis in which the tension between groups and individuals has been in evidence is in the

---

[101] *Id.* at 748. See also *Zundel, supra*, note 10 at 39-61, Cory and Iacobucci JJ., dissenting, emphasizing the importance of analyzing this issue in the context of ss.15 and 27 of the *Charter*.

[102] *Supra* at 497, citing *R. v. Red Hot Video Ltd.* (1985), 45 C.R. (3d) 36 at 43-44 (B.C.C.A.).

context of the minimal impairment branch of the *Oakes* proportionality test. As mentioned briefly above, the Court has adopted differing standards of scrutiny in this area. In some cases, the courts will be called upon to "strik[e] a balance between the claims of competing groups."[103] The Sunday retail restrictions cases are one example of this type of case. Many retail store owners and members of the public want stores to be open on Sundays, and undoubtedly some retail workers would like to be able to work on Sundays. Other members of the public including many retail workers and their families prefer to have one day each week to spend with each other pursuing common interests outside of work or shopping. In cases such as this, where competing groups in society have diametrically opposed interests, the Supreme Court has noted that

> the choice of means . . . frequently will require an assessment of conflicting scientific evidence . . . Democratic institutions are meant to let us all share in the responsibility for these difficult choices. Thus, as courts review the results of the legislature's deliberations, they must be mindful of the legislature's representative function.[104]

In such circumstances, the government will be required only to demonstrate that there is a "reasonable basis" for its conclusion that the impugned legislation or government action satisfies the minimal impairment test.[105] The "reasonable basis" test was applied in *McKinney v. University of Guelph* which dealt with the issue of university mandatory retirement policies. The majority noted that flexibility is needed when competing interests must be

---

[103] *Irwin Toy*, *supra*, note 22 at 993.

[104] *Ibid.*

[105] *Id.* at 994.

balanced by legislatures or government bodies. The court held that the academic excellence and freedom ensured by the tenure system for university professors could not be maintained without the faculty renewal provided by mandatory retirement policies. The court weighed the competing interests and determined that the government had met the "reasonable basis" standard.[106]

In contrast, in other cases, "rather than mediating between different groups, the government is best characterized as the singular antagonist of the individual whose right has been infringed."[107] For instance, in the criminal law context, the interests of the accused will generally be competing with the government's interests as a representative of the public. Thus where an accused alleges that his or her right to instruct counsel has been infringed, the minimal impairment examination will not require evidentiary inquiries of the scope necessitated in cases involving conflicting groups. Where the state is the "singular antagonist" of the individual whose rights have been infringed, judicial assessments whether the infringement minimally impairs the rights can be made with "a considerable measure of certainty, given [judicial] familiarity with the values and operation of the criminal justice system and the judicial system generally."[108]

Law in the final analysis comes down to the balancing of interests. In constitutional law, particularly questions involving fundamental rights and freedoms, the required balancing is even more evident and challenging. I hope that in this commentary I have conveyed an overview of what I regard as perhaps a uniquely Canadian contribution to entrenched bills of rights, namely the balancing of individual and collective rights and interests. As I have attempted to show, the methodology which has been adopted by the Supreme Court of Canada to be applied to the adjudication

---

[106] *Supra*, note 31 at 285-289.

[107] *Irwin Toy*, *supra*, note 22 at 994.

[108] *Stoffman v. Vancouver General Hospital*, [1990] 3 S.C.R. 483 at 521-22.

of *Charter* claims has attempted to promote those values sought to be protected by the entrenchment of the *Charter*. In particular, the emphasis on group rights and collective interests reflects a national commitment to respect cultural and linguistic differences present in our society, and to balance fairly and effectively collective and individual rights in carrying out that commitment.

HUMAN RIGHTS AND CONSTITUTIONAL REVIEW IN JAPAN

Itsuo Sonobe[1]

Translated by Masako Kamiya

PART A

THE SYSTEM OF CONSTITUTIONAL REVIEW IN JAPAN

I The Formation of the Supreme Court and the Japanese Constitution of 1946

In the fall of 1990, the Supreme Court of Japan celebrated the centennial of the birth of its modern judiciary. It was in 1890 that a modern system of courts of law was introduced. At the same time, a separate court of administrative law was also established. These modern courts were founded shortly after the promulgation of the Imperial Constitution (the Old Constitution) of 1889, which was drafted under the influence of Germany (Prussia).

The courts of law under the Imperial Constitution were fashioned after the European or continental model, in which courts

---

[1] The Supreme Court of Japan. Itsuo Sonobe taught administrative law at the Faculty of Law, Kyoto University and at other law faculties in Japan. Justice Sonobe served as a lower court judge and research official at the Supreme Court from 1970 to 1985 and has been Justice of the Supreme Court of Japan since 1989. His written works include "Comparative Administrative Law: Trends and Features in Administrative Law Studies (Japan)" (1986), 19 *Law in Japan* 40, in English.

The author's principle debt in the preparation of this study is owed to Professors Hideki Shibutani of Osaka Prefectural University and Masako Kamiya of Gakushuin University.

Footnotes 1,2,4,5,7,25,30,31,37,38,39,45 and 60 were supplemented by Professor Masako Kamiya who translated this article.

D.M. Beatty (ed.), Human Rights and Judicial Review, 135-174.

were placed under the authority of a department of justice and exercised their judicial power independently over civil and criminal matters. As for disputes in administrative law, there was one administrative court in Tokyo. It was a court of first instance and of last resort, placed under the authority of the executive branch of the government and with the exclusive jurisdiction over all cases filed. Matters which could be brought to that court were limited to those causes which were explicitly enumerated in the statutes.

The Constitution of 1889 did not contain any provision on constitutional review.[2] The courts themselves also held negative views on constitutional review by the judiciary.[3] The predominant views among academic lawyers also denied it. The reasons were that an assent of the monarch was an absolute guarantee of its constitutionality or that, apart from procedural defects, the legislature had the ultimate authority in the interpretation of the Constitution because of its centrality in governance. It is true that there was an opposing view, based on liberalism, alleging that the judiciary can and should exercise constitutional review, not just on issues of procedural defects but also on the substance of the matter, as part of judicial function to maintain legal order. Between 1925 and 1945, several scholars wrote introductory

---

[2] There were arguments in the academia as to whether, in spite of the lack of an explicit provision, there was any possibility of judicial review. Although the matter was phrased as the power to review the constitutionality of acts attributed to the State, the main concern was whether it was possible to question the constitutionality of the acts of the Imperial Diet. It is be necessary to note here that the administrative court was not barred from adjudicating on administrative actions executing legislation. But this review process was confined to the legality of administrative actions, i.e., whether the act of the government was ultra vires or not, much in the way judicial review is exercised in the United Kingdom. As that court was not a part of the judiciary, it could not have been judicial review.

[3] *Japan v. Shimada* (1913), 19 (7) Taishin-in Keiji Hanketsu-roku 790, the Grand Court of Judicature, judgment of 11 July 1913. *Mase et al. v. Suzuki* (1927), 38 Gyosei-saibansho Hanketsu-roku 1330, Administrative Court, judgment of 27 December 1927.

articles on systems of constitutional litigation in the United States and in European countries but those went no further than exercises in intellectual curiosity in the form of comparative legal studies.

As a result of the Second World War, which she lost, Japan experienced occupation by the Allied Forces. This naturally led to an overall reform of the legal system, including an amendment to the Imperial Constitution which was not the smallest of all the undertakings. There were many drafts and proposals for a new constitution presented both by the Government and by private individuals. Government-related projects included the Konoe proposal and the Matsumoto draft. It should be noted that Dr. Soichi Sasaki of Kyoto Imperial University, who drafted the Konoe proposal, advocated the establishment of a constitutional court and constitutional review, of both the abstract review and the adjudication of cases and controversies. None of the government-sponsored projects were adopted: either because its content did not live up to the expectations of the General Head Quarters of the Allied Forces in Occupation (GHQ) or because of the changes in the political situation.

The Constitution of 1946 was promulgated on 3 November 1946, after the GHQ handed the original draft (MacArthur draft) to the Japanese Government which, in turn, rewrote it as an amendment to the Imperial Constitution which was then ratified by the Imperial Diet. Article 81 of the Constitution states that "[t]he Supreme Court is the court of last resort with power to determine the constitutionality of any law, order, regulation or official act" and explicitly provides for constitutional review by the judiciary. The Government, from the very beginning, understood this to be limited to judicial review of the constitutionality of legislation or regulation which is to be exercised in the course of adjudicating cases and controversies. Although the Government, at first, indicated its understanding that the power of constitutional review would be limited to the Supreme Court, it changed its position at the time of the enactment of the Judiciary Law of 1947 following the GHQ suggestion. Since then, the Government has held the view that all courts of law have the power of constitutional review and has promulgated relevant statutes and orders to that effect.

The system of constitutional review in Japan was thus introduced and established by the constitutional amendment of 1946, with the understanding that it was modeled very much after the American system of judicial review. The courts were not only granted the power of constitutional review by the above-mentioned constitutional amendment. Their structure was fundamentally altered as well. The courts were made independent of the Department of Justice (the Ministry of Justice today). The Supreme Court and other lower courts are constitutionally equal in their status with the Diet and the Cabinet. Its jurisdiction extends not only to civil and to criminal cases but also to administrative cases. The administrative court was abolished and was integrated into the courts of law. A constitutional court, which would have adjudicated just constitutional litigations, was not established. As the result of this structural change, the newly established Supreme Court came to bear far greater burden in terms of the quality as well as of the quantity of cases in comparison to the Grand Court of Judicature, the highest court of law under the Imperial Constitution.

As I shall describe later, the Supreme Court of Japan, in the exercise of its judicial power of constitutional review, has the tendency to be extremely aware of and wary of its limitations. One of the reasons for this may be attributable to its historical structure, although a far more important explanation may be that, because the system of constitutional review was transplanted from elsewhere in the course of reconstructing a democratic state after the Second World War, rather than as a product of its own history to counterbalance the powers of the State or the legislature, as were the case in the Western countries, there is a tendency to emphasize the aspect of balance, that is, of harmony and collaboration, in applying the principle of checks and balances.

II The Structure of Constitutional Review and the Supreme Court

The Supreme Court of Japan consists of fifteen justices: one chief justice and fourteen associate justices. It has appellate jurisdiction over all civil, criminal and administrative cases. An ordinary case is dealt with by one of the three petty benches composed of five justices each. In cases where the constitutionality of a law, order, regulation or official act is at issue, when the Supreme Court decides to depart from its prior decision[4] or in other cases of great importance, a Grand Bench in which all fifteen members participate is convened.

Justices must retire at the age of seventy. As most justices are over sixty when they are appointed to their justiceship, the length of their service on the Bench rarely exceeds a decade. The background of justices before their appointment to the Court shows that a third (six justices at the moment) were career or professional judges of the lower courts, a third (four at the moment) were in private practice. Of the remaining five justices, two were career or professional public procurators, one was a career diplomat with the ranking of an ambassadorship, one was serving as a director-general to the Cabinet Legislation Bureau and the last was a law professor when they were appointed. The Cabinet has the power to designate a chief justice and to appoint associate justices. Because all justices are "reviewed by the people" at least once after their appointments,[5] they are subject to democratic control.

---

[4] Theoretically speaking, in a civil law country as in Japan, a decision of the highest court is not binding upon itself nor upon other courts of law. The decisions are not precedents in the strict sense of the word nor is the departure from a previous reasoning or a ruling an overruling.

[5] Popular review of each justice takes place at the time of the first general election following his appointment to the Supreme Court and every ten years thereafter. There are usually more than half a dozen names of justices at one ballot, most of whom had not been on the Bench long enough to leave any profound impression on the people at the time of the review. A voter is expected

The average percentage of votes of no-confidence at "popular review" have never been higher than twenty and no justice has ever been dismissed by receiving a majority of no-confidence votes.

The Supreme Court of Japan, unlike most European constitutional courts, does not deal exclusively with constitutional litigation nor does it have the scheme of case selection (discretionary disposal of petitions for writs of certiorari) as in the case of the Supreme Court of the United States. Therefore, the caseload of the Supreme Court is extremely large in comparison to the number of justices on the Bench. The Supreme Court allocates itself about thirty "research judges" in order to alleviate the heavy burden. These research judges are chosen from among excellent judges with fairly long experience in the lower courts.

III Matters Beyond Constitutional Review

1. ABSTRACT NORM CONTROL

Article 81 of the new Japanese Constitution which was promulgated in 1946 provides that the Supreme Court is the court of last resort with power to determine the constitutionality of any law, order, regulation or official act. Article 98 of the Constitution states that the Constitution is the supreme law of the nation and that no law, ordinance or other act of government contrary to the Constitution shall have legal force and validity. Article 99 of the Constitution prescribes that all public officials including judges have the obligation to respect and uphold the Constitution. The Supreme Court, in the *Theft Defendant* case (1948),[6] held that

---

not to mark except the names of justices s/he disapproves. With the majority votes of no confidence, the person shall be dismissed from justiceship immediately.

[6] *Japan v. Komatsu* (1948), 2 (8) Saiko saibansho Keiji Hanrei-shu, hereinafter cited as Keishu, 801, Supreme Court Grand Bench judgment of 8 July 1948.

even if the Constitution were without an Article 81, because of the supremacy clause of Article 98 and of Articles 76 and 99 binding the judges to respect and uphold the Constitution, one may satisfactorily deduce that the Supreme Court has the power of constitutional review as implied in the United States Constitution and established by numerous cases beginning with *Marbury v. Madison* (1803).[7] In another case, the Supreme Court stated that this power of constitutional review by the judiciary "does not include the power to decide whether laws, orders and others are constitutional in the abstract, without being applied to a concrete case" and announced that the Court is not a constitutional court exercising the power of abstract norm control, in the *Police Reserve Force* case (1952).[8]

2. ACTS OF GOVERNMENT AND AUTONOMOUS SOCIETIES

At the end of the 1950s and the beginning of the 1960s, the Supreme Court was given the chance to decide cases concerning the constitutionality of acts of the State which were highly political. In Japanese academia, theories pertaining to *actes de gouvernement* of France, *Regierungsakt* of Germany, acts of state of the United Kingdom and political questions of the United States had been discussed thoroughly for some time. The Court applied these theories to disputes arising out of: the highly political United States-Japan Security Treaty (as being part and parcel to the highly political and discretionary powers of the Cabinet and the Diet) (*Sunagawa* case (1959)[9]); the dissolution of the House of Representatives by the Cabinet (defining it as an act concerning the

---

[7] 1 Cranch 137.

[8] *Suzuki v. Japan* (1952), 6 (9) Saiko saibansho Minji Hanrei-shu, hereinafter cited as Minshu, 783, Supreme Court Grand Bench judgment of 8 October 1952.

[9] *Japan v. Sakata* (1959), 13 (13) Keishu 3225, Supreme Court Grand Bench judgment of 16 December 1960.

fundamental aspects of the Government of the State which is extremely political in its nature) (*Tomabeji* case (1960)[10]); and to the adequacy of the procedure observed in the process of an enactment of a bill in the Houses of the Diet (*Police Act Amendment* case (1962)[11]). In all these cases, the Court either excluded the matter as beyond the scope of its judicial review altogether, or showed extreme self-restraint in exercising its power. It is understood that the principle to exclude cases concerning acts of government or political questions from judicial review is a valid principle because it makes it possible for those justices who have not been elected directly by the people to remain neutral in political controversies when they have to adjudicate constitutional questions or administrative cases. Moreover, there is no doubt that this principle does not prevent the Court exercising its power of constitutional review and striking down an act of the Diet or of the Cabinet as being unconstitutional in cases where the act is so clearly and blatantly unconstitutional as to be null and void (See *Sunagawa* case (1959)).

Some hold the view that, even in cases where there is a constitutional issue arising between the State or a public authority and a private entity, if the violation of the person's interest is not concerned with the status of that person as a citizen, but with controversies within an autonomous society or organization, the dispute would not fall within the scope of judicial review. The Supreme Court has applied what could be called the theory of internal affairs of an autonomous society to a member of a local legislature (1960),[12] to the decision whether to grant credit at a

---

[10] *Tomabeji v. Japan* (1960), 14 (7) Minshu 1206, Supreme Court Grand Bench judgment of 8 June 1960.

[11] *Shimizu v. Governor of Osaka Prefecture* (1962), 16 (3) Minshu 445, Supreme Court Grand Bench judgment of 7 March 1962.

[12] *Ohtaki v. Yamashita Village Assembly*, Niigata Prefecture (1960), 14 (12) Minshu 2633, Supreme Court Grand Bench judgment of 19 October 1960.

national university (1977)[13] and to an internal dispute within a religious organization (1980),[14] thus marking the outer boundaries of judicial review by adopting a theory of exclusion from judicial review of matters falling within the sphere of internal affairs of autonomous societies.

3. DISPUTES AMONG PRIVATE ENTITIES

When it was alleged that to refuse to hire a person as a full-time employee when the candidate did not properly disclose or disclosed not exactly truthful information concerning his political creed at the time of his interview violated Article 19 (freedom of thought and conscience) and Article 14 (equality under the law) of the Constitution, the Supreme Court held that:

> "the purpose of the aforementioned provisions of the Constitution, like other provisions guaranteeing other fundamental liberties in chapter three, is to guarantee to an individual that person's fundamental liberty and equality against intrusive actions of the State or a public authority. These are intended to apply only to the relationships between an individual and the State or a public authority, and have not been expected to be applied directly to relationships between private entities."

According to the Court,

> "[i]n a private relationship, in which one entity

---

[13] *Fujita v. Toyama University*, the Dean of the Faculty of Economics (1977), 31 (2) Minshu 234, Supreme Court Third Petty Bench judgment of 15 March 1977.

[14] *Ogiwara v. Sodoshu, Inc.* (1980), 34 (1) Minshu 1, Supreme Court Third Petty Bench judgment of 11 January 1980.

> dominated the other, it is possible to correct the situation by legislative measures whenever specific intrusion into an individual's fundamental liberty or equality or the threat thereof exceed in manner or in degree that which may be tolerated within the society. There are ways to adjust and appropriately balance, in some cases, by appropriately applying general provisions restricting private autonomy such as Articles 1 and 90 or provisions of torts in the Civil Code, which makes it possible to honour the principle of private autonomy and the freedom of contract, and at the same time, to protect fundamental liberties and equality against any violation exceeding the limits which the society would not endure." (*Mitsubishi Resin* case (1973)[15])

In another case the Court ruled that:

> "[e]ven when one of the parties to a dispute between private entities publishes and sells a national daily newspaper with an extremely strong influence in gathering, controlling and dealing with information, it is obvious that the provision of Article 21 of the Constitution (freedom of expression) should not be read to apply directly giving grounds to the right to reply or to have a refuting article placed in the publication" (*Sankei Newspaper* case (1987)[16])

However, the Supreme Court has also held that part of a labour agreement which set the retiring age of female employees much earlier than that of male employees constituted

---

[15] *Takano v. Mitsubishi Resin Co.* (1973), 27 (11) Minshu 1536, Supreme Court Grand Bench judgment of 12 December 1973.

[16] *The Communist Party of Japan v. Sangyo Keizai Newspaper, Inc.* (1987). 41 (3) Minshu 490, Supreme Court Second Petty Bench judgment of 24 April 1987.

discrimination on the ground of being a female, and this should be declared null and void in violation of Article 90 of the Civil Code as unreasonable discrimination based solely on gender (citing Article 14 section 1 of the Constitution and Article 1-2 of the Civil Code) (*Nissan Automobile Manufacturing Co.* case (1981).[17]

All of these decisions reflect the view that the guarantee of human rights by the Constitution does not apply directly to the relationship between private entities. These decisions were based on the principle that, whenever there is a violation of constitutional rights of an individual, courts shall exercise the power of judicial review only in those cases where it was either the State or a public authority which actually and directly committed the violation. From obiter dicta in those decisions, however, it is clear that the court considers it important to have legislative measures to prevent violations of human rights as guaranteed in the Constitution and to make private remedies effective in case of violation.

As we have seen so far, the Supreme Court has marked the outer boundaries within which the judiciary shall exercise its power of constitutional review by referring to several principles. Next, we shall look into the methods in which the Constitution did apply.

PART B

METHODS OF CONSTITUTIONAL REVIEW

I Balancing Method (Principle of Minimum Necessity)

The balancing method is usually applied to cases on human rights when they conflict with public welfare. The important question in these cases is how far and in what manner the court can adjudicate by applying a balancing approach. In dealing with

---

[17] *Nakamoto v. Nissan Automobile Manufacturing Co.* (1981), 35 (2) Minshu 300, Supreme Court Grand Bench judgment of 24 March 1981.

the right of workers to engage in collective activities as provided by Article 28 of the Constitution, the Supreme Court stated that such matters must be decided with the objective establishing an appropriate balance between the two. It held that it was within the discretionary power of the Diet to determine the particulars and that, unless the degree of restrictions imposed upon human rights are such as to be disproportionately disruptive of the balance and are apparently unreasonable and in excess of the discretionary power of the legislature, the legislation would be presumed constitutional (*Wakayama Teachers' Union* case (1965)[18]). It also said, on more than one occasion that, while considering the appropriate interests to balance, the restrictions of the fundamental rights of workers "should be kept to the minimum which is necessary and reasonable" (see *National Postal Workers Union Tokyo Central Post Office* case (1966)[19] and the *National Union of Public Service in Agriculture and Forestry on Police Conduct Act* case (1973)[20]).

In criminal cases, as well, the Supreme Court has tried to strike a balance between fair trials and the freedom of the press to gather information. After balancing these interests, the Court upheld restrictions on the press to the extent that was necessary, a formula similar to the one already referred to.

> "In order to guarantee a fair criminal trial, in cases where materials obtained by the press through their information gathering activities became necessary to be introduced to the trial and admitted as evidence, occasions may rise in which the freedom to gather

---

[18] *Tanaka v. Board of Education*, Wakayama Municipality (1965), 19 (5) Minshu 1198, Supreme Court Grand Bench judgment of 14 July 1965.

[19] *Japan v. Sotoyama* (1966), 20 (8) Keishu 901, Supreme Court Grand Bench judgment of 26 October 1966.

[20] *Japan v. Tsuruzono* (1973), 27 (4) Keishu 547, Supreme Court Grand Bench judgment of 25 April 1973.

information would have to come under some restriction to a certain extent. However, even in such instances, it is necessary to weigh, on the one hand, the nature of the offence charged at the trial, the manner in which it was committed and its seriousness, the value of the materials accumulated by the press as evidence at the trial and its necessity or the indispensability in conducting a fair criminal trial, and on the other hand, the degree that the production of these materials to the court as evidence by court order would obstruct the freedom to gather information by the press and the extent of the impact it would have upon the freedom of the press and other considerations. It was said that the result should be reached by balancing these factors. Even if it were decided that there are compelling reasons to have the materials produced and admitted as evidence in the criminal trial, the court should give sufficient consideration so that any adverse impact that the press might suffer would be kept to the necessary minimum." (*Hakata Station Television Film Production Order* case (1969)[21]).

In the case of restrictions upon the freedom of pre-trial detainees to read newspapers and other materials, the same standard, that is that the restriction should be kept within the extent of what is necessary and reasonable, was applied.

"The provisions applicable here, Article 31 section 2 of the Gaol Law and rule 86 section 1 of the Rules and Regulations to Enforce the Gaol Law, are not in violation of Articles 13, 19 or 21 of the Constitution in that they authorize the restriction of the freedom of pre-trial detainees to read newspapers and other reading

---

[21] In parte RKB Mainichi Broadcasting Corp., ex rel. *Japan v. Kaneko* (1969), 23 (11) Keishu 1490, Supreme Court Grand Bench order of 29 November 1969.

materials for the purpose of maintaining order and discipline within gaol, so long as the restriction is limited to situations where it becomes quite probable that to permit the reading of certain materials under particular circumstances would cause difficulty to such degree which cannot be overlooked for the aforementioned maintenance of order and discipline, that is as long as these provisions are meant to limit the restrictions of the freedom to read only to the extent that is necessary and reasonable to prevent the difficulty." (*Deletion of the Newspaper Article on "Airplane Yodo Hijacking" to Pre-trial Detainees* case (1983)[22]).

II Constitutional-as-Narrowly-Interpreted Approach

Since 1966, the Supreme Court has applied a method known as "constitutional-as-narrowly-interpreted" approach in the interpretation of a statute. This approach requires that, when there is more than one possible interpretation of a provision in a statute or a rule, in which a strictly construed understanding would not imply any conflict with the Constitution but a less restrictive reading of it would give rise to questions of unconstitutionality, the courts should adopt the narrower understanding so as to render it constitutional. A typical example is the case of deleted and blackened newspaper articles (depriving their availability) to those held in pre-trial detention, mentioned earlier.[23] In this case, the Supreme Court said of the provisions in question, Article 31 section 2 of the Gaol Law and Rule 86 section 1 of the Rules and Regulations to Enforce the Gaol Law which made it possible to restrict the freedom of pre-trial detainees to read newspapers and

---

[22] *Fukuhara v. Japan* (1983), 37 (5) Minshu 793, Supreme Court Grand Bench judgment of 22 June 1983.

[23] *Id.*

other reading materials in order to maintain order and discipline within gaol that the application of these provision should be limited to circumstances where:

> "it would have been quite probable that, when all specific factors such as the personality and behaviour of the persons being detained, the particular conditions of the administration of the gaol and its security, the specific contents of newspaper articles and other reading materials are considered, to permit the reading of these materials under these particular circumstances would cause difficulty to a degree which cannot be overlooked for the maintenance of order and discipline within the gaol, and even in those cases, the degree of restriction should be confined within the extent that is necessary and reasonable to prevent the difficulty from arising."

The Court held that the provisions of the statute and regulation in question,

> "on their face, might appear to make it possible to restrict the freedom under fairly broad terms. Nevertheless, it is not only appropriate to understand that these provisions would be applied to permit restrictions upon the freedom to read only under the conditions and within the extent referred to already, but also possible as well. The provisions in question are not in violation of the Constitution."

Another case in which the Court applied the "constitutional-as-narrowly-interpreted" approach concerned the Fukuoka Prefectural Ordinance to Protect and Nurture Young Persons. Article 10 section 1 and Article 16 section 1 of the ordinance prohibited the performance of promiscuous or obscene acts against young persons by punishing the offender with imprisonment of two years or less or with a fine of one hundred thousand yen or less. The ordinance was challenged as unconstitutional on the ground that the meaning of the term "promiscuous" is not evident, in contradiction to the principle of prescription of crime and punishment by law as provided by Article 31 of the Constitution. In that case,[24] the Supreme Court stated that:

> "the term "promiscuous" should not be understood broadly to include all sexual conduct, generally speaking, performed against young persons, but should be limited either to intercourse and other similar conduct which were performed in an inappropriate manner by taking advantage of the mental and physical immaturity of a young person, such as by tempting, placing under duress, deceiving or embarrassing the young person or to intercourse and other similar conduct which defies all understandings other than that it could only have been performed so as to subject young persons merely to satisfy the perpetrator's own lust."

The Court rejected a less restrictive interpretation of the term "promiscuous" which applied it to all sexual conduct against young persons as well as less articulate understandings implying to include any unethical or improper sexual conduct. The method of interpretation applied here allows the courts to avoid deciding whether the provision in question is unconstitutional by interpreting it narrowly enough to uphold its constitutionality within reasonable limits.

This method of constitutional-as-narrowly-interpreted approach is used in instances where it is clear that had that approach not been taken, a court would have had to hold the provision unconstitutional. It is possible that narrowing the applicable scope of a statutory provision should be criticised in

---

[24] *Japan v. Shigefuji* (1985), 39 (6) Keishu 413, Supreme Court Grand Bench judgment of 23 October 1986.

cases where it is deemed to be constitutional even without resorting to a reasonably narrow understanding of it.[25]

Of the four decisions concerning labour disputes in the public service that the Supreme Court has decided, three were Grand Bench decisions. The *National Postal Workers Union Tokyo Central Post Office* case (1966),[26] the *Tokyo Metropolitan Teachers Union* case (1969)[27] and the *National Union of Court Workers Sendai Branch* case (1969)[28] held that "the act of public workers engaging in labour disputes and the act of agitating to so engage shall not be subject to criminal penalties as long as these acts are justly performed" and went on to say that when the meaning of the restrictions against the fundamental rights of workers are considered in accordance with the basic spirit underlining the Constitutional guarantee, the applicable statutory provision should be interpreted to limit its scope of application as stated above.

> "If we are to understand the intent and purpose of the fact that the Constitution itself is guaranteeing the fundamental rights of the workers as such, even in a case where there is a statute limiting the fundamental rights of the workers, the meaning of that restriction shall have to be understood in accordance with the basic

---

[25] If a statute were too narrowly construed when such narrowing was unnecessary to make it constitutional, such narrow interpretation would be so underinclusive vis-á-vis legislative aims as understood from its literal meaning that it would be against due process of law in that the prohibition would not give fair warning.

[26] *Supra*, note 19.

[27] *Japan v. Hasegawa* (1969), 23 (5) Keishu 305, Supreme Court Grand Bench judgment of 2 April 1969.

[28] *Japan v. Sakane* (1969), 23 (5) Keishu 685, Supreme Court Grand Bench judgment of 2 April 1969.

> spirit of the guarantee of the fundamental rights of the workers. This is especially true in a legal system where the guarantee of the right to a decent and cultured life is treated as one of the basic principles (of the Constitution) and where there is the (constitutional) guarantee to the workers of the right to work, to organize, to bargain collectively and to engage in labour disputes along with the right to property. In such a legal system, statutory provisions shall have to be interpreted appropriately and adequately so as to maintain the harmony and balance between these rights." (*National Postal Workers union Tokyo Central Post Office* case (1966))
>
> "All statutory provisions shall be interpreted reasonably, to the extent that is possible, in accordance with the Constitution so as to accommodate its mandate. From this perspective, the Court would have to reject the view which limits its understandings strictly to the wordings of the statute too literally and denounce it immediately to be unconstitutional without any other considerations." (*Tokyo Metropolitan Teachers Union* case (1969))

In contrast to these cases, the Supreme Court did not resort to the method of narrowing the interpretation in the *National Union of Public Service in Agriculture and Forestry on Police Conduct Act* case (1973).[29] The Grand Bench held the statute in question[30] constitutional and stated that "an ambiguously narrowed interpretation would be of disservice to the aspect of law which

---

[29] *Supra*, note 20.

[30] National Employees Law (Law No. 120 of 1947) section 98 stated that a national employee shall not engage in any strikes, slow-downs and other forms of labour disputes against the public as the employer being represented by the government. It proscribed employees engaging in any conduct which would adversely affect the efficiency of the government. Nor attempting to conspire, advocate or agitate others to engage in such acts.

guarantees that all the constituent elements of a crime shall have to be prescribed and might even cause some to doubt whether such narrowed interpretation would violate the principle against vagueness as required by Article 31 of the Constitution." This decision concluded that the restriction in question was constitutional, like the other three previous decisions of the Grand Bench.

This judgment has been criticised as having turned the clock backward in terms of the guarantee of the fundamental rights of the workers. However, the different approaches among these cases are based on differing views on the fundamental rights of workers in the public service. The *National Union of Public Service in Agriculture and Forestry on Police Conduct Act* (1973) case held the statute in question was constitutional without interpreting it narrowly. The decision did not signify the repudiation of the method to narrowly interpret a piece of legislation so as to render it constitutional.[31]

III Distinction Between the Objectives of Legislation and the Means to Accomplish those Ends

The methodology of distinguishing between the objectives, purposes, ends or aims of legislation and the content of the regulation or the means selected to achieve those ends was used

---

[31] There are several possible explanations as to why the Court decided not to follow the reasoning it once adopted. One is that the narrowing technique had gone so far as to be criticized as becoming utterly artificial and incomprehensible. Another is that the right-wing Liberal Democrat Party members of the Diet attacked the Court as being too pro-labour and leftist and that the Court acquiesced. The third is that there was a change in the composition of the Bench in between the first three decisions and the last.

consciously in the *Patricide* case (1973),[32] which was a criminal case. As described below, the Supreme Court, in its majority opinion, held that, although the purpose of the provision was constitutional, the means to achieve its end were not. Separate opinions in that case were written by those who considered that the purpose and the means were both unconstitutional and by one justice who thought both the purpose and the means to be constitutional.

This method has been used by the Court in civil matters as well. It was first applied to strike down a statute regulating the distance between two pharmacies in the *Pharmaceutical Law* case (1975),[33] as being in violation of Article 22 section 1 of the Constitution concerning the freedom to choose one's own occupation, and then in the *Forestry Law* case (1987).[34] In the latter case, the constitutionality of a statutory provision regulating the content of property rights was challenged as not being in accordance with the public welfare standard as stated in Article 29 section 2 of the Constitution. The purpose of the act to "prevent the dividing up of forest ownership into minuscule units so as to stabilize the management of forests, which in turn would promote the preservation and conservation of forests as well as to increase the productivity of the forestry industry, eventually contributing to the development of the national economy" was held to be in the public interest. But section 186 of the Forestry Law denying any request by an owner to divide a registered forest unit whose ownership is held in common (as in tenancy) whenever that title enabled one to claim half or less of the value of that land, lacks the reasonableness or the necessity in achieving the aforementioned

---

[32] *Japan v. Aizawa* (1973), 27 (3) Keishu 265, Supreme Court Grand Bench judgment of 4 April 1973.

[33] *Sumiyoshi Inc. v. Governor of Hiroshima Prefecture* (1975), 29 (4) Minshu 572, Supreme Court Grand Bench judgment of 30 April 1975.

[34] *Hiraguchi v. Hiraguchi* (1987), 41 (3) 408, Supreme Court Grand Bench judgment of 22 April 1987.

statutory purposes and is unconstitutional as exceeding the scope of the Diet's reasonable discretion.

From the decisions so far, one can detect the tendency of the Court is to accept the statutory objectives of the Diet as constitutional. In order to determine the constitutionality of the means being employed, it has applied the proportionality test (the least restrictive means of regulation) to ensure that the measures chosen are considered suitable to promote their ends.

PART C

THE DOCTRINES OF CONSTITUTIONAL REVIEW

I Reasonable Distinction/Unreasonable Discrimination

Article 14 of the Constitution states the general principle of equality under the law and explicitly prohibits discrimination in political, economic or social relations because of race, creed, sex, social status or family origins. There are also specific provisions for the equal rights of husbands and wives in their marriage and family life (Article 24), the equality of the right to vote (Article 44) and the equality in opportunity to receive an education (Article 26) as well.

In applying the principle of equality, the Supreme Court has adopted a relativistic approach, basically acknowledging the discretionary power of the legislature in determining whether certain differentiating treatment is reasonable. The Court has established what it refers to as the test of reasonable distinction/unreasonable discrimination and has indicated that only in cases where the legislative exercise of discretion fails grossly to be reasonable, exceeds its authority and is abused, does such discrimination become unconstitutional. Applying this test, in the *Patricide* case (1973)[35] the Court held that Article 200 of the

---

[35] *Supra*, note 32.

Criminal Code was in violation of Article 14 section 1 of the Constitution. Article 200 of the Criminal Code provided that those who were found guilty of killing one's own or one's spouse's parents or ancestors would be punished by death or life imprisonment. By contrast, those who committed the same type of crime as homicide in general could be punished under Article 199 by imprisonment from three years to life, or with death. The Court stated that Article 200 went beyond the necessary measures to achieve the legislative purpose, and treated an offender in an unreasonably discriminatory manner in comparison to the punishment that was prescribed in Article 199 of the Criminal Code. In its judgment the Court stated that there were reasonable grounds ("the feeling of reverence and respect to the ancestors is the basic morality of social life. It can be said that such natural affection or universal ethics is worthy of protection by criminal law") to impose more severe punishment for patricide (aggravated penalty on the ground of the victim's status), thereby upholding the objective of the provision as not being unconstitutional (the legislative purpose is constitutional), but the means adopted to achieve the end, by punishing the offender with an extremely heavy sentence went too far to justify the grounds for such an aggravated sentence and that it was therefore unreasonable discrimination (the means used were unconstitutional).

In considering the right to vote, the Supreme Court has also made use of a reasonableness test. In its decision in (*The House of Representatives Malapportionment Provision* case (1976)[36]) the Court held that

> "Article 14 section 1, Article 15 sections 1 and 3, and the caveat clause of Article 44 of the Constitution require that the content of the right to vote at the election of both houses of the Diet, that is the value of votes of each and every electorate, must be equal. If

---

[36] *Kurokawa v. Board of Election*, Chiba Prefecture (1976). 30 (3) Minshu 223, Supreme Court Grand Bench judgment of 14 April 1976.

> there is an inequality in the value of votes in the particular election scheme that the Diet provided, and if such inequality cannot be reasonably accepted as a result of important policies or for reasons which the Diet can properly take into consideration, the scheme is said to be in violation of these constitutional provisions."

The Supreme Court's decisions on malapportionment make it clear that the Court considers two factors as most relevant in determining whether the Diet exceeded certain limits to its reasonable discretion. One is whether the de facto ratio of electorates necessary to elect one member in the most populous district to the number of electorates necessary to elect one member from the least populated constituency is greater than three to one.[37] The other is whether a period longer than that which can be considered as reasonable has passed since the previous reapportionment. The Court has yet to indicate any specific figures for each of those factors. In the 1976 decision, the Court held that the schedule list distributing a specific number of seats to each

---

[37] An electorate is automatically registered as a qualified voter on becoming twenty years of age. It is up-dated by filing one's address to a local authority at every change of address. Except for one district which elects one member, the number of members elected from one district ranges from two to six. Reapportionment often includes the process of moving one seat from one district to another without changing the boundaries, which is extremely disturbing to an incumbent, rather than creating or carving a new district out of the existing one.

In *Koshiyama v. Tokyo Metropolitan Board of Election* (1983), the Supreme Court stated that the ratio of 2.92 to 1, as amended in 1975, constitutional. The Court found that the ratio of 3.94 to 1 at the time of the June 1980 general election was not constitutional, but, since the election was held within a reasonable period since the apportionment table was adjusted, the Court declared the election in question constitutional. 30 (9) Minshu 1243, Supreme Court Grand Bench judgment of 7 November 1983. Also in *Kanao v. Board of Election, Hiroshima Prefecture* (1985), 39 (5) Minshu 1100, Supreme Court Grand Bench judgment of 17 July 1985, the Court declared the apportionment table used at the December 1983 general election with the ratio of 4.40 to 1 as unconstitutional.

district was unconstitutional and that the challenged election in the district in question was illegal. But applying the "fundamental principle of general law",[38] the Court declared that, while the election held at that district was illegal, it would, at the same time, dismiss the claim seeking the Court to declare the election null and void. The Court stated that it had responsibility to adjudicate so as to avoid undue results arising from a declaration of a nullified election. Such a method, known as circumstantial judgments (upholding the status quo owing to its peculiar circumstances and where the court's declaration of unconstitutionality and/or illegality of an act has no direct consequences) came to be widely used in later decisions on malapportionment.[39]

II Public Welfare and Public Interests

Abstract notions such as public welfare and public interests are often cited in decisions as grounds to allow restrictions on fundamental human rights. In a series of cases, the Court has elaborated on the meaning of public welfare and on the factors determining whether a challenged restriction is necessary and reasonable. In *"Lady Chatterley's Lover"* case (1957),[40] for example, the Court ruled that the public welfare in "observing the

---

[38] Administrative Litigation Procedure Law section 31 section 1 first paragraph states that, the courts may choose not to nullify or cancel an administrative action even though that action is adjudicated to be illegal when the nullification or cancellation of such action would create a major obstacle to the public interest, and when, under certain circumstances, such nullification or cancellation would not be beneficial to the public welfare.

[39] E.g., *Kanao v. Board of Election*, Hiroshima Prefecture (1985), 39 (5) Minshu 1100, Supreme Court Grand Bench judgment of 17 July 1985.

[40] *Japan v. Koyama et al.* (1957), 11 (3) Keishu 997, Supreme Court Grand Bench judgment of 13 March 1957.

order and maintaining the minimum moral standards" justified the restriction on the sale of obscene materials. Similarly, in the *Sasebo Demonstration against USS Enterprise's Call of Port* case (1982),[41] the Court upheld an ordinance restricting a mass demonstration on the basis of the public interest in peace and order. In two cases dealing with regulations prohibiting handbills and posters being placed on utilities poles, the Court defined public welfare to include maintaining "the aesthetic view of the urban landscape" (*Osaka Municipal Ordinance Prohibiting Outdoor Advertisement* case (1968)[42]) and protecting a person's property right or the right to control against "undue invasion". (*Aichi Association Against Nuclear and Atomic Weapons* case (1970)[43]).

III Regulation of Economic Freedoms

1. REGULATION OF ECONOMIC FREEDOM TO ACHIEVE POSITIVE PURPOSES

In regulating economic freedom, the Supreme Court held explicitly, in the *Retail Market Licence System* case (1972),[44] that the Constitution allows affirmative business regulations and stated further that the regulatory schemes adopted by legislation ought to be within the extent necessary and reasonable to achieve an affirmative purpose. However, the Court also said that whether it

---

[41] *Japan v. Tanaka* (1982), 36 (11) Keishu 908, Supreme Court Third Petty Bench judgment of 16 November 1982.

[42] *Japan v. Arai* (1968), 22 (13) Keishu 1549, Supreme Court Grand Bench judgment of 18 December 1968.

[43] *Japan v. Yamagishi* (1970), 24 (6) Keishu 280, Supreme Court Grand Bench judgment of 17 June 1970.

[44] *Japan v. Marushin Industries, Inc.* (1972), 26 (9) Keishu 586, Supreme Court Grand Bench judgment of 22 November 1972.

is necessary to have legal regulatory measures against individual economic activities and, when necessary, whether the subject-matter, the method and the manner of regulation are proper and adequate, "the basic principle would be for the courts to leave the matters to the policy-making and technical discretion of the legislature, and the courts shall declare legislative measures constitutional and valid unless and only when it is extremely unreasonable and clear that the Diet has exceeded its discretionary power." The Court indicated that to this extent it would pay deference to the discretionary power of the legislature.

Based on this approach, the Supreme Court decided that the licensing scheme for retail markets as provided by the Retail Merchants Special Adjustment Measures Law was

> "a measure that the State has taken to protect small enterprises, and to develop plans for a harmonious development of social economy. [It stated] that one can assume the reasonableness of its purpose (finding of the presumptive reasonableness of legislative ends) and, on the manner and method of regulation, one cannot say that it was apparently clear that it was unreasonable (finding that the unreasonableness of means was not clear nor convincing)."

The distinctive feature of this judgment is that, while acknowledging, on the one hand, the time-honoured approach in adjudicating constitutionality on public welfare (public health, peace and order to national life, public morality, and so forth) as embracing what might be called negative regulation, it ventured into a new method of adjudicating constitutionality by referring to the so-called affirmative economic regulations.[45] It is important to

---

[45] The "old" and "time-honoured" approach assumed that all regulations are "negative" or prohibitive whereas the "new" approach acknowledges that there are some promotive regulations to enhance certain public good or to implement certain policy as well as prohibitive regulations to eliminate harms.

say that the Supreme Court has not gone to the extent of sharply distinguishing the two in terms of necessity and reasonableness. In the same case the Court held that:

> "legislative regulations against an individual's economic activities shall only be permitted in cases where such regulations are necessary and reasonable to remove or ameliorate harms passively (passive ends), when the harms arising from these economic activities that individuals freely engage cannot possibly be overlooked on grounds of the social and public safety and the maintenance of order"

while referring to "certain reasonable regulatory schemes" (which also are permissible if they are similarly within necessary and reasonable extent) as means to implement socio-economic policy (affirmative ends).

2. REGULATION OF ECONOMIC FREEDOM TO REMOVE NEGATIVE ELEMENTS

Three years later, the Supreme Court developed the ideas it discussed in the *Retail Market Licence System* case (1972) further. In the *Pharmaceutical Law* case (1975),[46] the Supreme Court stated that regulations of occupations range from those with affirmative purposes to promote certain ends and to implement certain policies to those with negative intent to remove certain harms. According to the Court not only do the purposes of those regulations vary greatly but the actual restrictions imposed to accomplish those purposes also differ very much according to each and every different circumstance, and that as a result the "authority and the responsibility" to select a specific regulatory scheme "fall primarily upon the Legislature". In the words of the Court, the courts

---

[46] *Supra*, note 33.

> "shall have to honour the judgment of the Legislature as a matter of legislative discretion, whenever the purposes of the regulation are in accordance with public welfare, so long as the decision concerning the actual content of the regulatory scheme to implement the objectives and the necessity and reasonableness of the scheme falls within the area of reasonable discretion. But, the extent or the scope of reasonable discretion depends very much upon the nature of the subject matter and the courts shall decide whether to defer (to the legislative discretion) in light of the nature and content such as the purposes, subject-matter and means of that specific regulation."

This decision, by affirming a positive/negative dichotomy, established the following test to be applied to occupational licensing systems. First of all, irrespective of what ends are sought, a more strict scrutiny would be applied to regulations restricting the freedom of choice of occupations (which would have to be balanced against interests promoting a more important public welfare) in comparison to regulations restricting the content and manner of activities to be engaged. Secondly, in the case of regulations with the negative purpose of preventing harms, in addition to a more strict scrutiny mentioned above, it would be necessary to show that more "lenient" regulations restricting the content and manner of activities (which is called a "more lenient restriction") would not have been sufficient to achieve the purpose of the regulation (principle of necessary and minimum regulation). As to the second part of the test, there are influential opinions in academia arguing that the Supreme Court has established a more demanding standard on reasonableness for regulations intended to remove certain harms, in comparison to regulations meant to achieve positive purposes. For the former regulations, it is expected to consider whether it would be possible to achieve the ends by less restrictive measures, also known as the less restrictive alternatives standard. In cases of regulations promoting certain policies rather than removing harms, it has been understood that the less rigorous test of apparent clarity would be employed as established by the *Retail Market Licence System* case (1972).

The 1975 decision dealt with a regulation which limited new entrants so as to achieve an even distribution of pharmacies. The Court acknowledged that "the licensing regulation which limits an opening of a new pharmacy based on its location (within a certain distance from existing ones) would have a great restrictive effect on the freedom to choose one's occupation" and that, more specifically,

> "in order for such preventive measures to be constitutional, it would not be sufficient simply to state that the regulation is not unnecessary for the health and welfare of the people (the test of necessity). The Court would have to be persuaded of the reasonableness of the allegation that, without such restrictive measures, there may be some risk to the health and welfare of the people (which would have to be balanced against the restriction on the freedom of occupation) (the test of reasonableness)."

It is true that when one observes such tests being applied, it appears that the Supreme Court was saying that in enacting regulations which are intended to remove harms for negative purposes in the exercise of police powers the legislature enjoys, in comparison to regulations for socio-political or economic policy purposes, a more limited discretion. But on both occasions the same test is being employed in the sense that if either kind of regulation was unnecessary or unreasonable in pursuing its legislative purposes and were ultra vires, the exercise of its discretionary powers would be judged as unconstitutional, being "beyond the extent of reasonable discretionary powers."

One may state that when the Supreme Court reviews regulations promoting social and economic policies, it allows the legislature wider discretion than when it reviews regulations which are aimed at removing harms. In the latter case, the discretion of the Legislature is narrow. However, it is relative and is not based upon a very precise, all or nothing standard of adjudication. For regulations promoting certain policies, the social and economic factors or legislative facts may range so widely that it is extremely difficult to refute the assumptions assuming the existence of those facts so that the only way the Court can approach it is to determine whether it is clearly obvious that it was extremely unreasonable. On the other hand, in the case of regulations removing certain harms, it is often much easier to understand the social factors and legislative facts in need of regulation than in the case of regulations promoting certain policies, so that it becomes easier to employ an approach which allows the Court to state that "judging from sound common sense there are no reasonable grounds" to it.

3. REGULATION OF PROPERTY RIGHTS

The Supreme Court has also tested the constitutionality of property laws against a principle of reasonable legislative discretion by adjudicating whether the means to achieve government's purposes were necessary and reasonable to attain their objectives: although again there are variations in the extent of legislative discretion the Court may allow. One example is the *Forestry Law* case (1987).[47] In that case, the issue was whether legislation restricting the content of property rights was in accordance with the public welfare standard in Article 29 section 2 of the Constitution. The Supreme Court had no doubt that, to prevent dividing up the forest ownership into minuscule units so as to stabilize the management of forests, which would promote the preservation and conservation of forests, increase the productivity of the forest industry and ultimately contribute to the development of the national economy, was in accordance with the public welfare. However, the Court also ruled that Article 186 of the Forestry Law, which denied any request by an owner to divide the forest-ownership when the ownership was held in common (as in

[47] *Supra*, note 34.

tenancy) and when that title enabled one to claim half or less of the value of that land, failed both the reasonableness and necessity standards, exceeded the scope of the legislature's reasonable discretion, and was therefore unconstitutional.

When one focuses on the distinction between regulations promoting certain policies and regulations removing certain harms, there are regulations whose characteristics are clearly apparent like the *Retail Market Licence System* case (1972) (positive purpose) and the *Pharmaceutical Law* case (1975) (negative purpose) and regulations which are less obvious. But it is also evident from the Court's judgments in the *Pharmaceutical Law* case (1975) and the *Forestry Law* case (1987), that the social grounds and purposes requiring regulations vary considerably and that there are some regulations which cannot easily be defined as either an affirmative or a negative type of regulation. In these cases, the Supreme Court has held that it should defer to the way the Legislature has balanced the competing interests that are involved. On this point, both the *Forestry Law* case (1987) and the *Pharmaceutical Law* case (1975) are agreed. Essentially, the Court will only strike legislation down as being unconstitutional when either the regulatory purpose of the legislation in question

> "cannot be said to have any social grounds or purpose and is clearly not in accordance with public welfare, or when the regulatory purposes are in accordance with public welfare but it is clear that the regulatory measures used fail in necessity or in reasonableness to be the means to achieve those ends, making it obvious that the judgment of the Legislature exceeds the scope of reasonable discretion."

Seen in this light, the *Pharmaceutical Law* case (1975) and the *Forestry* case (1987) both acknowledged that the power of judicial review extends toward both the legislative ends and the means used to achieve these ends. Both are using exactly the same approach in the sense that, in the case of legislative means, when the regulatory measures chosen fail in necessity or in reasonableness to be the means to achieve those ends, the judgment of the Diet exceeds the scope of reasonable discretion and would be determined as unconstitutional. The two cases can be understood to illustrate the approach the Court has consistently taken. That is, when it reviews the constitutionality of an economic regulation, it recognizes that the Legislature has a wide discretion in choosing the purposes the regulation shall accomplish and would strike down only those whose purposes are clearly inconsistent with the public welfare. The Court would also hold any regulation unconstitutional even though its purposes may be in accordance with the public welfare, when the measures chosen to achieve such purposes cannot be justified in their necessity or reasonableness and the Legislature has exceeded in the exercise of its reasonable discretion. (If the purposes are deemed as negative regulations to exercise police powers and to eliminate harms, the Legislature is given much narrower discretion and is expected to select a less restrictive method against the regulated activity.)

One can summarize the way the Court applied these principles and methods of review as follows. Because the *Retail Market Licence System* case (1972) involved a typical affirmative regulation, the Supreme Court applied the principle of clarity whereas the *Pharmaceutical Law* case (1975) was a typical negative regulation, and so it was possible for the Court to look into legislative facts in deciding the case. In the *Forestry Law* case (1987), while, acknowledging that it was not easy to clearly classify the purposes of the regulation compared with the aforementioned two cases, the opinion of the Court was that it fell with the affirmative purpose (the development of national economy) and held that, although the purpose was in accordance with Article 29 section 2 of the Constitution ("property rights shall be defined by law, in conformity with the public welfare."), and, since the regulatory purpose was stated in the abstract, the Court adopted the method to scrutinize legislative facts on the necessity and the reasonableness of the regulation.

IV Discretion of the Legislature

It should be clear from the cases already mentioned, that the Supreme Court of Japan has been acutely sensitive to the fact that the Diet is the highest organ of State power (Article 41 of the Constitution) and to the principle of the separation of powers. In order to accommodate these notions, it has paid much deference to the discretionary powers of the Diet. Firstly, as we have seen, the Court categorizes the legitimate range of subject matter of the regulation. In cases in which the Court regards the discretion of the Legislature more narrowly (e.g. when it passes a law to prevent some harm), it will deny the reasonableness of a statute and therefore the presumption of the constitutionality of its regulations when it is based on legislative facts which lack reasonable grounds based on sound common sense or which cannot supply sufficient materials to support those grounds. In cases where the Court allows the Legislature wider discretion, the Court will deny the reasonableness of legislation and therefore the presumption of the constitutionality of the regulation only when there are sufficient facts to indicate clearly and convincingly that the legislative discretion was exercised extremely unreasonably.

Regulation of economic activities is not the only area where the Court has deferred to legislative judgments. This inevitably has meant that only a few cases have been held to be unconstitutional. They are *Confiscation of Property of a Third Party* case (1962),[48] the *Patricide* case (1973),[49] the *Pharmaceutical Law* case (1975),[50] the *Malapportionment of the House of Representatives* case (1976)[51] and the *Forestry Law* case (1987).[52] In the first

---

[48] *Japan v. Nakamura* (1962), 16 (11) Keishu 1593, Supreme Court Grand Bench judgment of 28 November 1962.

[49] *Supra*, note 32.

[50] *Supra*, note 33.

[51] *Supra*, note 36.

case, the Supreme Court held that the Customs Law providing for the forfeiture of property of a third party used in a crime without giving any notice, hearing or chance to defend their interests was in violation of Article 31 of the Constitution guaranteeing procedures established by law. In the second case, as noted earlier the Court held that the law providing for aggravated penalties because of the status of the victim was in violation of Article 14 section 1 of the Constitution guaranteeing the principle of equality. In addition to these two criminal cases, the Supreme Court narrowly interpreted legislative discretion in the other three civil cases and, applying the test of reasonableness and necessity, held that the Legislature had exceeded the valid exercise of its discretion.

As we have seen, the approach which the judiciary has applied towards legislative discretion in adjudicating the constitutionality of legislation differs according to the type of law or regulation being adjudicated. In addition to the cases we have already examined, it should be noted that in the case of legislation which requires fiscal considerations, such as those concerning the rights to living and to education, there has been a tendency for the Court to recognize very wide discretionary powers of the State. For example, in the *Food Rationing and Control Law* case (1948),[53] the Supreme Court stated that

> "even if it were conceded that the provisions of the Law were not adequate to achieve the purposes of the law as has been alleged, and therefore, to guarantee sufficiently the right to maintain living as defined by Article 25 of the Constitution, such allegation only challenges the inadequacy or the failure of the legislation and does not indicate any grounds for the existing law to

---

[52] *Supra*, note 34.

[53] *Japan v. Nakano* (1948), 2 (10) Keishu 1235, Supreme Court Grand Bench judgment of 29 September 1948.

> be an unconstitutional legislation in conflict with and in violation of Article 25 of the Constitution whose purposes the present Foods Rationing and Control Law shares."

In other words, since Article 25 of the Constitution does not define, in any particular way, the measures to be taken in order to accomplish the purposes, it was left to the Diet to decide what measures it would take. The inadequacy and failure of the legislation was a matter of legislative policy.

In the *Free Textbook* case (1964),[54] in which plaintiffs claimed that the cost of textbooks for the primary and the compulsory secondary education should be born by the State, the Supreme Court held that Article 26 section 2 of the Constitution providing for a free (compulsory) education only meant that the State cannot collect fees for "public education." With respect to other costs, the Court wrote,

> "it is no doubt desirable for the State to take into consideration to some extent and to endeavour to lighten the burden of those responsible for children concerning the cost of textbooks and other materials. But the issue has to be solved as a matter of legislative policy by taking into consideration the fiscal condition of the State and other factors, as the aforementioned constitutional clause does not explicitly state the provision of such matters."

In the *Asahi* case (1967),[55] the Court decided that

---

[54] *Kato v. Japan* (1964), 18 (2) Minshu 343, Supreme Court Grand Bench judgment of 27 February 1964.

[55] *Asahi v. The Minister of Health and Welfare* (1967), 21 (5) Minshu 1043, Supreme Court Grand Bench judgment of 24 May 1967.

> "Article 25 section 1 did not . . . directly guarantee specific rights to the individuals (see the *Food Rationing and Control Law* case (1948)). It should be understood that such a right was conferred for the first time by the Livelihood Protection Law which was enacted with the intent to realize the objectives of the constitutional provisions. The right in question should be understood to consist of a right to receive such assistance as is stipulated in the schedule would be sufficient to maintain minimum standards of living. The authority to determine what constitutes the minimum standard of wholesome and cultured living (as provided by Article 25 of the Constitution) is, in principle, vested within the discretionary power of the Minister of Health and Welfare. Although it might lead to political debate on an issue of propriety and political responsibility of the Government, his decision may not directly create an issue of illegality unless the Minister exceeded the limits of or abused the discretionary power given."

In a more recent decision dealing with entitlement to multiple social assistance benefits the Court reaffirmed this approach. In the *Horiki* case (1982),[56] the Supreme Court held that Article 25 of the Constitution guarantees a national "the right to maintain a minimum standard of wholesome and cultured living" but "section 1 does not provide that the State is liable to individual nationals in concretely and realistically having the aforementioned duty fulfilled (citing the *Foods Rationing and Control Law* case (1948)". Again, the Court stated that the specific content of the provision must be decided according to the fiscal conditions of the State and the professional and technical consideration and the policy judgment of these factors. Such matters are left to the wide discretion of the Legislature. Unless the exercise of that discretionary power

---

[56] *Horiki v. Governor of Hyogo Prefecture* (1982), 36 (7) Minshu 1235, Supreme Court Grand Bench judgment of 7 July 1982.

becomes extremely unreasonable, and exceeds or abuses its powers, it would not be in violation of Articles 25 and 14 (principle of equality) of the Constitution.

V Equitable Remedies

The Japanese judiciary faces a very difficult situation whenever it entertains the possibility of creating remedial procedures independently, without a statutory basis, because the foundation of its judicial remedies derives from the civil law system. Constitutional litigation is considered part of the legal framework of civil (including administrative) and criminal procedures, which makes it impossible to depart from the type of procedure that the original party had chosen and to change to a procedure which would be more suitable in terms of the constitutional remedies appropriate in a case. Administrative litigation is limited to certain types of cases contesting official action whose structure confines itself to deal with a typical case asking courts to nullify official actions. The Court cannot, by its own discretion, hear a case which asks it to issue a court order forcing the Government and other authorities to perform accordingly, because there is no statutory provision to allow it to act in such a way.

In spite of such restrictions, however, the Supreme Court has managed to create two special remedial procedures in order to redress unconstitutional conditions. First, litigation to annul an election, as provided by the Public Office Election Law, was used to challenge the malapportionment of seats. In this case, the Court created a formula, similar to a declaratory judgment, by ruling that the provision of the Public Office Election Law on the allocation of seats of the House of Representatives to certain districts to be unconstitutional but, at the same time, held that the challenged election to be in force (the doctrine of circumstantial judgment)

(*Malapportionment of the House of Representatives* case (1976)[57]). The Supreme Court has also interpreted Article 37 section 1 of the Constitution, which guarantees the right to a speedy trial, in a way which allows courts to guillotine a trial as an emergency measure on an ad hoc basis when the trial of a particular criminal case has been exorbitantly delayed to such an extent that it makes holding a speedy trial impossible (*Takada* case (1972)[58]).

VI The Role of Constitutional Review in Japan and its Assessment

The Supreme Court of Japan has ruled on many constitutional issues in the course of adjudicating ordinary appellate cases. Since it acquired the power of constitutional review in 1947, the Court has published the Constitutional Case Reports in which the number of decisions on constitutional issues is indicated at about seven hundred criminal and one hundred and fifty civil (inclusive of administrative) cases. Of those, as we have seen, in only five, has the Court held legislation to be unconstitutional: two criminal and three civil cases. Because of this, the Supreme Court of Japan is often described in academic literature and elsewhere as judicially passivist or restrained.

To my understanding, the description that the Japanese courts are taking "a very careful and cautious approach"[59] toward constitutional review seems to be more preferable and appropriate. The Supreme Court has been careful and cautious, especially toward political decisions of the Diet and the Cabinet (acts of government), and toward legislative discretion (notably when that

---

[57] *Supra*, note 36.

[58] *Japan v. Pak* (1972), 26 (10) Keishu 631, Supreme Court Grand Bench judgment of 20 December 1972.

[59] Professor Beatty's letter dated April 28, 1992.

discretion was based on specialized and technical knowledge) by the Diet (Legislature) which is the highest organ of the State. It has been discrete and, unless the alleged unconstitutional situation concerns the direct relationship between a private individual and the State or other public authorities, has actually been reluctant to intervene in controversies arising out of relationship between private individuals or entities or of an autonomous act of a private entity. As we have so far noted, the courts in Japan, for both political and policy reasons, have thought it wise to defer to the discretionary decisions of other branches of the Government or to autonomous decisions in private relationships, and, on the whole, have kept a delicate balance between securing the area of fact-finding and legal adjudication as an area most suited to the courts and of not intruding into other areas. It is because of its delicate sense of balance, that the Court has made use of such an approach as constitutional-as-narrowly-interpreted in its adjudication of issues requiring constitutional judgment.

As to the specific exercise of the power of judicial review, the courts have been keen to balance many competing claims. Such a tendency is especially apparent when the public welfare and restrictions on human rights are balanced, or when the principles of reasonableness and necessity are applied toward legislative discretion. In its not too long history of judicial review, the courts in Japan have succeeded in establishing a set of principles and method of reasoning which guide it in distinguishing laws which are constitutional from those which are not. These principles have been applied to almost all areas of the Constitution. As a result, most of the newly filed constitutional litigation may be dealt with by citing previous decisions of a similar nature. Compared with the first fifteen years since the establishment of constitutional review, there are fewer decisions of constitutional significance today. The only exception seems to be in the area of freedom affecting democracy and self-government where certain principles for constitutional review have yet to be established.[60] It has been the expectation of many to see the Supreme Court take on appropriate cases and to adjudicate accordingly in this area as well.

[60] The Supreme Court has held no laws and regulations unconstitutional in the areas such as freedom of expression and of assembly so far. In spite of the statements paying higher regard to such freedoms as of conscience, of expression of assembly and of petition than to economic freedom, all restrictions have been upheld in the name of competing public welfare. The implication here appears to be that the public interest and public welfare, whatever they may be, are given greater weight in balancing these competing claims.

THE JURISPRUDENCE OF HUMAN RIGHTS

B.P. Jeewan Reddy*
Rajeev Dhavan**

1. Historical Background

There was both hope and despair. In 1947, India became independent, but was partitioned into two sovereign states. A peaceful administrative transition of power was marred by massive upheavals, as killings and massacres accompanied the mass exodus from one territory to another. Against these haunting images, the newly founded Pakistan chose to be an Islamic republic, whilst India - wisely so - created a strong, democratic and secular constitution to pledge together its diverse people who belonged to many faiths, spoke and wrote different languages in a multitude of dialects and scripts and lived hugely varied lives in uniquely different settings. Faced with this dauntingly challenging task, India's elected Constituent Assembly (1946-49) prefaced its deliberations by endorsing an Objectives Resolution of 1947[1] which gave compendious expression to the various demands of rights articulated during the independence movement since 1895 as well as the promise of the Karachi Resolution of 1931 that free India would grant substantive equality and a redistributive social

---

* B.P. Jeewan Reddy is a Judge of the Supreme Court of India. He has formerly been the Chief Justice of the High Court of Allahabad of the State of Uttar Pradesh and a Judge of the High Court of Andhra Pradesh.

** Rajeev Dhavan is an Advocate of the Supreme Court of India and Hony and a Professor of Law at the Indian Law Institute. He has taught at various universities and written several books, monographs and articles on public law.

1 The Objectives Resolution was piloted by Nehru in the Constituent Assembly see 1 *Constituent Assembly Debates* (hereafter *C.A.D.*) 57-65 to be followed by a rigorous debate. 1, *CAD* 65-109, 113-130, 133-153, 166-7, 269-289, 291-324. The Resolution effectively found its place as the Preamble of the Constitution on which see X *C.A.D.* 430-456 (17 Oct. 1949).

D.M. Beatty (ed.), Human Rights and Judicial Review, 175-226.

and economic justice to all.[2] Not just a political text which institutionalized and disciplined the democratic power of the people within a rational structure, the Constitution was also projected as a social document. Along with its diversity, India inherited abject poverty and a mal-distribution of power, resources and wealth. In the contemporary wisdom of the day, the answers seemed to lie in creating a strong interventionist State which would prevent chaos, indiscipline and greed and re-distribute wealth, power and opportunity.[3] But, what if it did not? If the discipline of the Constitution failed, there was always a danger that the massive empowerment of the State would invite its own abuse and wear down the civil liberties of the citizen to the advantage of those able to corrupt State processes. This would only deepen the "life of contradiction" into which the republic was launched whereby a formal political equality granted equal electoral value to each individual, but denied such equality to most of the citizens in their everyday social and economic lives.[4]

What, then, was the answer? If the Constitution failed to

---

2 The various formal documents relevant to the discourse on human rights before Independence in 1947 can be found in 1 SR. 3-122, BR Study 1-92 (SR denotes the four volume anthology of historical archival material edited by B. Shiva Rae (et. al). *The Framing of India's Constitution* (Delhi 1968) preceded by the volume number and followed by the page. The fifth study volume is referred to as 'SR Study').

3 Such a belief may trace its origins to Nehru's views of 'Law and Development' that the State must be massively empowered to achieve social change (see R. Dhavan "If I contradict myself, well, then I contradict myself..." Nehru, Law and Social Change in R. Dhavan et al. (ed.) *Nehru and the Constitution* (Delhi 1992) 45-62. But, however bonafide its antecedents, such a premise can, and does, result in acquiring power for its own sake and to feed the greed and ambitions of those associated with the State.

4 This image of the life of contradiction into which independent India would be born is taken from B.R. Ambedkar's closing speech in the Constituent Assembly, XI *CAD* 979-980.

redeem what Nehru called its "tryst with destiny", the people would turn away from it to find their own solutions in the tumult of civil society. Yet, there were no instant answers other than to provide a viable structure of governance which would stabilize its existence and move towards achieving its goals as systematically, swiftly and honestly as possible.

Although familiar to us today, the Constitution makers evolved what was then a novel constitutional device which classified entitlements into 'fundamental rights' which were justiciable in a court of law and 'directive principles of state policy' which, though not judicially enforceable, were nevertheless fundamental in the governance of the nation.[5] During the discussions, many dismissed these principles as pious wishes. But - even if lacking in symmetry - they represent constitutional aspirations to ensure that the resources of the nation subserve the common good, amidst conditions of social and economic equality which enable humane conditions of life, livelihood and work to all, a uniform civil code, protection of agriculture and animal husbandry and good international relations. Too much can be made of the apparent conflict between fundamental rights and the directive principles which, in the main, enlarge rather than diminish the quality of the fundamental rights. What created

---

[5] Article 37 (Constitution of India) makes Directive Principles non-justiciable but nevertheless fundamental in the governance of the nation. The main discussions in the Constituent Assembly can be found at VII *C.A.D.* 473-606 (19 Nov. - 25 Nov. 1949); and summarized in SR Study 319-333) with a powerful potential for both politics and judicial interpretation. Several amendments to the Constitution (25th Amendment) Act 1971 and Constitution (42nd Amendment) Act 1976 ousted the jurisdiction of the courts in respect of legislation which sought to achieve the mandates of the Directive Principles. But the courts while accepting the importance of the Directive Principles (*Kesavananda v. State of Kerala* AIR 1973 SC 1461) were not prepared to accept an ouster of its judicial review in matters concerning fundamental rights (*Minerva Mills v. Union of India*) AIR 1980 SC 1789; *Sanjeev Coke v. Bharat Coking Coal* AIR 1983 SC 239); *Bhim Singhji v. Union of India* AIR 1981 SC 234; *State of Maharashtra v. Basantibai* (1986) 2 SCC 516)).

complications and necessitated judicial resolution was the demand (incorporated in the form of constitutional amendments) that all State action to fulfil the directive principles was immune from judicial review and the discipline of the main provisions of the fundamental rights chapter. This was a tall order which could not, itself, escape judicial scrutiny.

The fundamental rights chapter of the Constitution was sculpted after great deliberation. It was designed to discipline the State and review all those actions which threaten or transgress fundamental rights beyond the permissible limitations defined by the Constitution. But, since so many of the guaranteed rights were couched in universal terms[6] and not specifically addressed to the State and so many 'laws' including custom and usage[7] fell to be tested within the regime of this chapter, serious consideration had to be given as to whether the dispensation of fundamental rights applies only to State action or also - and if so in what way - to non-State action. The substantive content of India's chapter of protected rights and freedoms is different but not unique. The right to equality protects equality before law and equal protection of all laws. But the detailed provisions not only restrain the State from discriminating on grounds of caste, descent, place of birth and residence in addition to race, religion and sex but also guarantee access to public places to people of all castes, religions, races and sex. Far from being blind to predicaments to the disadvantaged, the Constitution enables special treatment of particular historically disadvantaged groups and other backward classes.[8] The right of free speech and expression, assembly, association, free movement, property and choice of residence, profession, occupation or business are all subject to "reasonable

---

6 E.g. Constitution of India, article 17 (untouchability) and articles 23 and 24 (forced labour).

7 Constitution of India, Article 13.

8 Constitution of India, Articles 14-18 dealing with equality.

restrictions" in the public interest.[9] During the deliberations of the Assembly, the due process clause was watered down in the light of American warnings. In its place, the Assembly approved an "any procedure" clause so that the life and liberty of a person could be restrained by "any procedure established by law".[10] Specific provisions dealt with retroactive crimes, double jeopardy, self-incrimination, imprisonment without being informed of the grounds of arrest, the right to counsel on arrest and magisterial supervision of imprisonment beyond twenty four hours.[11] But, at the same time when many of these salutary provisions were introduced, other extraordinary provisions were also included which constitutionalized administrative detention without trial, with the detenu being given a right to representation and have his case examined by an Advisory Board where such detention exceeded three months unless Parliament dispensed with such an examination in particular classes of cases.[12] Novel provisions protected the

---

9 Constitution of India, Article 19.

10 Article 21 - Constitution of India. Beginning life as a due process clause (see II *SR* 75, 79, 86, 119-20), the Drafting Committee opted for a "any procedure established by Law" clause in the Draft Constitution of 1948 (Article 15) which, despite angry protest (VII *CAD* 842-859 (6-7 December, 1943) 99-100 (13 Dec. 1948)), remained until 'due process' was injected into it by the Supreme Court (following *Maneka Gandhi's* case (*infra* n.71)).

11 Article 20 (no retroactive punishments, double jeopardy and self incrimination). The right to counsel and magisterial supervision of pre-trial detention (Article 22(1) and (2)) were inserted as compensation for a due process clause (see Ambedkar's speech introducing these clauses IX *C.A.D.*, 1496-1498 (15 Sept. 1949)).

12 The preventive administrative detention clauses (article 22(2) to (7) were introduced at the last minute (IX *C.A.D.* 1496-1570) 15-16 Sept. 1949)) and have grown along with a rigorous jurisprudence examining the validity of the reasons for detention and the procedure followed. This pattern of review was progressively developed in *A.K. Gopalan v. State of Madras*, AIR 1950 SC 27; *State of Bombay v. Atma Ram* AIR 1951 SC

individual from various forms of forced labour.[13] The freedom of religion clauses guaranteed religious thought, belief, practices and institutional existence, subject not just to public order and morality and the right to regulate the secular aspects of any religion but also to effect social reform and compel public Hindu temples to open their doors to all classes and sections of Hindus.[14] These seemingly far reaching intrusions were introduced so as to secure the abolition of untouchability and provide for gender justice. Each distinct religious, linguistic and cultural group was given the freedom to establish institutions to preserve their culture, language or script provided they did not discriminate against others on grounds of religion, race, caste or language when admitting students to such institutions if they received grants from the State.[15] The original Constitution guaranteed a right to property and to obtain compensation for property acquired by law for a

---

157; *Ram Kishan v. State of Delhi* AIR 1956 SC 476; *A.K. Roy v. Union of India* AIR 1982 SC 710.

13 Articles 23 and 24, Constitution of India.

14 The right to religion clauses (Constitution of India) turned out to be a reasonable compromise between the secular reformists who empowered the State to throw open temples and restrain religious education without consent in State aided institutions and the no less secular traditionalists who wanted to guarantee religious thought, belief and practices and the institutional existence of all faiths (see VII *C.A.D.* 817-840 (3 Dec. 1949) 859-891, (7 Dec. 1949)). The courts have continued to effect a reconciliation between religious demands, public accountability and the public interest (see R. Dhavan "Religious Freedoms in India" (1987) 35 *American Journal of Comparative Law* 209).

15 Constitution of India, Articles 29-30. For the constitutional discussions see VII *C.A.D.* 891-92 (7th Dec. 1948). The provisions have been the subject of fertile litigation since they affect school and college education. The latest decision permits aided denominational institutions which impart general education to give preferential admission to students from their own religions or other community to the extent of 50% (*St. Stephen's College v. University of Delhi* (1992) 1 SCC 558).

public purpose except in those crucial areas of agrarian reform earmarked for land re-distribution.[16] While Parliament could modify the application of fundamental rights to members of the armed forces[17] and provisions enabled the suspension of fundamental rights during an emergency,[18] there was a right to petition the Supreme Court directly to enforce fundamental rights.[19]

At first, institutional disagreements between the judiciary and the executive over the interpretation of fundamental rights were resolved by the legislature enacting constitutional amendments. Nehru felt entitled to use legislative majorities for this drastic step

---

16 Constitution of India, Article 31. Subsequently, Articles 31A and B were added by the Constitution (First Amendment) Act 1951 which were amended and added to by the Constitution (Fourth Amendment) Act 1954; Constitution (Seventeenth Amendment) Act 1984; Constitution (Twenty-Fifth Amendment) Act 1971; Constitution (Twenty-Fourth Amendment) Act 1971; Constitution (Twenty-Ninth Amendment) Act 1974; Constitution (Thirty Fourth Amendment) Act 1975; Constitution (Thirty-Ninth Amendment) Act 1975; Constitution (Fortieth Amendment) Act 1976; Constitution (Forty-Second Amendment) Act 1976; Constitution (Forty-Fourth Amendment) Act 1978; Constitution (Forty-Seventh Amendment) Act 1984; Constitution (Fiftieth Amendment) Act 1984; Constitution (Sixty-Sixth Amendment) Act 1990; Articles 31C and D were added and amended by the Constitution (Twenty-Fifth Amendment) Act 1971 and Constitution (Forty-Second) Amendment Act 1976. Article 31D which was directed at "anti-national" activities was repealed by the Constitution (Forty-Third) Amendment Act 1977. The effect of all these was to immunize particular statutes or species of legislation or executive action from scrutiny by courts to test infringements under various clauses of the fundamental rights chapter.

17 Constitution of India, Article 33.

18 Constitution of India; articles 358 and 359. This is in addition to provisions whereby Parliament can immunize persons who infringe rights whilst restoring order under conditions of martial law.

19 Constitution of India, Article 32.

because he felt that lawyers had "purloined the Constitution."[20] and the judiciary could not be allowed to stand in the way of progress. The less controversial amendments were over the power of the State to restrain free speech within reasonable limits in the interests of public order and the sovereignty and integrity of India and not just to defend the security of state.[21] More controversial were the amendments which started as an effort to save some agrarian reform legislation,[22] but, in fact, went beyond this limited objective. A constitutional technique was devised whereby all legislation listed in a separate Schedule of the Constitution was immunized from scrutiny on fundamental rights grounds (the Ninth Schedule Immunity).[23] Several years later, another set of amendments went further to introduce a similar immunity to

---

20 J.L. Nehru XII-XIII *Parliamentary Debates cols* 8832 (16 May 1951).

21 *Romesh Thappar v. State of Madras*, AIR 1950 SC 124. *Brij Bhushan v. State of Delhi* AIR 1950 SC 129. This resulted in a clarification through the Constitution (First Amendment) Act 1951 which added 'public order' to the list of reasonable restrictions on free speech and expression in Art.19(2) of the Constitution.

22 *Surya Pal Singh v. State of U.P.* AIR 1951 All. 677. *Kameshwar Singh v. State of Bihar* AIR 1951 Patna 91- on appeal see *State of Bihar v. Kameshwar Singh* AIR 1952 SC 252. Later, in *State of West Bengal v. Bella Banerjee* AIR 1954 SC 170 the Supreme Court staked a claim to review the adequacy of compensation. All this resulted in the Constitution (First Amendment) Act 1952 and the Constitution (Fourth Amendment) Act 1954. This, too, did not stop judicial review. (*Vajravelu v. Sp. Dty. Collector* AIR 1965 SC 1017; *R.C. Cooper v. Union of India* AIR 1970 SC 564) which resulted in further amendments (Constitution (Twenty-Fourth) Amendment Act 1971 until a dignified status quo was achieved in *Kesavananda v. State of Kerala* AIR 1973 SC 1461 which allowed legislatures to determine compensation levels under an ultimate scrutiny by courts.

23 Introduced by article 31B of the Constitution. However, after *Kesavananda v. State of Kerala* AIR 1973 SC 1461 such an en masse ouster of judicial review is no longer possible (see further n.27 *infra*).

protect statutes which purported to give effect to the policy of securing some - and, later, any or all - of the Directive Principles (the Directive Principles immunity).[24] Taken to their logical outer limits, such immunities are capable of rendering the judicial protection of fundamental rights entirely otiose. In 1973, in the celebrated Fundamental Rights case,[25] the Supreme Court placed the basic structure of the Constitution beyond the power of amendment.[26] Room was left for the constitutional amendment of fundamental rights because each fundamental right as originally conceived was not necessarily a part of the basic structure. But, judicial review was part of the basic structure and could not be ousted.[27] After the fundamental rights case, the Schedule immunity of pre-1973 Statutes was preserved, but would not

---

[24] This was first introduced in the Constitution (Twenty Fifth Amendment) Act 1971 which provided an immunity in respect of one sub-clause in the Directive Principles (art.39(b) and (c)) dealing with material resources and monopolism). Later the Constitution (Forty-Second Amendment) Act 1976 extended the immunity to all the Directive Principles. However, judicial review extends to considering whether there is a nexus between the legislation and the 'directive principles' it purports to achieve.

[25] *Kesavananda v. State of Kerala* AIR 1973 SC 1461. See also *Shankari Prasad v. Union of India* AIR 1951 SC 458; *Sajjan Singh v. State of Rajasthan* AIR 1964 SC 845; *Golak Nath v. State of Punjab* AIR 1967 SC 1643.

[26] For an analysis of the case see R. Dhavan, *The Supreme Court and Parliamentary Sovereignty* (Delhi 1976).

[27] *Minerva Mills Ltd. v. Union of India* AIR 1980 SC 1789; *Waman Rao v. Union of India* AIR 1981 SC 271; *S.P. Sampat Kumar v. Union of India* AIR 1987 SC 663; *Subhash Sharma v. Union of India* AIR 1991 SC 631; *Khota Hoolohon v. Zachilhu* (1992) 1 SCC 309 (even though this last decision rests, in the main, on the procedural failure that the constitutional amendment ousting the jurisdiction of the courts was not ratified by the State legislatures).

extend to any further additions to the Ninth Schedule.[28] A similar formula was evolved for the statutes that fell within the Directive Principles immunity. In the latter case, the pre-1973 amendments sought immunity from fundamental rights scrutiny only in respect of specified directive principles dealing with monopolism and measures to subserve community resources. These amendments were saved to the extent that judicial review would be limited to examine whether there was a real substantial nexus between the status sought to be protected and the directive principles in question.[29] But, post-1973 amendments which sweepingly immunized all legislation purporting to fulfil any directive principle are subjected to the full rigour of the fundamental rights chapter. Irrespective of these amendments, the directive principles remain pivotal to the interpretation of the Constitution. But, once it is accepted that judicial review can never be ousted, there is little to be gained by confining judicial scrutiny to examining whether there is a reasonable nexus between impugned legislation and the directive principles it purports to fulfil. Limiting judicial scrutiny to such a limited nexus test would do no more than test the declared bonafides of the legislature, but abdicate that more stringent investigation into the transgression of fundamental rights which the Constitution makers so assiduously assigned to the

---

28 As it is, Ninth Schedule immunity extended to the statutes but not subsequent amendments or orders under it (M/S *Prag Ice and Oil Mills v. Union of India* AIR 1978 SC 1296; *State of Maharashtra v. Man Singh* AIR 1978 SC 916; *State of Maharashtra v. Madhavarao* AIR 1968 SC 1395; *Godavair Sugar Mills v. S.B. Ramble* AIR 1975 SC 1193); However, after *Kesavananda's* case (*supra* n.23) the validity of such en masse ouster of judicial review by the legislature is in doubt. However, judges continue to talk of the protective umbrella of the Ninth Schedule (*Dattarava v. State of Maharashtra* AIR 1589 SC 1796 pr.3 p.1797; *Ambalal v. State of Gujarat* AIR 1982 SC 1090). Yet statutes placed in the Ninth Schedule after *Kesavananda* (*supra* n.23) are subject to the discipline of the Fundamental Rights chapter (*Waman Rao v. Union of India*) AIR 1981 SC 271; *Kalimata v. Union of India* AIR 1981 SC 1030).

29 See *Minerva Mills* (*supra* n.27) and *Sanjeev Coke* AIR 1983 SC 239.

judiciary.[30] It may, perhaps, be appropriate to develop a jurisprudence which neither accepts any immunizing ipse dixit of government or Parliament nor prevents the courts from considering the full totality of fundamental rights protections in the light of the directive principles. Any other interpretation would fail to give effect to the goals of the Constitution which include, perforce, the protection of fundamental rights.

The Constitution does not forbid - nor have the courts stood in the way of - empowering State agencies to fulfil the positive mandates of the Constitution towards the poor and the disadvantaged and subserving the common good.[31] But such

---

30 However, this formula is, itself, a limitation. There is a vast difference between determining whether a piece of legislation bears a nexus to the achievement of a Directive Principle (and then calling on the judiciary to adopt a "hands off" approach) and examining the issues de novo and adjudging them on the basis of relevant human rights constitutional criteria. The former may well stultify judicial review and make it mechanical so that a government certificate may oust judicial review *Navnit R. v. R.R. Kamani* AIR 1939 SC 9) or limit its scope (see State of *Tamil Nadu v. Abu Kavur Bai* AIR 1984 SC 326; *Bhim Singh v. Union of India* AIR 1981 SC 234; *Vellore Electric Corpn Ltd. v. State of Tamil Nadu* AIR 1989 SC 1741; *Maharashtra State Electricity Board v. Thana Electricity Supply Co.* AIR 1990 SC 153; *Tinsukhiya Electric Supply Co. v. State of Assam* AIR 1990 SC 123). Although the Supreme Court has categorically stated that it will lift the veil of a government certificate that the legislation necessarily conforms to and fulfils the Directive Principles (see *Assam Sillimanate v. Union of India* (1990) 3SCC 182), the nexus doctrine limiting the scope of the Courts' inquiry seems to have gained some ground.

31 For an interesting and comprehensive survey of the political discourse see F. Frankel: *India's Political Economy* 1947-1977 (Princeton 1978). However, the developments created self serving trends which consumed the State (see the insightful but overwritten P.S. Jha: *India's Political Economy of Stagnation* Delhi 1980)). The impact of this on the constitutional system was to undermine the very foundations which require public power to be used for public and not private purposes (see R. Dhavan: "The Constitution as the situs of struggle" in L. Beer (ed.)

empowerment does not, and cannot, exist for its own sake. Nor can it be granted on terms that immunize the arbitrary exercise of power. In the complex vision of the Constitution, there is no inherent conflict between the socialist goals of the nation and the civil liberties of individuals and groups. That adjustments have to be made does not obviate the need for a careful scrutiny which mediates accountability from those who wield power - not just by verifying whether the blood group of the power exercised corresponds to the purposes for which it was given, but, also, by considering whether the social and political goals of the Constitution are being achieved in a humane and just manner. Inevitably, those who fight for fairness must themselves be fair.

II. Scope of the Constitution

The rights and liberties granted by the Constitution inhere in individuals and groups. Some rights are granted only to citizens whilst others are granted to groups and may be claimed by individuals and citizens. But, against whom are the rights to be claimed? If at first, it appears that fundamental rights afford protection only against any action by the State, there is enough in the text of the Constitution to suggest a much wider dispensation. This is not - as we shall see presently - just because the term 'State' has been widely defined (Art.12) or that the laws which are subjected to human rights scrutiny include "any ordinance, order, by-law, rule, regulation, notification, custom or usage having in the territory of India the force of law" (Art.13(3)(A)) but because many of the rights have been articulated in the universal form. How else does one interpret the article which decrees: 'Untouchability' is abolished and its practice in any form is forbidden. The enforcement of any disability arising out of 'untouchability' shall be an offence punishable in accordance with

---

Constitutional Systems in Late Twentieth Century Asia (London 1992) 373-461).

law".[32] But what happens if there is no legislation implementing this declaration, which was the case between 1950 and 1955? Or, if the legislation is inadequate and does not cover all actions and practices that are forbidden by the text of the Constitution? Would the courts intervene to provide a remedy against a private person who defied this constitutional injunction against untouchability. Likewise, another article declares that "traffic in human beings begar and other similar forms of forced labour is prohibited and any contravention of this provision shall be an offence punishable in accordance with law". Yet another provides that "no child below the age of fourteen years shall be employed to work in any factory or mine or engaged in any hazardous employment".[33] To restrict the sweep of such articles to action or inaction by the State does not do justice to either the intent or text of the Constitution. These articles are clearly earmarked to operate in civil society. While certain fundamental rights specifically mention the State, a fair measure of them do not. Thus, aspects of equality, the fundamental freedoms, the right to life and liberty, freedom of religion and the right of minorities are all phrased widely enough to provide protection from transgressions from non-State action. If they are not addressed to the State alone, careful consideration had to be given as to whether they give rise to a cause of action, by way of an actionable constitutional wrong, and are judicially enforceable. It would, perhaps, be a great leap forward if juristic ways and means are found to take the message of the fundamental rights chapter beyond state action to discipline relations between groups, institutions and men and women in their everyday lives. This is all the more pressing in the case of some of the fundamental rights in the Indian constitution which specifically address civil society and not just institutions of governance.

The Indian State is expected to fulfil a wide range of constitutional responsibilities which flow not just from specific

---

32 Article 17, Constitution of India.

33 Articles 23-4, Constitution of India.

mandates in the fundamental rights and directive principles chapters, but more generally from governance. For whatever reason, the institutions of State in India have grown both quantitively and in their variety. The legal form of this expansion has varied. Some of the tasks of governance have been directly performed by the designated bureaucracies of the States, others have been entrusted to other State institutions. Not all these institutions, agencies and functions have been authorized by the legislature. In a very far-reaching decision of 1955,[34] the Supreme Court extended the executive power of the Union and States to extend to all matters within their legislative competence even in the absence of supportive authorizing legislation. This doctrine, which leads to the ironical circumstance that the less legislation there is, the greater the power of the executive, could potentially result in a cruel blow for civil liberties and human rights, but for a salutary caveat which interposes the restraint that the fundamental rights can only be transgressed by duly enacted legislation and not mere executive action.[35] This has not prevented the executive power from being widely used to create government companies and an enormous variety of programmes and agencies to discharge various governmental, regulatory, programmatic and welfare functions.

The fundamental rights provisions of the Constitution define the State widely to include the Government and Parliament of the Union and Constituent States and all local and other authorities within the territory of India "or under the control of the Government of India."[36] Accordingly, there is little difficulty in

---

34 *Ram Jawayya Kapur v. State of Punjab* AIR 1955 SC 549.

35 See *Ram Jawayya* (*supra* n.34), *M/S Bishambbar Dayal v. State of U.P.* AIR 1982 SC 33; *Narain Das v. State of U.P.* AIR 1974 SC 1232.

36 Article 12, Constitution of India. Strangely enough the addition was introduced to cover such territories which the United Nations might entrust to India under a mandate or trusteeship (see VII *CAD* 607 (25 No. 1949)).

subjecting various state bureaucracies, local government and, indeed, the judiciary itself to the regime of fundamental rights. But could one go further? Once statutory corporations, such as electricity boards, which perform commercial functions,[37]were included there was little reason for not extending the inclusionary definition of 'state' to other non-statutory commercial bodies run by the State.[38] But which ones? What has emerged from various decisions of the Supreme Court may appear, prima facie, to be puzzling. Whilst regional engineering colleges set up by the government,[39] statutory government companies,[40] the Indian Statistical Institute and the Indian Council of Agricultural Research[41] and government owned nationalized industries[42] have been included within the definition of 'State' for fundamental rights purposes, the Indian Council of Scientific Research,[43] the Institute of Constitutional and Parliamentary Studies[44] and the National Council of Education, Research and Training[45] have not

---

37 *Rajasthan State Electricity Board v. Mohan Lal*, AIR 1967 SC 1857.

38 *Som Prakash v. Union of India* AIR 1981 SC 212.

39 *Ajai Hasia v. Khalid Mujib* AIR 1981 SC 487.

40 *Sukhdev v. Bhagatram* AIR 1975 SC 1331.

41 *B.V. Minhas v. Indian Statistical Institute* AIR 1984 SC 362; *P.A. Ramachandra Iyer v. Union of India* AIR 1984 SC 541 (Indian Council of Agricultural Research).

42 *Supra* n.38.

43 *Sabhajit Tewary v. Union of India*. In 1975 SC 1329 (Indian Council of Scientific Research).

44 *Tekraj v. Union of India* AIR 1988 SC 469.

45 *Chandra Mohan Khanna v. National Council of Education, Research and Training* (1991) 4 SCC 578.

been so included. These decisions rest on a catalogue of tests which examine the extent of State funding and control and consider whether the functions which these institutions and agencies perform can be ascribed as the responsibility of the State.[46] But, since various decisions have enjoined the State from arbitrariness even in their ordinary contractual dealings, the discipline of the fundamental rights chapter applies with equal force to licensing and the commercial dealings of the State.[47] Equally, there has been a concomitant expansion of the fundamental rights expectations so that the right to life and liberty includes, amongst others, the right to livelihood, environment and education.[48]

Inevitably, the broader the sweep of the fundamental rights, the greater the responsibility of the State to ensure that these

---

46 A resume of the tests can be found in *Ajai Hasia* (*supra* n.39).

47 *Shrilekha Vidyarthi v. State of U.P.* (1991) 1 SCC 212. *Dwarkadas v. Board of Trustees of the Port of Bombay* (1989) 3 SCC 293; *Mahabir Auto Stores v. Indian Oil Corporation* (1990) 3 SCC 752.

48 *Olga Tellis v. Bombay Municipal Corporation* (1985) 3 SCC 545 (right to livelihood); *C.E.S.C. Ltd. v. Subhash Chandra Bose* (1992) 1 SCC 441 (medicine and health); *Unnikrishnan v. State of Bihar* (1993) 1 SCC 645 (to education). In this ruling, Jeewan Reddy J. put pragmatic limits on the right to education as a fundamental right so that the inclusion of the "right to education" as part of the enforceable right to 'liberty' in Article 21 of the Constitution is to be read along with the Directive Principles of State Policy which place a premium on universal education up to the age of 14. No doubt, all educational schemes must be reasonable, fair and just. To that end, in this case, the Court gave schematic directions in respect of both State and private colleges providing opportunities for technical education. The detailed scheme declared by the Court visualizes a distribution of seats between 'payment' and 'free' seats, admission to both of which will be on merit judged by objective criteria such as, for example, a common entrance examination. This case illustrates the manner and extent to which a Court may need to go to ensure that conditions of equality and fairness are maintained by all those who provide important opportunities and privileges to differentially placed persons in an unequal society.

enlarged elements are also not transgressed. Therefore, it is possible to argue that the content of State responsibility is also determined by the rights it is obliged to protect and not just from some ideological notions about what the State ought to be doing.[49] This takes us back to the larger question whether the courts can simply stand by to watch the transgression of fundamental rights by private persons and entities who, when all the facts and circumstances are considered, are expected to respect the guaranteed human rights. There are many instances where the State imposes regulatory control to ensure that the obligations of the State are discharged through private institutions. The question may be asked: should not these private institutions be amenable to remedial judicial review if they fail to respect the dispensation of the fundamental rights chapter? In an important and significant decision, a totally privately owned company was included within the definition of 'State' for fundamental rights purposes because it failed to discharge its statutory obligations and permitted the emission of gases which were inimical to the welfare of human

---

49 The State's delineated duties in relation to fundamental rights are specifically mentioned in articles 12 (definition of State), 13 (definition of law), 14 (equality), 15 (non-discrimination), 16 (equality of opportunity in public employment), 18 (abolition of titles), 31A, B, C (property and social reform). The State's powers are circumscribed in articles 15(3)(4), 16(3)(4)(5) (equality); 18 (abolition of titles), 19(2) to (6) (reasonable restrictions to the seven freedoms), Articles 25(2), 26, 28 (social reform in relation to religious rights), 30(1A)(2) (restrictions on minority rights). The State is clearly the intended 'respondent' in articles 20 and 22 (criminal due process and preventive detention). State intervention by way of aid or otherwise is the reason for the reconstruction of the rights in question in articles 28, 29(2), 30(2) (aspects of compulsion in the matter of religious education, non-discrimination in admitting students and fair distribution of State Funds). Yet the articles dealing with untouchability (article 17), fundamental freedoms (article 19), due process (article 21), anti-exploitation (articles 23-4), religious and cultural rights (articles 25, 26, 29, 30) are declaratory and, arguendo, can be claimed against anybody without necessarily establishing a nexus with State action.

beings and the environment.[50] In another case, the right to education was recognized as a justiciable fundamental right. Consequently, private educational institutions were also expected to observe the discipline of the fundamental rights chapter because 'inter alia' it is through such institutions that the State discharged its duty to provide educational opportunities for people.[51] These decisions would avoid intricate political and ideological confrontations on the legitimate functions of State. Accepting the wide range of activities of State, they explicate that all kinds of statutory and non-statutory, state-owned and private agencies which are linked to the State or entrusted with or discharge its widely defined functions are subject to fundamental rights accountability where it is clear that the effect of the activities of such agencies is to directly and inevitably affect any fundamental right.

We have already noticed that judicial review is not restricted to statutorily enacted laws but extends to custom or usage.[52] The Supreme Court has been unequivocal in accepting that a "custom must yield to a fundamental right".[53] But, since custom and usage have not been enacted by the State, the fact that the Constitution makes them vulnerable to fundamental rights scrutiny leaves open the vast possibility for a private person to legitimately complain that the rights given by custom or usage to another private person

---

[50] *M.C. Mehta v. Union of India* AIR 1987 SC 1086.

[51] *Mohini Jain v. State of Karnataka* (1992) 3 SCC 666. To some extent, the discipline of the fundamental rights chapter had already been made applicable to "societies" imparting education subject to the framework of regulation (*Ajai Hasia, supra* n.39). There has never been any doubt that a private business acting in the public interest can be regulated by State action and subjected to the regime of the fundamental rights chapter (*Deepak Theatre v. State of Punjab* (1992) Supp.(1)SCC 684). See also *Unnikrishnan v. State of Bihar supra* n.48.

[52] Article 13, Constitution of India.

[53] *Rama Rao v. State of Andhra Pradesh*, AIR 1961 SC 564 at pr.9, p.570.

are discriminatory, unfair, unreasonable or otherwise contrary to the fundamental rights guaranteed to him. Indeed, if a custom or usage sanctions untouchability or exploitative bonded labour, the courts can surely declare such a custom or usage unconstitutional. In similar circumstances, the Supreme Court had little hesitation in invalidating statute-backed and custom-based rights of pre-emption on grounds of vicinage even though they affected private sales between individuals.[54] This goes beyond enlarging notions of public policy that private transactions which are contrary to the fundamental rights chapter are illegal, void and unenforceable. Much further they extend constitutional expectations into civil society where custom or usage silently but effectively reconstitute the power that human beings exercise over each other in frightening disproportion to the respect that human beings owe each other. Thus, the Court has intervened to prevent private contractors used by the State from indulging in exploitative labour practices.[55] Having come thus far, we are not too far from those crucially significant areas of religious and other personal law which redefine relationships within the family and other personal institutions in which so much of our lives are spent. For the present, the courts seem to have taken the view that in contradistinction to custom and usage, the fundamental rights chapter 'does not touch upon the personal laws of the parties.'[56] Yet, there is room for considering whether the Constitution, in all its plenitude, does not just protect religious or other personal laws, but also pledges them to strive towards gender justice and fairness within the family. It may seem anomalous, that personal religious laws, unlike other customs and usages, wholly escape the equality and due process texts of the fundamental rights chapter.

---

54 See *Bhau Ram v. Baij Nath* AIR 1962 SC 1476; *Ram Sarup v. Munshi* AIR 1963 SC 553; *Sant Ram v. Labh Singh* AIR 1965 SC 314.

55 *Sanjit Roy v. State of Rajasthan* AIR 1983 SC 328; *Peoples Union of Democratic Rights v. Union of India* AIR 1982 SC 1473.

56 *Krishna Singh v. Mathura Ahir* AIR 1982 SC 686 at pr.17, p.712.

We have travelled a great deal from the limited notion that fundamental rights are available only against the State. Apart from defining the State widely for fundamental rights purposes to include India's sprawling public sector as well as various private agencies, Indian courts have given serious thought to bringing private transactions and customary relationships within the human rights catchment of the Constitution. Aspects of these incremental developments remain forbearingly undefined because the Constitution leaves individuals and groups free to pursue their version of the good life while stepping in to regulate and discipline those aspects of power and authority in civil and political society and governance which threaten the mutual respect and concern which the Constitution decrees is owed to all.

III. Defining Rights and Freedoms

There is good reason to universalize the collective predicament of all human rights as a shared concern and celebrate human rights in their global incarnation. International human rights texts exude this concern which, in turn, is reflected in a standard menu of civil and political (and, to a much lesser extent, economic and social) rights being found in most national charters. This identity of concern is impressively matched by the rigour of juridical discourse which has produced an impressive international jurisprudence. But, there is room for the inevitable caution that people and societies do vary in the way in which they recognize and comprehend the worth of various human priorities. If India has cross-fertilized its jurisprudence with cosmopolitan learning, it has retained innumerable moral and other intuitions about the nature of its human rights enterprise.

Indian courts have interposed a tentative preliminary interdiction that certain claims should be excluded from constitutional protection because they are morally unworthy even though they might fall within the normal ambit of the fundamental rights in question. An example will elucidate. The Constitution guaranteed the freedom to practise any profession or to carry on any occupation, trade or business. Widely phrased, it is all inclusive. But, it would seem diabolical if this was interpreted without any moral reserve to include, say, the rights of a professional murderer to kill for money. No doubt, an expanded interpretation of the permissible restrictions on professional freedom would extend to prohibiting the professional murderer from practising his trade at all. In each case, the end result may be the same. But, there is a vast difference between treating murderers as constitutional lepers and recognizing their trade as constitutionally reprehensible and according constitutional protection to the trade of professional murderers but easing it out of the protective umbrella of the Constitution by prohibiting its exercise altogether. While all Bills of Rights must recognize the bewildering variety of human expression and avocations, they are not an invitation to every pimp, thug and thief to claim constitutional respectability. Not everything that is dreamt or in one's philosophy is necessarily the object of constitutional worth. Yet, this leaves open the possibility that the collective intuition of judges might not just silence, prohibit and censor but delegitimate many causes and pursuits on the basis that a majoritarian understanding expressed through judicial discourse finds them morally offensive. This is why judicial discourse on the inherent moral worth of human rights claims merits rigorous scrutiny.

There are several instances where Indian courts have transposed the preliminary condition of constitutional worthiness so as to exclude from the purview of a constitutional right such claims or activities which the courts find morally unworthy or reprehensible. While it may be an overstatement to suggest that the courts have generally accepted the principle that they will "protect such rights as they think are worthy of protection",[57] the jurisprudence of the Supreme Court seems to suggest that moral worthiness is a factor to be borne in mind; and, further, that the

---

57 See R. Dhavan: *The Supreme Court of India: A Socio-Legal Analysis of Its Juristic Techniques* (Bombay 1977) 142-3; R. Dhavan: "The morality of trade: A Socialist Supreme Court's animadversions to rural debt collectors" (1973) 1 SCC 10 (Journal).

categories of moral worth are never closed. In one of its very early cases, the Court had no difficulty in denying that a citizen has an inherent right to carry on trade in intoxicating liquors, but disposed of the issue by relying on the police power of the State to restrain and prohibit noxious trades.[58] While subsequent cases were wary about treading the high moral ground that the liquor trade was constitutionally unworthy per se, the Supreme Court seemed to be in little doubt that "gambling" was "(n)ever intended to form any part of this country's trade and commerce".[59] This rested on the much wider principle that "those activities which encourage a spirit of reckless propensity for making easy gain by lot or chance and which lead to a loss of hard earned money of the undiscerning, improvident and common man and thereby lower his standard of living and eventually disrupt the peace and happiness of his home, could (not) possibly have been intended by our Constitution makers to be raised to the status of a trade, commerce and intercourse and to be made the subject of a fundamental right".[60] Yet if the underlying logic of this decision were taken further, many forms of speculative business activity which spell ruin for the unfortunately improvident person would be excluded from constitutional protection. Once excluded from the constitutional domain, they would automatically become unconstitutional forms of human endeavour irrespective of whether they are prohibited by statutorily enacted law. Applying the moral constitutional worth doctrine (although it was never quite articulated as a general self standing principle as such), certain advertisements for curing sexual disorders were excluded from the purview of constitutionally protected free speech in a manner partly reminiscent of the American Supreme Court excluding

---

58 *Coverjee v. Excise Commissioner* AIR 1954 SC 220.

59 *State of Bombay v. R.M.D.C. Chamarbaugwala* AIR 1957 SC 699.

60 *Ibid.*, at pr.42, p.720.

obscene libels from the mantle of constitutional protection.[61]

So far, the courts have confined these prohibitions to areas such as obscene speech and gambling, which are also recognized by the common law as being contrary to public policy; and, the liquor trade which is, if nothing else - at least, frowned upon by the directive principles of State. In that sense, the Rural Debt case of 1977[62] marks out a fresh terrain by declaring that "anti-social, usurious, unscrupulous money lending to economic weaker sections" is not a constitutionally protected trade. Since the Supreme Court refrained from formulating the moral constitutional worth doctrine as a precise constitutional principle to be reasoned from and applied, the preemptive exclusionary filter to sift constitutionally righteous rights from those which are unworthy remains unpredictably large. That may not be a reason for dispensing with the moral constitutional worth doctrine altogether since constitutional interpretation cannot shirk the moral task of, say, telling a murderer that his trade is much too offensive to be worthy of constitutional protection. At the same time, the anti-exploitation components of the tests in the Gambling and Rural Debt cases present open-ended opportunities for judges to impliedly exclude what the Constitution does not expressly prohibit. Using the directive principles as a guide, there might be a case for confining the moral worth test to those unequivocal categories of public policy which should, as a matter of principle, be excluded from legal protection altogether. Arguably, credit transactions - still less, those which are crucial to the social economy of the village - are not per se obnoxious. The rural money lending trade may be both necessary and worthy. But a law controlling the terms of rural money lending or writing off some or all onerous debts would be a reasonable restriction on the right to rural money lenders to pursue their trade with an extraordinary vigour but a limited conscience. Normally, each

---

61 *Hamdard Dawakhana Wakf v. Union of India* (1960) 2SCR 671.

62 *Fatehchand Himmat Lal v. State of Maharashtra* (1977) 2 SCC 670.

fundamental right should be as widely defined as possible, subject to some obvious exceptions whose inclusion would shock the public conscience.

But our problems with defining fundamental rights are far from over. The constitutional texts which formulate rights within manageable definitions are open-textured. They acquire contextual meanings from conventional understandings derived from their use in the system of governance as a whole. But the task of constitutional interpretation cannot be wholly pre-determined by lawyers, judges and those who articulate and manage the discourse of governance. It has to be taken further to enlarge the human rights enterprise in a manner consistent with the welfare of all and not remain trapped forever within conventional meanings. Before 1978, the Constitution protected the right to 'acquire hold and dispose property'. In India, this could cover many claims.[63]It was relatively easy to elaborate conventional legal understandings to include within the conspectus of this right "those well defined types of interests which have the insignia and characteristics of property rights".[64]So, property rights were what earlier legal discourse predetermined them to be. But, were prior legislative definitions to be applicable to the Constitution; or, was the Constitution to go further to enlarge its protections to cover that wide range of interests which are essential to peoples' well-being and worthy of protection? It was relatively easy to include the right of the shareholder to the enjoyment of his shares as falling within the notion of a constitutional property right.[65]But, what about the right of a religious functionary to a lucrative hereditary office or the right of a neighbour to make a pre-emptive purchase

---

[63] See R. Dhavan: *Supreme Court of India* (*supra* n.57) 140-6 for various examples arising uniquely from the Indian situation.

[64] *Commissioner, Hindu Religious Endowments v. L.T. Swamiar* AIR 1954 SC 282 at pr.12 pp.283-9.

[65] *Chiranjit Lal v. Union of India* AIR 1951 SC 41; *Dwarka Dass v. Sholapur Spg. and Wvg. Co. Ltd.* AIR 1954 SC 119.

of land (which has been included in the definition of property) or the right of a quasi permanent allottee of evacuee property, rights under an executory contract of immoveable property or a right of a bare license (which has not been so included)?[66] The answers to these questions do not just require the mechanical application of conventional meanings. Inevitably, constitutional interpretations tread, howsoever warily, into social and political questions requiring judges to choose between weighty competing options. That judges must make principled decisions which transcend the immediate result involved only makes constitutional choices more arduous and complex.

The manner in which principled decisions have to be made over defining the scope of fundamental rights can be illustrated by examining how the Indian Supreme Court has approached claims relating to freedom of religion. Faced with a constitutional text which protects 'freedom of conscience and the right freely to profess, practise and propagate religion', Indian courts have been called upon to consider whether the ambit of a person's religion is as wide as a person declares it to be or whether the court can go behind this personal declaration to consider whether any particular claim is genuinely a part of that person's faith or not. If the Indian courts were simply to accept what a person claimed his faith to be, they would be flooded with an enormous wave of piquant and barbarous claims in the name of religion. As it is, claims have been made in civil society that it is a part of the Hindu faith that widows immolate themselves at their husband's funeral pyre. Theoretically, there would be little difficulty for courts to accept such a practice as part of the Hindu faith but prohibit it as

---

[66] E.g. *Commissioner v. L.T. Swamiar* (*supra* n.64 - on the management rights of a manant (priest) as a property right); *Amar Singh v. Custodian, Evacuee Property* AIR 1957 SC 599 (Property right of a quasi permanent allotted of evacuee property in the wake of the creation of Pakistan); *Ananda Behera v. State of Orissa* AIR 1956 SC 17 (immoveable property); *Firm Chotabhai, J. Patel & Co. v. State of M.P.* AIR 1953 SC 108; *Mahadeo v. State of Bombay* AIR 1959 SC 735 (bare licencee).

contrary to public order and morality. The end result would be the same. The practice would be denuded of constitutional protection. Such a course would, however, precipitate a head on confrontation between religious claims and the police power of the State.

But, the Indian Constitution goes beyond restraining religion for reasons of public order, morality and health. It not only permits the State to make laws to regulate or restrict "any economic, financial, political or other secular activity which may be associated with religious practice" but also empowers the State to enable "social welfare..., reform (and)...the throwing open of Hindu religious institutions of a public character to all classes and sections of Hindus".[67] It is in this context that Indian courts have been called upon to separate truly religious practice from those 'secular' aspects of a religion which are amenable to State regulation. Rather than accept any claimant's version, the Supreme Court has enunciated the principle that the Constitution protects only such practices which are an "essential" part of a religion.[68]Unenviably, the Supreme Court has been asked to decide whether a sect called the Swami Narayans are part of the Hindu faith when the litigating adherents claimed they were not or whether it was a part of the Muslim faith to slaughter cows, or whether it was truly the case that a Jehovah's witness was enjoined

---

67 Article 25(2), Constitution of India.

68 *Commissioner v. L.T. Swamiar* (*supra* n.64). Although the "essential practices" test appears to have been accepted by the Court and the commentators as emanating from this judgement, on closer reading, in the *Swamiar* case, the Court rejected the argument that the constitutional obligation of the Courts extended only to those practices which are proved to be "essential", treating it as much too broad and cautioned that any inquiry into the practices of any faith must derive sustenance from the faith and not any judicial version of it.

by his religion from singing the national anthem.[69] The judges have diligently tried to discharge their constitutional inquiries about the essential practices of any faith by actually examining the historicity of any claims and considering them in the overall philosophy of the faith in question. Yet, they have been placed in the position of high priests, academics, judges and social reformers.[70] It is possible to treat the "essential practices" doctrine as part of a bonafide rule to weed out irresponsible and irreverent claims, but it is much wider than any simple version of such a rule. In its complexity, the "essential practices" doctrine takes us into that imprecise realm of juristic discretion where the factual inquiry as to the religious status of a social practice and the normative determination as to whether it deserves constitutional protection overlap mightily.

Enthusiastic judicial interpretation may have overlooked the fact that the constitutionally permissable 'police power', 'secular regulation' and 'social reform' restraints on the right to religion purport to discipline the external expression of faith to enable conformity to universal constitutionally recognized standards and reasonable demands of objective necessity; and, not to reform the faiths themselves. The constitutional dispensation does not set up a confrontation between religion and the Constitution, elevating the latter to the status of a transcendent faith empowered to subsume and subvert religious beliefs and practices. It is not enough to evolve a balance between the two but to ensure that State action is not insensitively subsumptive of religion to a point that it belittles or undermines religious claims by cornering and confining them into little constitutionally protected enclaves. There are good

---

69 *Yagnapurushdasji v. Muldas* AIR 1966 SC 1119; *Mohammad H. Qureshi v. State of Bihar* AIR 1958 SC 731. *Bijoe Emmanuel v. State of Kerala* AIR 1987 SC 748.

70 E.g. M. Galanter: *Law and Society in Modern India* (Delhi 1989) 237-258; J.D.R. Derrett: "Hindu - a definition wanted for the purpose of applying personal law" (1968) 70 *Zeitschrift fuer vergleischende rechtswissenschaft* 110.

reasons for Indian courts not to accept what people claim their faith to be and, thereby precipitating a dangerous confrontation between religious orthodoxy and State reformism. Much rather, they have chosen to inspire - and, where necessary, impose - restraints on faiths drawn from an examination of the interior philosophy and practices of the faiths themselves. This has made the tasks of the courts complicated and difficult. But, it has also provided them with an opportunity to find Indian compromises instead of perpetrating head-on conflict between unmediated religious claims and the State's right to prohibit practices inimical to the public interest and social reform. The Constitution, thus, recognizes the need for an interactive learning process for those who adhere to a faith and are simultaneously obliged to accept a commonality of constitutional norms applicable to adherents of all faiths.

Amidst other examples, a benign reformism concerned with social welfare is evident in the Supreme Court's interpretation of the guarantee (Art. 21) that "no person shall be deprived of their life and liberty except by procedures established by law". This clause was de-radicalized by the Constituent Assembly which substituted the original due process clause with the present formulation which protects 'any process' as long as it is prescribed by a duly enacted law. This provides only limited protection from executive caprice but not legislative majorities. Limiting the definition of 'life' and 'personal liberty', the Court took an uncomfortably restricted view that this fundamental right guaranteed no more than the right not to be detained other than by a prescribed statutory procedure.[71] This posed logical difficulties. As part of the ensemble of the seven protected freedoms, (Art. 19) the freedom of movement of a citizen could not be restrained unless such restriction met the dual test of being both enacted by law and a 'reasonable restriction' in the public interest.

---

71 See *Gopalan v. State of Madras* AIR 1950 SC 27. This interpretation was re-examined and found wanting in *Maneka Gandhi v. Union of India* AIR 1978 SC 597.

Incongruously, a total deprivation of liberty by incarceration was not subjected to inquiry into the reasonableness of the executive or legislative action, whereas a partial deprivation of the liberty of movement was subjected to stringent constitutional tests. The argument that the guarantee of the seven fundamental freedoms were available only to persons who were otherwise free led to the frightening result that prisoners were not entitled to any of the fundamental freedoms including the right of free speech and expression, protest, property and to intellectual pursuits. In addition to safeguarding prisoners' rights, Indian courts have expanded the meaning of 'life' and 'liberty' to include the sum total of those rights which a person requires for their well being, including right to privacy, livelihood, a good environment, health and education.[72] It may well be the case that such an interpretation goes beyond the supposedly original intent of the Constitution makers. Even so, it captures the spirit of what was intended in a manner consistent with the human rights and social justice enterprise of the Constitution as a whole. By interpreting 'life and liberty' as including the total well being of a human being, the Constitution has cast a protective umbrella around the everyday concerns of ordinary life. This definitional expansion has necessitated a transformation of the 'any process' clause into a due process clause.

---

[72] See *Maneka Gandhi* (*supra* n.71) at pr.54 pp.620-22. Thus there is an expanded interpretation of personal liberty to include: the right to privacy *Kharak Singh v. State of U.P.* AIR 1963 SC 1295; *Govind v. State of M.P.* AIR 1975 SC 1378; *State of Maharshtra v. M.N. Mardikar* AIR 1991 SC 207; livelihood *Olga Tellis v. Bombay Municipal Corporation* (1985) 3 SCC 545; *Delhi Transport Corporation v. D.T.C. Mazdoor Congress* AIR 1991 SC 101), environment *Rural Litigation and Entitlement Kendra v. State of U.P.* AIR 1985 SC 652, 1259), health *C.E.S.C. Ltd. v. Subhash Chandra Bose* (1992) 1 SCC 441, education *Mohini Jain v. State of Karnataka* (1992) 3 SCC 666), consumer protection *Common Cause v. Union of India* (1992) 1 SCC 707) and the judicial system *All India Judges Association v. Union of India* (1992) 1 SCC 119).

But, even after having identified the broad inclusionary scope of a fundamental right, various further questions continue to tease constitutional discourse. Does every right have a 'core' content which alone is enforceable as a fundamental right, or does the mantle of constitutional protection extend to various concomitant rights which are crucial to the exercise of the right in question? The Constitution guarantees the right to form associations and unions. But, such a right would be meaningless if it simply assured legal existence to any association that was formed but crippled the association into not functioning in an effective manner. And, if the association is a workers' union formed for the purpose of defending members' rights, is the right to strike part of freedom of association? In denying the right to strike as a fundamental right, the Supreme Court cautioned against interpreting fundamental rights to invite an uncontrollable sprawl so as to protect rights concomitant to fundamental rights and "by a series of ever expanding concentric circles in the shape of rights concomitant to concomitant rights" extend this protection virtually ad infinitum. This it was felt, would "lead to a grotesque result".[73] Anxious to ensure that particular fundamental rights should not be enlarged out of shape, the Court has refused to "accept the theory that a peripheral or concomitant right which facilitates the exercise of a named fundamental right or gives it meaning and substance or makes its exercise effective is itself a fundamental right."[74] However, in a series of cases dealing with freedom of the press, the Court has protected such aspects of this freedom without which the right, itself, would become non-existent or meaningless.[75] The government has, for example, been

---

[73] *All India Bank Employees Association v. National Industrial Tribunal* AIR 1962 SC 171 pr.20, p.180.

[74] *Maneka Gandhi* (*supra* n.71), pr.81, p.642.

[75] *Express Newspapers v. Union of India* AIR 1958 SC 578 (conditions of work of journalists); *Sakal Papers Pvt. Ltd. v. Union of India* AIR 1962 SC 305 (price and page control); *Bennett Coleman & Co. v. Union of*

prevented from imposing restrictions on the price and pages of newspapers or imposing unjustified and onerous taxes on the press or controlling the supply of newsprint. The concomitant rights doctrine is a brake on extravagant claims masquerading as human rights. But, it was never intended to define fundamental rights so restrictively that claimants - especially the disadvantaged - are not able to present and protest just claims as the objects of constitutional protection.

These various quandaries over the definition of fundamental rights are strong reminders that human rights issues do not lend themselves to narrow textual interpretation. Constitutional interpretation must view the definition of human rights with an expansive wisdom to interpret the text purposively so as to preserve the right of all human beings to mutual respect and concern.

IV. Limitations on Constitutional Guarantees

When the Constitution was being drafted much criticism was levelled that the derogations were so expansively drawn that they would swallow up the rights themselves. Soon after the Constitution came into effect, a Supreme Court judge dissentingly warned that it must not be overlooked that it is the rights that are fundamental and not the restrictions.[76] Wise as caution, the warning seems to have been less reliable as prescient wisdom of what the courts did do in fact.

India AIR 1973 SC 106 (newsprint); *Indian Express Newspapers (Bombay) Pvt. Ltd. v. Union of India* (1985) 1 SCC 641; *Prabha Dutt v. Union of India* AIR 1982 SC 6 (journalists' rights of access to a prison). But there is no full-fledged recognition of the institutional rights of the press other than the freedom of speech and expression guaranteed to every citizen. B.P. Jeewan Reddy J.'s judgment in *The Printers (Mysore) Ltd. v. Asst. Commercial Tax Officer* JT 1994 (1) SC 692 resolves ambiguities by unequivocally accepting that the freedom of the press is implicit in the guarantee of freedom of speech and expression.

[76] *Ram Singh v. State of Delhi* AIR 1951 SC 270 at 276.

Defining each right separately, the Constitution articulated an identifiably distinct regime of limitations for each right. But were the limitations so disparate as to elude a coherent and consistent theory of constitutional limitations? The equality provisions were wide enough to give the courts a considerable leeway to evolve a balance between governance and the State's duty to respect the individuality of every human being and group. Written into the scheme of equality were special provisions to prevent untouchables being denied access to public places and the creation of preferential programmes for women, untouchables, tribals and backward classes. These have to be understood in the context of the overall constitutional enterprise and the past history of India to which they were a response. The seven basic freedoms were subject to 'reasonable restrictions' in the public interest. Introduced by a back bench member in the Constituent Assembly, the open textured nature of the phrase 'reasonable restrictions' was an invitation to the judiciary to evolve principled criteria. The right to life and liberty could be restricted by any "procedure established by law". The latter phrase sought to exclude judicial review, leaving it to the legislatures to formulate any procedure they thought fit. There was some recognition of aspects of criminal due process, but at the same time the Constitution specifically sanctioned administrative detention without trial. The anti-exploitation provisions were plainly prohibitive, abolishing forced labour and employing children under 14 years of age in hazardous jobs. In the absence of any specific restriction on these rights, it was up to the courts to decide what constituted forced labour or hazardous employment. The freedom of religion provisions opened with the derogation that religious freedoms would be subject to "public order and health" and went on to espouse the case for social welfare and reform, opening Hindu, Buddhist and Sikh public temples to all believers and strictly regulating the economic, financial, political and other secular activity associated with religious practice. With specific protection given to the right of Sikhs to wear a kirpan (dagger) as part of their faith, the Constitution enunciated a partial separation of State from religion. In exchange for State funds, religious and minority educational institutions would have to accept a wider duty to other communities and refrain from forcing religious instruction on them. The right to property (abolished in 1978) was converted into a complex code which guaranteed compensation for property acquired by the State. But there were massive derogations from such protections in areas of agrarian reform.

What does one make of this ensemble of constitutional limitations? What was the link, if any, between the equality provisions, the concept of 'reasonable restrictions', the seemingly ad hoc statements on criminal due process, the guarantee against 'forced labour', the police power and social reform caveats attached to the right of religion and culture and the maze of limitations around the property article? Was there any connecting link? If so, where was it to be found? Would it be something that judges would invent as they go along? Or, was the scheme of constitutional limitations to be slowly but sedulously drawn out from India's distinctly goal based Constitution which had to be located within its Indian context to find solutions to India's unenviable, but challenging quest for social justice.

Initially, the Court treated each right as a code in itself.[77] But this created anomalies because each right did not operate in an exclusive sphere; and, it meant that while one aspect of a right was subject to one regime of limitations, another aspect of the same right was differentially subjected to some other regime. We have already noticed that while the total liberty of a human being could be taken away through imprisonment by any statutory procedure, freedom of movement was subject to laws which had to be shown to be reasonable restrictions in the public interest. The right to hold, own and dispose of property could be subject to reasonable restrictions but the property itself could simply be acquired by any statutory procedure. The right to propagate religion was subject to public order, health morality and social reform, but free speech was subject to "reasonable restrictions" to defend those aspects of

---

[77] *Supra* n.71.

the public interest which were listed in the Constitution itself. Over time, the Supreme Court was persuaded that individual fundamental rights cannot be wholly treated disjunctively from each other and that the earlier "assumption...that certain articles in the Constitution exclusively deal with specific matters cannot be accepted as correct".[78] And, if the rights - especially life and liberty - overlapped with others, some common ground had to be explored to consider the case for some kind of unified theory of constitutional limitation.

A first step in this regard was to merge the implied limitations in the equality clause against arbitrariness with the concept of 'reasonable restrictions' which circumscribed the exercise of the basic freedoms (Art.19) and, then, to read both of these into the "any procedure" clause (Art.21) by which alone life and liberty could be taken away. There have been occasions when the Court has reflected on general unifying principles. Thus, it has declared that "the substance of American due process has been introduced into the conservative text of the Constitution".[79] Again, it has observed that "(i)n fact the concept of reasonableness and non-arbitrariness pervades the entire constitutional scheme and is a golden thread which runs through the whole fabric of the Constitution".[80] What has emerged - and will, undoubtedly mature - is not a single concept but strands of an increasingly related bundle of constitutional protections located in various parts of the chapter on fundamental rights which will partly retain their identity as separate tests but also inter-connect to provide a comprehensive constitutional scheme.[81] An assimilationist theory

---

78 *R.C. Cooper v. Union of India* AIR 1970 SC 564.

79 *Ranjan Dwivedi v. Union of India* AIR 1983 SC 624 at pr.8, p.627.

80 *Ajai Hasia v. Khalid Mujib* (*supra* n.39) at 499.

81 *Maneka Gandhi v. Union of India* (*supra* n.71) at pr.56.

of constitutional limitations[82] should not crowd out more specific jurisprudential journeys into aspects of the social and public interest which provides the basis for simultaneously restricting specific fundamental rights and encouraging their creative and purposeful use.

Indian constitutional law has interpreted each one of the limitations in an engagingly rigorous way. In order that the equality clause may not stand in the way of the State classifying persons, procedures and situations for differential treatments, the courts accepted a broad power of classification. For example, special criminal procedures could be devised to provide for the speedy trial of particular criminals.[83] Similarly, the poor and the rich had a right to be treated as separate categories for welfare and tax purposes. On this basis, it could be said that even if no special constitutional provisions existed for women, children and the disadvantaged, the State could make preferential discrimination schemes in their favour. But the doctrine of classification could easily provide the basis of conferring a vast amount of unregulated power to the State if judicial inquiry stopped as soon as the courts accepted any particular classification as a valid constitutional classification. The dangers of this were eloquently pointed out by a dissenting judge in 1963 (and later affirmed by the Court) when he said:

> The doctrine of classification is only a subsidiary rule evolved by courts to give a practical content to the (equality)...doctrine...Overemphasis on the doctrine of classification or an anxious or sustained attempt to

---

82 Note the views of Beg and Bhagwati, JJ quoted in (1992) 1 SCC 225 at 249-50.

83 *A.P. Antulay v. R.S. Nayak* (*supra* n.79); *State of Maharashtra v. Sukde Singh* (1992) 3 SCC 700 at 748.

> discover some basis for classification may gradually and imperceptibly deprive the (equality) article of its glorious content. That process would inevitably end in substituting the doctrine of classification for the doctrine of equality. The fundamental right to equality before the law and equal protection of all laws may be replaced by the doctrine of classification.[84]

In a trilogy of landmark cases,[85] the Supreme Court itself recognized the need for and gave a "new dimension" to the equality article. One judge later opined that "the propositions applicable to cases arising under (the equality article) have been repeated so many times that they now sound platitudinous".[86] Equality had "a high activist magnitude" which cannot be "imprisoned within traditional and doctrinaire limits". The doctrine of classification "is not (a) paraphrase of (equality; but)... merely a judicial formula for determining whether the legislative or executive action is arbitrary and, therefore, a denial of equality." The 'new' test is that in order to pass muster against the equality provisions, State action must be rigorously tested for anti-arbitrariness so that "(w)henever there is arbitrariness in State

---

84 *Lachmandas v. State of Punjab* AIR 1963 SC 222 at pr.50, p.240; quoted in *A.S. Iyer v. V. Balasubramanayam* AIR 1980 SC 377 at pr.57, pp.468-9; see also *Mohd Shujat Ali v. Union of India* AIR 1974 SC 1631 at 1653.

85 *R.D. Shetty v. International Airports Authority* AIR 1979 SC 1628; *E.P. Royappa v. State of Tamil Nadu* AIR 1974 SC 555; *Ajay Hasia v. Khalid Mujib* AIR 1981 SC 487.

86 *In Re: Special Courts* AIR 1979 SC 478 at 508.

action... (the equality) article springs into action".[87]

But what exactly does the new 'anti-arbitrariness doctrine' mean? There is a broad "well recognized distinction between power to be exercised within defined limits in the reasonable discretion of designated authority and the vesting of an absolute and uncontrolled power in such authority".[88] Unlike Dicey's famous propositions on the rule of law, there is no objection to the grant of power of "wide discretionary authority",[89] but the power and its exercise must be subjected to and exercised by reference to objective, identifiable and understood guidelines.[90] This is subject to the caveat that where the authority is a high ranking public, statutory or constitutional authority that, by itself affords some "guarantee that the power will be used and with a sense of responsibility".[91] Under the new doctrine, each law, rule or action would have to be tested so that some rational explanation can reasonably explain the need for, nature and exercise of that power. This new doctrine impliedly transcends the earlier and more stringent requirement in equality cases that not only must there be a discrimination but that it must be hostile, intentional or purposeful.[92] Now, under the equality doctrine the State must be shown to have acted reasonably. This requirement of reasonableness under the equality clause does not have the same meaning as the substantive doctrine of reasonableness under the

---

87 *Ajay Hasia v. Khalid Mujib* (*supra* n.39).

88 *Suman Gupta v. State of J.R.* AIR 1983 SC 1235 at pr.6, p.1236.

89 A.V. Dicey: *Introduction to the Law of the Constitution* (London, 1885).

90 *Supra* n.82.

91 *Organo Chemicals v. Union of India* AIR 1979 SC 1803 at pr.12, p.1807.

92 See *Budhan Chowdhry v. State of Bihar* AIR 1955 SC 191 at 195. *State of J. & K. v. Ghulam Rasool* AIR 1961 SC 1301 at pr.6, p.1302; *Narain Das v. Improvement Trust, Amritsar* AIR 1972 SC 865 at pr.6-7, p.871.

general freedoms clause.

Some commentators have assumed that such a doctrine opens the doors for the Court to substitute its own subjective notion of reasonableness.[93] While that danger is always present and to be guarded against in all exercises of judicial review, 'reasonableness' as part of an anti-arbitrariness doctrine is concerned with whether there is a rational explanation that the procedure followed and the power exercised are relevant and appropriate to the ends to be achieved. There may well be a thin, but significant line between testing State action for relevance and appropriateness on grounds of rationality and a general assessment of the desirability of State action on wider grounds. The equality doctrine eschews desirability questions for it is not the intention of judicial review to take over State decision making but simply to review it. Indeed, as far as the equality article is concerned, any action "is not unreasonable in the legal sense because the court thinks it is unwise".[94]

This does not mean that the equality doctrine does not have substantive content. It is as much a concern of equality to root out disadvantage as it is to prevent arbitrariness. Courts have, therefore, enforced the 'equal pay' doctrine[95] and - quite apart from the specific provisions permitting positive action - evolved doctrines (such as the doctrine of source) whereby particular ameliorative or preferential treatment may be given to identifiable

---

93 T.R. Andhyarajuna: *Judicial Activism and Constitutional Democracy* (Bombay 1922).

94 *G.B. Mahajan v. Jaigaon Municipal Council* AIR 1991 SC 1153.

95 See *P. Savita v. Union of India* AIR 1985 SC 1124; *Randhir Singh v. Union of India* AIR 1982 SC 879; *Grih Kalyan Kendra Workers v. Union of India* AIR 1991 SC 1173.

classes in fulfilment of these dual goals of equality.[96] When it comes to looking at the substantive dimensions of equality, the Court is aware that it cannot, by itself alter indefensible social inequalities in civil society, but it can within limits permit or, in certain circumstances, even mandate strong affirmative action where the exigencies of a situation demand it. Interpreting constitutional provisions which permit the reservation of quotas in public employment for 'untouchables', tribal people and other backward classes, the Court has evolved both a principled and pragmatic resolution of the demands of redressing social imbalances and promoting efficiency. Importing greater rigour into defining those entitled to preferential treatment (inter alia, by excluding from consideration the creamy layer of successful persons who are otherwise identified with or part of any targeted beneficiary group), the Court, in a significant judgment, has allowed reservations of quotas of up to 50 percent at the stage of initial appointment (but not promotion).[97] Juristically, this kind of structuring of the areas of permissible State action is both necessary and proper so that policymakers have clear guidelines before them and future judicial decision making proceeds within an identifiable framework and is not left to decisions on the basis of case by case intuitions.

The constitutional limitations testing the reasonableness of restrictions on the seven fundamental freedoms (Art.19) look at governmental action differently. Here the task of the Court is to determine whether the impugned action or legislation is a "reasonable restriction" in the interests of the general public. Some articles particularize the interest that is to be safeguarded. Thus, freedom of speech can only be reasonably restricted in the interests of the sovereignty and integrity of India, security of state,

---

96 *Chitra Ghosh v. Union of India* AIR 1970 SC 35; *D.H. Chanchala v. State of Mysore* AIR 1971 SC 1762; *Nidamarati v. State of Maharashtra* (1986) 2 SCC 534; *Deepak Sibal v. Punjab University* (1989) 2 SCC 145.

97 *Indira Sawhney v. Union of India* (1993) Supp. 3 SCC 215.

friendly relations with foreign states, public order, decency or morality or in relation to contempt of court, defamation and incitement to an offence. Likewise, freedom of residence is also subject to the need for the protection of the interests of any Scheduled Tribe. Freedom of profession, occupation and trade is specifically subject to the right of the State to impose professional and technical qualifications; or, for the State itself, to carry on any trade, business, industry or service to the exclusion of private citizens.[98] A very powerful statement of the concept of reasonableness in the fundamental freedoms article was elegantly enunciated by the Supreme Court in 1952:

> ...(F)rom the point of view of reasonableness, the Court should consider not only factors such as the duration and the extent of the restrictions, but also the circumstances in which and the manner in which their imposition has been authorized. It is important in this context to bear in mind that the test of reasonableness, whether prescribed, should be applied to each individual statute impugned and no abstract standard or general pattern of reasonableness can be laid down as applicable to all cases. The nature of the right alleged to have been infringed, the underlying purpose of the restriction imposed, the extent and urgency of the evil sought to be remedied thereby, the disproportion of the imposition, the prevailing conditions of the time

---

[98] Article 19, Constitution of India.

> should all enter into the judicial verdict. In evaluating such elusive factors and forcing their own conception of what is reasonable in all the circumstances of a given case, it is inevitable that the social philosophy and scale of values of the judges participating in the decision play an important part, and the limit to their interference with legislative judgment in such cases can only be dictated by their sense of responsibility and self restraint and the sobering reflection that the Constitution is meant not only for people of their way of thinking but for all, and that the majority of the elected representatives of the people have, in authorizing the imposition of the restrictions, considered them to be reasonable.[99]

The purpose behind this description of the judicial function when examining the reasonableness of a restriction in fundamental freedom cases is not to substitute judicial arbitrariness for legislative partiality or executive caprice. Bearing in mind the democratic backing behind State action, the Court must, nevertheless, consider whether the State action is in the public interest in terms of its purpose, direct and indirect effects, the procedures to be followed, the persons or institutions empowered, the people, interests and causes affected and the constitutional backdrop of human rights and social justice against which all constitutional action must be mirrored. To some extent, there is bound to be a considerable overlap between the anti-arbitrariness

99 *State of Madras v. V.G. Rao* AIR 1952 SC 196 at 200.

doctrine in equality jurisprudence, the process requirements in the life and liberty clause and the reasonableness doctrine applicable to the fundamental freedoms. But the latter doctrine is more expansive and requires the Court to be satisfied that the constitutional ends of human rights - which are subserved by both the fundamental rights and directive principles chapters - are, in fact, satisfied.

Despite the strong interventionist flavour of its earlier 1952 statement on the judicial role, critics have alleged that the Supreme Court has been somewhat mechanical in its approach to constitutional limitations, skirting the more meaningful questions about the reasonableness of State action and limiting its inquiry into considering whether the impugned actions falls within the specific excepted constitutional limitation. Such a 'typological' approach[100] fails to fulfil the role which the Constitution assigned to the judiciary. In determining, for example, free speech issues, the Court is not just asked to consider whether the restriction in question falls within the category of contempt of court, defamation, official secrecy or any other designated exception. Rather, its task is to examine whether the law of contempt of court or defamation or official secrecy (and so on) itself constitutes a 'reasonable restriction' on the freedom of speech and expression. One of the very earliest decisions of the Court used the 'typological' approach creatively by insisting that laws relating to public order did not fall within the constitutional category of security of state.[101] This necessitated an amendment of the Constitution whereby 'public order' was also included in the list of constitutional limitations.

However, this kind of use of the typological approach has

---

100 R. Dhavan: *Only the Good News; On the Law of the Press in India* (Delhi 1987).

101 See *Romesh Thappar v. State of Madras* AIR 1950 SC 594; *Brij Bhushan v. State of Delhi* AIR 1950 SC 129. But note the Supreme Court's own retrospective reflection in *State of Bihar v. Shailabaladevi* AIR 1952 SC 329 at pr.4, p.330.

failed to find consistent expression in the jurisprudence of the Court. For a long time, the Court accepted that if the 'pith and substance' of any impugned action fell into a constitutional category, it would back off. Later, the Court accepted that the "...(t)he pith and substance doctrine looks only at the object and subject matter of State action...(whereas) what the Court must consider is the direct and inevitable consequence of the State action, (o)therwise, the protection of the fundamental rights chapter would be subtly but surely eroded".[102] But, even this movement away from a pure mechanical approach to considering examining the 'direct and inevitable effect' of State action is a limited move in a wider direction. In the myriad of instances where the Court has considered fundamental rights challenges to State action, it has examined the pros and cons of State action, but it has held back from enunciating the determinate and indeterminate elements of the constitutional criteria to be used. One reason for this may well be that the heavy pressure of constitutional amendments immunizing vast categories of legislation from fundamental rights scrutiny has intuitively counselled judicial restraint. But, given the enormity of prima facie justifiable complaints, the Court is giving increasing consideration to following a more detailed and principled approach to the 'reasonableness' doctrine which remains insufficiently explored as explicable doctrine.

By contrast after 1978, the "procedure established by law" clause (Art.21) has been reinterpreted to incorporate the anti-arbitrariness doctrine of the equality clause and aspects of the reasonableness doctrine of the fundamental freedoms clause.[103] Having benefitted from such infusion, the Court has also taken the view that "procedure established by law" does not just admit of a descriptive meaning but, even independent of the equality and fundamental freedom clauses, must be interpreted as prescribing

---

102 *Maneka Gandhi* (*supra* n.71) at pr.68, p.635,

103 *Maneka Gandhi*, *supra* n.71.

a reasonable and fair procedure for all infringements of life and personal liberty. The Court has taken the view that this article read as a whole is concerned with the fullest development of an individual and ensuring his dignity through the rule of law.[104] Every procedure must seem to be 'reasonable, fair and just'.[105] The right to life and personal liberty has been interpreted widely to include the right to livelihood, health, education, environment and all those matters which contributed to life with dignity. The test of procedural fairness has been deemed to be one which is commensurate to protecting such rights.[106] Thus, where workers have been deemed to have the right to public employment and its concomitant right to livelihood, a hire-fire clause in favour of the State is not reasonable, fair and just[107] even though the State cannot affirmatively provide livelihood for all. Under this doctrine the Court will not just examine whether the procedure itself is reasonable, fair and just, but also whether it has been operated in a fair, just and reasonable manner. This has meant accepting, for example, that the right to speedy trial[108] and legal aid[109] are part

---

104 For the sweep of this article see *supra* n.72.

105 *Hussainara Khatoon v. State of Bihar* AIR 1979 SC 1360 at pr.5, p.1365.

106 *Supra* n.39.

107 *Delhi Transport Corporation v. D.T.C. Mazdoor Sabha* AIR 1991 SC 101.

108 *A.R. Antulay v. R.S. Nayak* (1992) 1 SCC 225.

109 *Ranchod Mathur v. State of Gujarat* AIR 1974 SC 1143; *M.H. Hoskot v. State of Maharashtra* AIR 1978 SC 1548; *State of Haryana v. Darshana Devi* AIR 1979 SC 1360, 1369; *Gopalanachari v. State of Kerala* AIR 1981 SC 674; *Sheela Barse v. State of Maharashtra* AIR 1983 SC 378; *Ranjan Dwivedi v. Union of India* AIR 1983 SC 624; *Suk Das v. Union Territory of Arunachal Pradesh* AIR 1986 SC 991; *Center for Legal Research v. State of Kerala* (1986) 2 SCC 706; *Kishore Chand v. State of H.P.* (1991) 11 SCC 286.

of any reasonable, fair and just procedure. The process clause is comprehensive and applicable in all areas of State action covering civil, criminal and administrative action. Inclusive of doctrines of natural justice which afford affected parties a chance to be heard, the process clause assimilates within its grasp the doctrines of administrative law and provides them the niche of constitutional protection.[110] It remains to be seen whether the courts will further extend the requirement of a reasonable, fair and just procedure by critically examining the provisions of the Criminal Procedure Code and other well established statutes; and, having done so go further to add to the minimal due process which the Constitution prescribes in the matter of preventive administrative detention.[111]

The dilemmas of interpreting the scheme of constitutional limitations travel beyond any simple application of the anti-arbitrariness doctrine (drawn from the equality article), reasonableness (taken from the basic freedoms article) and 'reasonable, fair and just procedure' (derived from the life and personal liberty provisions). Characteristically, each fundamental right stipulates its own complex archaeology. The religious freedom clause permits the regulation of economic, financial, political and other secular activity. Such limitations cannot be pronounced on in the abstract. Taken to alternative logical conclusions, there would be nothing left of either the right to religious freedom or the limitations respectively. Yet, by devising the 'essential practice' test to determine which aspects of religious belief and practice merit constitutional protection, the Court has

---

110 Inquiries into the abuse of power and denial of process no longer just flow from the courts' prerogative writ jurisdiction but, in the light of the anti-arbitrariness cases (*supra* n.85), as a part of the guaranteed fundamental rights as well.

111 The articles on preventive detention form a quasi-separate code. Although they have been broadly interpreted to admit a wide ranging judicial review (*supra* n.12), such review has travelled on its own textual steam rather than the new due process.

allowed leeway to all kinds of religious practices while retaining the right to decree on non-essential and doubtful assertions.

It might be argued that the Courts should confine their investigation into the bonafides of an assertion to ensure that trumped up assertions do not masquerade as religious claims. But, should it go further? Even if the 'essential practices' test has been interpreted with a responsible judicial statesmanship, the Supreme Court could be accused of combining the role of a constitutional custodian with that of an all-purpose high priest for all faiths. Yet an accommodating, inoffensive and sensitive interpretation of various religious faiths have simultaneously provided an expansive and generous protection to various beliefs and practices while at the same time enabling a greater financial, administrative and social oversight of powerful religious institutions which have been subjected to the discipline of the Constitution.[112] Again, where the State has to define the 'backward classes' entitled to preferential treatment, or the extent to which minority education institutions can be forced to accept non-minority students if that institution accepts State aid, the Court cannot devise easy formulae as to what is constitutionally acceptable, but has to look at the constitutional enterprise as a whole in the light of existing practices.[113] It is here that the interpretation of the Constitution needs to fully comprehend the socialist and secular aims of India's Constitution (which was devised for a people with a diversity of social and economic backgrounds and possessed of many faiths and beliefs) and promote these goals consistently with its egalitarian

---

112 *Commissioner...v. L.T. Swamiar* (*supra* n.64). For a further account of the Supreme Court's jurisprudence on Hindu religious endowments see R. Dhavan: The Supreme Court and Hindu Religious Endowments 1950-1975, (1978), 20 JILI 52-102.

113 On the complexities of the positive discrimination programme see *Indira Sawhney v. Union of India* JI (1992) (6) SC 273; On minority institutions see *St. Stephens v. Union of India* (*supra* n.15); Both areas serve as excellent examples of a juristic flexibility and doctrinal resilience in finding specific answers to complex social questions.

and libertarian commitments which are, indubitably, fundamental and part of the basic structure of the Constitution. While respecting plurality, the Constitution is pointed in the direction of achieving substantive and real equality as expeditiously and comprehensively as possible within the rule of law. The constitutional limitations are not to be read as independent texts but as an overall programmatic constitutional scheme of social justice.

Our review of various juristic problems connected with creating a human rights jurisprudence for India have identified various exploratory facets including: the identification of the institutions and agencies of State vulnerable to fundamental rights discipline; the yielding of customs, practices and personal lives to fundamental rights claims; the definition and extent of fundamental rights and the delineation of claims which were not worthy of constitutional protection; the relationship between fundamental rights inter se as part of the constitutional scheme; and - amongst other things - the interpretation of the constitutional limitations. In all cases, there is an insistence on the rule of law. In the context of India's human rights jurisprudence, the rule of law includes both the formal requirement that rights can only be taken away by duly enacted laws as well as the broader prescription that any empowerment to infringe a fundamental right must be necessary in the public interest, rationally connected to the purposes for which it is given, exercised with due consideration of relevant factors and after affording an opportunity for participatory decision making and based on a bedrock of principles which defend the dignity of all human beings and provide them genuinely equal opportunities. No doubt these principles have to be superimposed on the untidy claims of everyday life in societies that are unequal.

This is where the judicial task begins. It may be necessary to correct the impression that the judicial discretion is large enough to contain multitudes. Judges often use open textured concepts to define their discretion. But, this makes judicial decision making less of an opportunity and more of a responsibility. At times, such responsibility entails prescribing detailed schematic rules to universally govern State action. This was manifest in the cases dealing with preferential quotas for the disadvantaged in the matter of State employment. This was also the case in the controversial issue surrounding the demand for fairness and justice for those seeking admission to colleges offering technical education.[114] Even if - both in form and substance - such schemes appear as judicial legislation, they are founded on principled considerations and, undoubtedly, within the judicial remit. As the Court transits over time, each discretion giving concept, that guides judicial decision making, finds elucidation so that judges do not just find their answer at any point on a scale of preference but devise categories of inclusion, exclusion and emphasis to shape future decision making. The fact that interpretations vary over time cannot belittle any contemporary effort to give a structure meaning to the various juristic techniques employed in human rights jurisprudence. It may, however, be useful to remember that it is the rights that are fundamental, yielding to the various degrees and kinds of necessity that make the co-existence of persons and nature possible, fair and just.

V. Epilogue

To condense the principles of constitutional interpretation should not result in their oversimplification. The Indian Constitution does not specifically give a preferred status to one fundamental right over another. But, inevitably, where there is a threat to the person of a human being the courts will act swiftly and decisively. A great deal of the work of the higher judiciary in fundamental rights cases has been to consider the kind of interlocutory relief that must be given.[115] Almost as much of the

---

114 *Indira Sawhney v. Union of India ibid.*; *Unnikrishnan v. State of A.P.*, *supra* n.48.

115 For an account of some of the statistical data see R. Dhavan, *The Supreme Court Under Strain: The Challenge of Arrears* (Delhi 1979) 56-59; and *Litigation Explosion in India* (Delhi 1984) 82-83.

Court's time is taken up in determining these matters of immediate relief as it is in making principled decisions supported by final judgments. Although one of the leading Constitution makers said on the floor of the Assembly that the Constitution had discarded the village and made the individual the basic unit of the Constitution, the Constitution sought to preserve the rights of individuals as well as the collectivities and group life which characterize the life of a nation.[116] The Constitution in its own circumspect way did seek to cleanse many traditional group formations of many practices founded on entrenched notions like caste which resulted in the unwarranted domination of human beings by each other. It was also solicitous that the nation should not proceed on the exploitative basis that one part of it prospers at the expense of another. Since the Constitution envisaged that the State would be an important, though not the only, instrument of social change, a theory of constitutional limitations was devised which granted the State a considerable amount of power to regulate the political economy and introduce welfare schemes which would benefit the least advantaged. Over the years, successive governments claimed that they were acting to achieve human rights consistent with social justice for all, even if in the course of effecting this distributive justice, the rights of some were taken away. The Court was prepared to allow the State to empower itself to undertake this exercise without putting too many limitations in the grant of such powers. Yet, the Court was unprepared to allow the State to usurp and exercise these powers without being accountable for it through the aegis of judicial review and subject to the discipline of the fundamental rights dispensation of the Constitution. If until 1973, the Court agreed to abdicate judicial review by accepting wide ranging ouster clauses in the area of agrarian reform and social welfare, after

---

[116] B.R. Ambedkar: VII CAD 38-9 (4th Nov. 1948). Yet the associational freedoms guaranteed in the Fundamental Rights chapter can be, and usually are, claimed as individual rights. Equally, clusters of individual rights are often claimed collectively as the rights.

1973, the Court refused to accept such blanket ousters of its jurisdiction.

The highest judiciary can never be shunted out from the first base of judicial review to examine whether the exercise of a valid constitutional power was genuine and bore a nexus with the purposes for which it claimed. But, having entered into such an examination, the Court is duty bound to consider the extent to which the fundamental rights are trespassed, in what way and to what effect. In a very broad sense - and, this is without reference to any particular competing claims - it cannot be argued that human rights issues are invariably and necessarily antithetical to the socialist or social justice aims of the Constitution. This false dichotomy is artificial in nature and was responsible for plaguing discourse on the Indian Constitution into an unhealthy stagnation. In recent years, the Court seems to have made it clear that socialist regimes are expected to be as sensitive to human rights disciplines as any other, after due recognition is given to the fact that the demands of individuals have to be balanced against those of social justice. The fact that power is sought to be exercised for the public good is no reason for not subjecting it to rigorous judicial scrutiny to ensure its bonafide use consistent with human rights.

What has enabled an expansive view of human rights and State responsibility has been an unrelated series of litigation which has been collectively called 'public interest' or 'social action' litigation.[117] The Supreme Court greatly liberalized the rules of locus standi so that public spirited citizens may bring justiciable public causes before the higher judiciary in defence of either diffused public interests which affect a large section of the public or the interests of identifiable beneficiaries including, especially,

---

117 For a general review see U. Baxi: "Taking Suffering Seriously: Social Action Litigation in the Supreme Court of India" in R. Dhavan et al *Judges and the Judicial Power* (Bombay 1925) 289-315. R. Dhavan: "Law as Struggle" (Public Interest Legal Support and Research Centre (PILS.RC) Working Paper No. 10 (1992)).

the disadvantaged and weaker sections of the community.[118] Even a mere letter is enough to initiate the jurisdiction of the courts except in such cases where such an initiative is not bonafide or cloaked a private interest.[119] Faced with such challenges, the Court has devised new procedures to appoint investigating commissions to cull facts or make recommendations and provide schematic relief beyond declaring action invalid, passing injunctive orders or making damage awards.[120] By their very nature, public interest cases are less concerned with individuals and more with collective entitlements and responsibilities. Under pressure from these demands, the nature and extent of fundamental rights have been recast with consequential effects not just on the remedies available but on the human rights enterprise of the Constitution as a whole.[121]

But the constitutional interpretation of fundamental rights in India cannot be wholly understood without comprehending the human situation in which the demand for rights is made. The human condition speaks of poverty at levels of penury where basic needs and livelihood are not assured. There is homelessness, illiteracy and a structural reinforcement of privilege and power. There are manifold problems of housing, health, environment and

---

118 *S.P. Gupta v. Union of India* AIR 1982 SC 149.

119 Generally Pathak, J. in *Bandhua Mukti Morcha v. Union of India* AIR 1984 SC 802; *State of H.P. v. A. Parent* AIR 1985 SC 910; *Forward Construction v. Prabhat Mandal* (1986) 1 SCC 100; *Janata Dal v. B.S. Chaudhry* (1991) 3 SCC 756.

120 E.g. *Bandhua Mukti Morcha... (ibid.* n.51) and also (1991) 4 SCC 174, 177; *Mukesh Advani v. Union of India* AIR 1985 SC 1363 (bonded labour); *Sheela Barse v. Union of India* (1983) 2 SCC 96 (prison); *Mohan Lal Sharma v. State of U.P.* (1989) 2 SCC 600 (reinvestigation of crime); *Delhi Judicial Services Association v. State of Gujarat* (1991) 4 SCC 406; *Tarun Bharat Singh v. Union of India* AIR 1992 SC 514; *Banwasi Seva Ashram v. Station of U.P.* (1986) 4 SCC 753.

121 *Supra* n.72.

exploitation. All this is of immense dimension, including in their number a large number of the poorest of the poor. It is an oversimplification to argue that the essential principles of constitutional interpretation rotate around ensuring a basic equality in how individuals are conventionally treated by their governments and the imposition of a discipline so that the powers claimed are not disproportionate to the purposes for which they are to be used. The constitutional quest for a human rights jurisprudence is something more than getting government to respect the rule of law. Even where the rule of law may be satisfied, the humanity of Indian constitutionalism cannot stop short of a ceaseless quest to raise the level of constitutional concern beyond the negative requirement of disciplining the State to a more positive assertion of finding a more substantial equality in civil society, stimulating a greater capacity for the assertion of one's dignity, evolving a more equitable opportunity of choice, supporting levels of individual and collective creativity and securing a more equitable civil and political society in which the values of democracy and social equality leave both individuals, their collectivities, and society at greater peace with each other. Part of India's experiment with human rights has been to develop a jurisprudence which does not protect us just from State excesses but exacts accountability and responsibility from those who exercise power in civil society and the State. As such, its human rights jurisprudence is part of the struggle of those who strive to protect their dignity and are entitled to equal treatment, respect and concern.

METHODS AND CRITERIA OF JUDGMENT ON THE QUESTION OF RIGHTS TO FREEDOM IN ITALY

Enzo Cheli* and Filippo Donati**

I. Introduction

This essay proposes to illustrate the procedural and substantive methods, as well as the decision-making criteria (*rationes decidendi*), most commonly applied by the Italian Constitutional Court in the exercise of its powers of control over the constitutionality of laws, when this control touches the sphere of the fundamental freedoms of citizens and social groups.

The description and the evaluation of these methods and criteria will dwell particularly on the following points: a) the historical development of Italian constitutional case-law on the theme of freedom; b) the way in which judicial practice has progressively detached itself from the model adopted by the Charter of 1948, by interpreting the model in an evolutionary way; c) the possibility of identifying recurrent and predictable criteria, that do not depend on the circumstances of the individual case, from the types of arguments that most frequently occur in the Italian Court; d) the current trends and possible predictions that can be formulated with respect to the future development of Italian constitutional justice.

The analysis of these points requires as a first step, some reminders of the model of constitutional justice adopted in Italy by the Constitution of 1948 and of the practical experiences in the development of this model from 1956 onwards - the year in which the Italian Constitutional Court was established.

II. The Birth of the System of Constitutional Review in Italy

A complete system of constitutional justice appeared for the

D.M. Beatty (ed.), Human Rights and Judicial Review, 227-265.

first time in Italy with the Republican Charter of 1st January 1948.[1] The idea of entrusting constitutional control to an *ad hoc* organ was, in fact, completely foreign to previous experience of the Italian State. This was so both for the liberal period governed by the Albertine Statute (based on the pre-eminence of Parliament and the monarch), and also for the authoritarian period of the fascist regime (based on the pre-eminence of the executive and Head of Government).

The idea of introducing a system of constitutional justice thus came to fruition in the Italian legal order during the period of formation of the Constitution of 1948. There was a requirement for guarantees that placed the necessity of avoiding the risk of recent authoritarian experiences amongst the primary objectives of the new order. In short - in the light of the debate that developed in the Constituent Assembly between 1946 and 1948 - the reasons for the adoption of a system of constitutional justice in Italy can be reduced to three fundamental objectives: to guarantee the "rigidity" of the Constitution, by protecting it against the possibility of being hijacked by transient political majorities; to introduce a "judge of freedoms" to whom the defence of the human rights, that the new Constitution had outlined in its first part, could be entrusted; and

---

*Professor of Constitutional Law at the University of Florence, Law School, and Justice of the Constitutional Supreme Court since 1987. Author of many monographs, essays and articles dealing with fundamental issues of Constitutional Law, he mainly directs his scientific interests in the following fields: Governmental activity, sources of law, regional Governments, and rights related to mass media.

**Constitutional Law Researcher and Lecturer and the University of Florence, Law School. He has studied various aspects of Constitutional case-law. Presently his scientific interests are mainly directed at the issues of constitutionality in the process of conforming to EEC legislation.

[1] For reading on the establishment of the Constitutional Court in Italy, cf. G. D'Orazio, *La genesi della Corte Costituzionale*, Milano 1981 and C. Mezzanotte, *Il giudizio sulle leggi*, vol. I, *Le ideologie del costituente*, Milano 1979.

to identify a body that could adjudicate on the controversies between the different organs of the State, and between the State and the new regional bodies.

These three objectives were realised in the Charter of 1948 with the creation of a centralised organ of constitutional justice (the Constitutional Court) invested with the tasks of judging: a) on controversies related to the constitutional legality of the laws of the State and of the Regions; b) on the distribution of the competencies of the State, between State and Regions, and between Regions; c) on the criminal responsibility of the Head of State for treason and violation of the Constitution, and over Ministers for crimes committed in the course of their functions (Article 134 Constitution).[2]

To these competencies there was subsequently added a fourth, relating to the control of the admissibility of abrogative referendums, requested by 500.000 votes or 5 Regional Councils (Article 75 Constitution and Article 2 of the Constitutional Law of 11th March 1953, n° 1).

III. Peculiarities of the Italian Model for the Control of the Constitutionality of Laws

When the members of the Italian Constituent Assembly made their choice, their models were those of Austria and the United States. In the end, the model which prevailed was the Austrian and this led to the choice of a "centralised" organ of constitutional justice endowed with a power of annulment *erga omnes* of unconstitutional laws. This model would normally also have implied direct access to the Court. However, it came to be

---

[2] This last competence was suppressed by the constitutional law 1/1989, which granted the jurisdiction over ministerial crimes (*reati ministeriali*) to the authority of the ordinary judge.

'corrected' - if this can be said - by the US model. The provision of access to the Court was not direct - it was not to be a court of first instance - but always by way of another judicial body. It was established, as a consequence, that questions relative to the constitutionality of laws could only be presented to the Court in the case where, in the course of proceedings, a judge (ordinary or administrative) considered it necessary to present to the Constitutional Court a preliminary question of the constitutionality of the law to be applied in that same case. Moreover, the judge must have considered the question - raised by himself or at the request of the parties - to be "relevant" to the resolution of the original proceedings and "not manifestly unfounded" in its content. The combination thus produced, between the Austrian and the United States' models, marks out the Italian system of constitutional justice as unique among the Western systems of constitutional control.[3] In short, constitutional control in Italy is, on the one hand, marked by an abstract judgment on the rules which focuses on the confrontation between the limits represented by the constitutional rules and the ends represented by the ordinary rules; but, on the other hand, while the judgment is abstract, it is concretely anchored to the existence of a controversy and the presence of a judge who is called upon to apply the contested norm in the solution of a specific case.

The "mixed" character of the Italian model led, as a consequence, to the Constitutional Court being put in a very special position, bordering between government bodies and society. At constitutional level there has been established, then, a parallel series of relations between, on the one hand, the Constitutional Court and the legislative power and, on the other, between the

---

[3] For a description of the different systems of constitutional justice, see in the Italian literature, in particular, M. Cappelletti, *Il controllo giudiziario di costituzionalità delle leggi nel diritto comparato*, Milano, 1970 and *La giustizia costituzionale in Europa: dai modelli alla prassi*, in *Quaderni costituzionali* 1982, no. 3 and *Costituzione e giustizia costituzionale nel diritto comparato*, edited by G. Lombardi, Torino 1985.

Constitutional Court and the judicial power.[4] Given this position at the point of convergence between politics and the judiciary, the Italian Constitutional Court has historically found itself in an optimal situation to carry out a double role: at times addressing the political sphere with social requests deriving from its contact with the judicial world; at others upholding the demands and interests of the political world when confronting the judicial sphere.[5]

---

[4] On the positioning of the Court in the Constitutional system see amongst others P. Barile, *La Corte costituzionale organo sovrano: implicazioni pratiche*, in *Giur. cost.*, 1957; A. M. Sandulli, *Sulla posizione della Corte nel sistema degli organi costituzionale dello Stato*, in *Riv. trim. dir. pubb.* 1960: AA.VV., *La Corte costituzionale tra norma giuridica e realta sociale*, edited by N. Occhiocupo, Bologna 1978; *Corte costituzionale e sviluppo della forma di governo in Italia*, edited by P. Barile, E. Cheli and S. Grassi, Bologna 1982; C. Mezzanotte, *Corte costituzionale e legittimazione politica*, Roma 1984; M. Luciani, *La Corte costituzionale nella forma di governo italiana*, in *La Costituzione italiana quarant'anni dopo*, Milano 1989.

[5] For the best explanation of this point, see Cheli, *La Corte costituzionale nella forma di governo in Italia*, in *Quaderni no.1 dell Associazione per gli studi e ricerche parlamentari*, Milano, 1991, 125et seq.

For comprehensive treatment of constitutional justice in Italy cf. V. Crisafulli, *Lezioni di diritto costituzionale, II, L'ordinamento costituzionale italiano: le fonti normative. La Corte costituzionale*, Padova 1984; A. Pizzorusso, G. Volpe, F. Sorrentino and B. Moretti, *Garanzie costituzionale: artt. 134-139*, in *Commentario della Costituzione*, edited by G. Branca, Bologna-Rome, 1981 e G. Zagrebelsky, *La giustizia costituzionale*, Bologna 1988. Otherwise see the numerous essays collected in *Scritti sulla giustizia costituzionale in honour of Vezio Crisafulli*, Padova 1985; in *Strumenti e tecniche di giudizio della Corte costituzionale*, Milano 1988, as well as in the proceedings of the seminars organised by the Constitutional Court and collected in the volumes *Effetti temporali delle sentenze della Corte costituzionale anche con riferimento alle esperienze straniere*, Milano 1989; *Giudizio "a quo" e promovimento del processo costituzionale*, Milano 1990; *La Corte costituzionale tra diritto interno e diritto comunitario*, Milano 1991; *Le sentenze della Corte costituzionale e l'art. 81, u.c., della Costituzione*, Milano, 1993, and finally *Il principio di ragionevolezza nella giurisprudenza della Corte costituzionale. Riferimenti comparatici* (forthcoming).

IV. The Limits of Control Deriving from the Model

In order to preserve a degree of autonomy of both the legislative and judicial powers, a preliminary requirement of the new model of constitutional control adopted by the Charter of 1948 was to identify certain limits to the Court's powers of constitutional review.

In an initial period, these were principally:

a) The type of judgment on constitutionality with which the Italian Court is invested, as we have already stated, is an abstract decision that refers to laws that are in conflict with constitutional rules. In principle therefore, and this is how it initially took shape in the Italian legal order, it was said that the judgment on constitutionality should not exceed the limits indicated by a strict technique of comparing the norms of positive law with the constitution, without involving the values and interests underlying those norms.

b) The means of access to the Court adopted by the constitutional model excludes a power of initiative on the part of the Court in the proposing or choosing of the questions to be examined. All the activities of the Court, according to the model, in fact depend on the initiative of external actors and, in particular, on the initiative of the other judicial bodies. It was intended by the members of the Constituent Assembly that this limitation on access should mitigate the possible "political" connotations of the Constitutional Court, emphasising instead its "judicial" functions.

c) As well as abiding by the model, in judgments on the constitutionality of laws, the Italian Court had to remain within the limits of the following alternatives. It could either admit a question and annul the unconstitutional law, or reject it, thereby leaving the law unchanged, and thus to the free interpretation of the judges and other persons applying the law. Since there are no other alternatives, it is therefore outside the ambit of the model for the Constitutional Court either to give a binding authoritative interpretation of the norms in question, or to vary their content.

d) An ongoing problem concerning the definition of the model, was how to prevent the Constitutional Court from straying onto the terrain of the political choices of the legislator. As a result, it was established by the law, that the Court's control of legality "excluded any evaluation of a political nature and any control of the use of the discretionary powers of Parliament" (Article 28, *legge* 11th March 1953, n° 87). But this norm, as we shall see, met with little success in Italy, to such an extent that it seems never to have been applied at all in practice or, at least, has long since fallen into desuetude.

V. Methods of Broadening the Control

As the Court has gained experience with its powers of constitutional review, it has moved away from the limits derived from the original model. We shall now briefly describe how this process came about.

a) In the first place, in practice, the judgment of constitutionality has been increasingly transformed from a decision "*su regole*" into a decision "*su argomenti*".[6] That is to say, it has changed from being a decision on rules to being a decision on principles.[7] Consequently, it has been noted that there is a

---

6 R. Bin, *Diritti e argomenti. Il bilancio degli interessi nella giurisprudenza costituzionale*, Milano 1992.

7 R. Dworkin (*Taking Rights Seriously*, Duckworth, 1978), has observed that, "Rules are applicable in all-or-nothing fashion. If the facts a rule stipulates are given, then either the rule is valid, in which case the answer it supplies must be accepted, or it is not, in which case it contributes nothing to the decision" (page 24). Principles, on the contrary, "have a dimension that rules do not - the dimension of weight or importance. When principles intersect ... one who must resolve the conflict has to take into account the relative weight of each. This cannot be, of course, an exact measurement, and the judgment that a particular

tendency on the part of Italian constitutional justice not to treat the content of the Italian constitution as absolute rules, but rather as principles, aiming at the protection of certain interests or expressing certain values. As a consequence these are then open to being balanced against the interests and values put into play by the law whose legality is being challenged.[8]

b) To overcome the limits deriving from the fact that the question of constitutionality cannot be raised independently, but must necessarily be raised by a judge in the course of proceedings, the Court has tended to reinterpret the terms of the question proposed, with a certain freedom in its evaluation, thus stretching, in certain cases, the strict connection between the question raised by the judge and the content of the subsequent constitutional judgment. In practice, the Court frequently tries to widen its room for manoeuvre. Sometimes it expands the reference to the constitutional parameters operated by the judge *a quo* by means of interpretation. At others it puts forward a systematic reconstruction of the law under review. At others again - and this is the most characteristic departure from the original model - it may raise before its own jurisdiction a preliminary question of constitutionality in relation to the judgment of the other question. In this case, the Court becomes its own judge *a quo*, and can consequently direct its control in directions that were not foreseen in the original referral that gave rise to the question.

---

principle or policy is more important than another will often be a controversial one. Nevertheless, it is an integral part of the concept of a principle that it has this dimension, that it makes sense to ask how important or how weighty it is. Rules do not have this dimension. We speak of rules as being *functionally* important or unimportant...But we cannot say that one rule is more important than another within the system of rules, so that when the two rules conflict one supersedes the other by virtue of its greater weight" (page 26-27).

8 On the balancing of interests and values, see *infra*, para. XI.

A further method of widening the control of constitutionality, which is foreseen by the same law, regulating constitutional procedure (Article 27 Law 11th March 1953, n° 87), is the process whereby the Court, in its decision accepting the question of constitutionality, is allowed to extend the scope of the annulment, by defining precisely "which are the other legal rules, whose illegality follows as a result of the adopted judgment".

c) The methods of extending control of constitutionality have found their most relevant and incisive expression at the level of the types of judgment. Here, in fact, the Court has long departed from the scheme of the alternatives between acceptance and rejection, sanctioned by the constitutional model, a long time ago, and has in many cases adopted "interpretative" judgments which at times amount to changes in substantive law. To be more precise, the practice of the Italian Constitutional Court has led to the formulation of: 1) judgments of "interpretative rejection" ("*interpretative di rigetto*"). These refuse a question *in quanto* but interpret the constitutional norm or the law in question in terms different from those advanced by the judge *a quo* in their referral. In other words, they declare that the question of constitutionality is unfounded, but only insofar as the law can be interpreted in a different way, that is consistent with the Constitution.[9]

---

[9] In practice, a judge raises the question of the constitutionality of a law on the basis of a certain interpretation, which he holds to be unconstitutional. The Constitutional Court, on the contrary, rejects the claim holding that the law must be interpreted in a different manner, which is considered to be consistent with the Constitution.

By way of example, according to the Italian Code of Criminal Procedure, prior to its reform, penal procedure could be divided into two stages: the preliminary investigation stage (carried out by judicial police forces), and the full investigation stage (carried out essentially by judges, according to rules guaranteeing full respect for the right of defence). Article 392 of the former Code of Criminal Procedure provided that the norms of the full investigation stage were to be observed simply "insofar as applicable". In a claim brought

These judgments bind the judge that has raised the question, but have no authority for other judges, because the interpretative power over the law remains in the hands of the ordinary judges and, in particular, the supreme judicial body, the Corte di Cassazione; 2) "manipulative" judgments that lead to the formation of a new statute.

"Manipulative" judgments can take different forms. The first relates to the so-called "*interpretative di accoglimento*", where the Court judges that only a certain interpretation of the law is unconstitutional. Consequently, the law remains formally unchanged, but the interpretation which has been declared unconstitutional can no longer be applied.[10]

A second case is that of the so-called "*sentenze additive*", whereby the Court declares a law to be unconstitutional "in the part in which" it

---

before the Constitutional Court, a judge alleged the unconstitutionality of Article 392 of the former Code of Criminal Procedure, insofar as it didn't allow the full right of defence to be guaranteed to the preliminary investigation stage. The Court rejected the judge's claim of unconstitutionality, holding that the former Article 392 had been misinterpreted. According to the Constitutional Court, Article 392 did in fact allow for full respect of the right of defence at the preliminary investigation stage, as it was normally guaranteed at the full investigation stage, and was therefore consistent with the Constitution (Case n° 11/1965).

[10] In substance, "interpretative di accoglimento" do not judge the law itself to be unconstitutional, but only a particular interpretation of that law. Here, by way of example, we can refer to the events described in the previous note, where the Court had to declare that its interpretation continued to be ignored by judges. The judges, as such, continued to hold that Article 392 of the Code of Criminal Procedure, did not guarantee the defendant the rights of defence during the preliminary examination. Consequently, the Court later declared unconstitutional the interpretation of the former Article 392, according to which the guarantee of the right of defence foreseen at the full examination stage did not also apply to the preliminary stage (Case n° 52/1965).

fails to provide for something considered to be essential for it to be considered constitutional. The effect of this type of judgment is to enhance the contents of the law, with respect to the original version.[11]

A third case covers the so-called "*sentenze sostitutive*", in which the Court declares unconstitutional a law, which makes provision for something instead of something else. The effect of this judgment is to impose upon judges, the application of a norm defined by the Court, in place of the one which has been declared unconstitutional.[12]

Of these new types of judgments, the "additive" ones have assumed a particular importance, especially in the field of social rights, because they are the ones in which the Court has used the basic constitutional principles to redress the omissions and lacunae of the legislator. The "additive" judgments can, moreover, bind the legislator with different degrees of intensity. There exist in practice, in fact, "self-applying" additive judgments, that completely reformulate a new norm (and also have a direct effect at the level of public

---

11 For example, in Case n° 190/1970, the Constitutional Court declared the former Article 304-bis of the Code of Criminal Procedure to be unconstitutional, insofar as it did not give the defendant the right of assistance during questioning.

12 For example, in Case n° 15/1969 the Constitutional Court held the former Article 313 of the Criminal Code, concerning the grant of permission to prosecute for contempt of the Constitutional Court, to be unconstitutional, insofar as it attributed the right to grant such permission to the Ministry of Justice, instead of to the Constitutional Court itself.

spending),[13] and "non-self-applying" additive judgments that introduce a new norm, whose implementation is remitted to the legislator (especially at the level of allocation of funds).[14]

In the same area of the expansion of the decision-making tools of the Court, one can include those judgments that declare the "supervening illegality" of the law, or those fixing a deadline,

---

[13] In this respect, Case n° 219/1975 is exemplary. Here, the Court declared unconstitutional a law, concerning the remuneration of high ranking civil servants, insofar as it did not extend such rights to university professors. This judgment thereby introduced equality of pay between university professors and (the highest) salaried management level civil servants. This, subsequently gave rise to the problem of financing the additional cost to the State of the highest salaried professors.

The financial repercussions of the Court's judgment caused much controversy and heated doctrinal discussion. Such judgments, in fact, lead to new increased expenditure to the State without providing the appropriate means for covering such additional costs. In this respect, Article 81 Constitution, provides that every law that incurs new expenditure or reduces revenue to the State, must indicate the means of covering its costs. This therefore led to the question of whether such an obligation, to cover additional State expenditure, could limit the discretion of the Constitutional Court insofar as such judgments give rise to financial obligations.

For ample detail, in this respect, see the collected essays in the volume entitled, *"Le sentenze della Corte constituzionale e l'art. 81, u.c., della Costituzione. Atti del seminario di studi tenutosi a Roma, palazzo della Consulta nei giorni 8 e 9 novembre 1991"*, cit.

[14] For example, in Case n° 479/1988, the Court held a law to be unconstitutional insofar as it did not provide for protection against inflation in the compensation offered against redundancies to a certain category of workers, whereas, on the contrary such a system was available for other categories. In the case in question, however, the Court held that the task of providing for such a system of protection for that particular category fell to the legislator. This judgment, in contrast to the case discussed in the previous note, did not have direct effects on the State budget. In this manner, the Court allowed for the legislator to review the unconstitutional section, taking account of the actual means of the budget.

after which the terms of the judgment must take effect. Through this type of judgment the Court has sought to relax the "rigidity" of the temporal effects of the judgment of acceptance under Article 136 of the Constitution. This declares that the unconstitutional norm should cease to have effect from the day following the publication of the judgment, with the ensuing obligation on judges not to apply the norm that has been declared unconstitutional in proceedings that are pending (and that would exclude, by the same principle, the possibility of the Court laying down different terms for the effects of its own judgments).

The techniques referred to, are all based on the premise, elaborated in scientific terms, that draws a distinction between the notion of "*disposizione*" (that describes the formal linguistic expression of the law) and the notion of the "*norma*" (that expresses the way in which the law is interpreted and applied in individual circumstances).[15] As a result, it is obvious that the types of judgments, as have been illustrated, and particularly the "manipulative" judgments, are those that affect the "*norma*", that is to say, simply a particular interpretation derived from the law.[16]

---

15 On the distinction between "disposizione" and "norma" cf V. Crisafulli, *Disposizione (e norma)*, in *Enc. dir.*, Milano 1964; more recently see R. Guastini, *Dalle fonti alle norme*, Torino 1990.

16 Judgments on the question of constitutionality can refer simply to the law itself. In such cases, the Court can either reject the question of constitutionality, thereby leaving it as a matter of discretion before the judges to decide upon the most appropriate interpretation in the circumstances; or alternatively, the Court can declare the law unconstitutional, thereby rendering it inapplicable and to this extent incapable of being interpreted.

The "*interpretative di rigetto*" and "*manipolative*", on the contrary, regard

Thus, there has been a marked evolution, with respect to the model originally provided for, under Article 136 of the Constitution, which stipulated that judges could not continue to apply a law once it had been declared unconstitutional, without making any provision for the various possible interpretations, in this respect.

d) We referred above to the rule of law that prohibited the control of the Parliament's use of its discretionary powers, and we pointed out that this rule has never been applied in practice. In reality, constitutional review by the Italian Court has frequently affected the sphere of discretion of the legislator, when such control has regarded the aims, internal coherence, consistency of laws, and other aspects connected to their "reasonableness" ("*ragionevolezza*"). In other words, even if the Italian Court has never explicitly maintained that

---

a certain interpretation attributed to the law. As such, they presuppose that a law may be subject to various interpretations. If, for example, a law "L" can be interpreted in ways, "I"(1) and "I"(2), but not "I"(3), this may give rise to the following type of judgments.

a) "*interpretative di rigetto*": the judge has raised the question of constitutionality, holding that "L" must be interpreted in the way "I"(1) and that "I"(1) is unconstitutional; the Court does not declare that "L" itself is unconstitutional insofar as "L" must be interpreted in way "I"(2), which is in conformity with the Constitution. The interpretation given by the Constitutional Court, however, is not binding on judges of lower courts (since the principle of "stare decisis" is not known to the Italian legal system).

b) "*interpretative di accoglimento*": the Court declares that "L" to be unconstitutional only with regard to "I"(1);

c) "*additiva*": the Court declares "L" to be unconstitutional in the section which fails to make provision for something that ought to have foreseen. This judgment does not repeal "L", but imports a different interpretation "I"(3) to be attributed to it by judges;

d) "*sostitutiva*": the Court declares "L" to be unconstitutional in the section which provides for something instead of something else. As a result, the judges must apply "L" in a way, "I"(3), other than was previously determined prior to the constitutional judgment.

For more detailed analysis, cf. R. Guastini, *op. cit.*, 227 et seq.

it could also extend its control to the "excess of legislative power" (such as that exercised by the administrative judge for the review of the excess of administrative power), it has, in fact, always exercised this type of control. It has done this either by reviewing the aims of the law when these are bound by the Constitution (as in the case of delegated legislation adopted by the Government under the terms of Article 76 of the Constitution,[17] or by the "*riserva di legge*" (areas reserved to the legislator by the Constitution), strengthened by certain aims that the legislator is obliged to respect in that area by the Constitution;[18] or by reviewing the "reasonableness" of the laws, on the grounds of the application of the general principle of equality established by the Article 3 of the Constitution, according to the methods that will be illustrated in the following section.[19]

VI. Constitutional Jurisprudence on the Question of Freedom: Premises and Developments

If we move to consider the historical development of the

---

17 Article 76 of the Constitution provides that legislative tasks cannot be delegated to the Government, except insofar as is determined by principles and directions, and in any case only for a limited period and within defined aims. The Court may be required to verify whether or not the Government has effectively limited its intervention to the sphere of activities determined by the Parliament; in the event of a negative decision, the Court declares the "Government law" in breach of Article 76 of the Constitution and therefore illegitimate.

18 For example, Article 43 of the Constitution only consents to the nationalisation of a certain type of company, by way of a law which seeks at achieving ends judged to be in the public interest. In cases of nationalisation, the Court must therefore ensure that the law is in conformity with the aims imposed by the Constitution.

19 See, in this respect, paragraphs VIII-XI and examples drawn therefrom.

constitutional case-law on the theme of freedom, it can be argued that the Italian Court, in the course of its experience - that now spans a period of 36 years - has developed more its "political" than its "judicial" characteristics in its powers of review. It operates predominantly as the moving agent of processes of innovation and reform more than as a "custodian", in the sense of preserving the constitutional values in a conservative way.

This development in the constitutional case-law - which can be considered as a constant throughout the changing historical circumstances of the Italian Republic - has been encouraged by some of the structural conditions of the Italian political and institutional system. Firstly, there has been the presence of a Constitution that offers strong guarantees of the basic human rights, not only in the field of traditional civil and political freedoms but also, especially, in social rights.[20] Secondly, this

---

[20] The discipline of social rights contained in the Italian Constitution is considered to be amongst the most extensive and detailed of contemporary constitutions (Cf. instances given in A. Baldassarre, *Diritti sociali*, in *Enciclopedia giuridica*, Roma, 1989, 13 e 28). It is not possible here to give a detailed account of the structure of social rights drawn from the Italian Constitution (for further information, cf. E. Cheli, *La Constitution face au progres economique et social: le case de l'Italie*, Rapport italien au IIIe Congrès mondial de l'Association internationale de droit constitutionnel, Varsavia 2-5 September 1991). Nevertheless, it is clear, as can be seen from the text of the Constitution, that the keystone to its classification is the human being and this disciplines the various relationships between the individual and different social strata, through which personality takes its form. Within this perspective, socio-ethical and economic relationships are classified into distinct categories, including in the first-mentioned category, family rights (Articles 29-31), health (Article 32), and education (Articles 33-34); in the second category one finds labour rights (Articles 35-50), company and property rights (Articles 41-44), cooperation (Article 45), collaboration with company management (Article 46), credit and savings (Article 47). More specifically, the social rights contained in the Italian Constitution are advanced as direct instruments, which can either guarantee the full enjoyment of classical freedoms, or achieve the so-called principle of substantial equality, that is the limitation of "hindrances to economic and social order, which prevent the full development of the human being and effective participation of all workers in the political, social and economic

was caused by the wide gap in the initial phase of the activity of the Court, between a Constitution that was very advanced in the field of freedoms and human rights and the preceding legislation that was characteristic of liberal and fascist Italy. Thirdly, and finally, there was the distinct absence of unity and the particular fragmentation of the Italian political system that has caused slowness and waste in the formation of political decisions. This has encouraged the judicial organs, by contrast, to supply the defects of the political organs charged carrying out the same with the same functions.

This group of factors taken together has stimulated the Court to promote itself. On many occasions it has made itself the direct interpreter, in competition with the institutions of the political system, of the demands emerging from the social body, but not recognised by the party system. This has brought about a strong "activism" by the Constitutional Court in many phases of Italian history - especially in relation to rights to freedom. This has touched the most diverse areas and has gone through various phases of development.

In an initial phase, the Court engaged in the process of the 'clearing out' of the illiberal legislation of the fascist period. This was done through judgments that rendered the principles of the Constitution of 1948 effective against this legislation, especially in the areas of personal freedoms, political rights and freedom of expression.[21] In a second phase the Court used the principle of

---

organisation of the country" (Article 3.2 Constitution). From this perspective, it has been stressed that social rights aim to create the effective conditions for the achievement of "equal freedoms" amongst citizens (A. Baldassarre, *op. cit.*, 12).

[21] In its first judgment, Case n° 1/1956), the Constitutional Court defined its own competence to scrutinise laws adopted prior to the Constitution. By this assertion, it dismissed the submission whereby such laws were to be repealed due to the effects of the adoption of the Constitution, with whose norms they were regarded as incompatible. In that perspective, it therefore remained to the judiciary to declare whether or not the prior law were inconsistent with the

equality, that is Article 3 of the Constitution, to its maximum to spur the legislator on the interpretation of social rights in the areas of work, welfare, health, family and education.[22] This is the phase in which – as we have stated above – the technique of "additive" judgments was asserted, which aimed to fill the delays and omissions of the legislator. Finally, in a third phase the Court occupied itself in the encouragement of the recognition of new rights, not expressly laid down in the text of the Constitution but that could be inferred from the implicit development of the other rights described in the Constitution. This manifested itself, for example, in relation to the right to privacy,[23] the right of information,[24] the right to a clean environment[25] and the right to

---

Constitution, without raising a question of constitutionality before the Constitutional Court. It is not possible to go into detail on this complex matter, but it is noteworthy that, in the historical judgment made in 1956, the Court overthrew a body of judicial opinion (constituted during the fascist period), which opposed the integral application of new legal principles being sanctioned by the Constitutional Court. The resultant extension of the Court's competencies, has paved the way for the removal of numerous fascist laws from the statute books as unconstitutional. To give but one example from a wealth of possibilities, in this respect, the Case n° 2/1956 held Article 157 of the Code of Public Safety to be unconstitutional, as it made provision for "arrest" for an unspecified period, of persons simply defined as "suspects".

22 On the developments which have taken place with regard to the principle of equality, cf. infra. paras. VIII et seq. For some examples of case-law of the Constitutional Court in the field of social law, cf. notes (25), (26), (28), (29), (30).

23 In the Case n° 38/1973, the Constitutional Court, also referring to Articles 8 and 10 of the European Convention on Human Rights, considered as inviolable rights, amongst others, the right to "dignity, honour, self respect, privacy, intimacy and reputation".

24 On several occasions, the Constitutional Court has recognised the existence of the right to information, which can be traced to Article 21 of the Constitution (cf. cases 49/1971, 105/1972 94/1974). In this respect, for example, the Court held that it was necessary for the television broadcasting network to be

housing.[26]

The possibility of further development along these lines, today, appears to be connected to a great extent, to the interpretation that could be given to Article 2 of the Constitution, which talks of "the inviolable rights of man both as an individual and in the social organisations wherein his personality is developed". There is theoretical discussion of this normative formulation over the question of whether the rule should be considered as referring only to the rights explicitly enumerated in the text of the Constitution (representing those rights as a closed category), or if instead it should be considered as a formula open to progressive expansion in relation to the evolution of the economic and social fabric. The Italian Court - even without ever having explicitly tackled the problem - seems for the time being to be heading towards the first solution that allows the admission of "new rights", but only insofar as those rights can be derived, by means of interpretation, from the rights explicitly sanctioned by the text of the Constitution.[27]

---

structured in such a way as to guarantee consumers plurality of opinion, in order to grant citizen the freedom of choice between various sources of information. (cf. Case n° 826/1988).

[25] On the basis of its evaluation of Article 32 in relation to Article 9 of the Constitution, the court acknowledged the citizens' right to a healthy environment (cf. amongst others, Cases n° 210/1987 and n° 641/1987).

[26] The Court has recognised the right to a home, in connection with the right to dignity of the human being. In this respect, the Court has recognised the right of the partner "more uxorio" of the tenant, to remain in the house in the event of cessation of cohabitation, either where the primary tenant dies, or moves away (Case n° 404/1988). Similarly, the Court has declared unconstitutional a law which denied certain subjects the right to financial participation in the acquisition of a first home (Case n° 217/1988).

[27] For an interpretation of Article 2 as an "open clause" ("clausola aperta") cf. A. Barbera, *Commento all'article 2*, in *Commentario della Costituzione*, edited by G. Branca, Bologna- Roma 1975; on the argument that the "new

In its various phases the action of the Court, thus, anticipated the interventions of the Parliament and the Government and directed them towards reforms of great economic and social relevance. This happened in a more or less intense and direct form, in relation to laws ranging from agricultural reform, fiscal reform, town planning, rent controls, exercising the right to strike, the organization of broadcasting as a mixed system (constructed on the basis of competition between the public and private sectors), the new family law, to the recent reform of the code of criminal procedure.

In some of these fields, by its judgments, the Court, has in fact taken the place of the normal tasks of the legislator.[28] In

---

rights" are always, either explicitly or implicitly, derivable from the "established" rights, see among others A. Baldassarre, *Diritti inviolabili*, in *Enciclopedia giuridica*, Roma 1989. Notwithstanding a certain oscillation, the constitutional jurisprudence supports the line that Article 2 of the Constitution "in the recognition of the inviolable rights of man must be connected back to the constitutional norms concerning individual rights and fundamental guarantees, at least in the sense that there do not exist other fundamental inviolable rights that do not necessarily follow from those foreseen in the Constitution" (Case n° 98/1979).

[28] For example, Article 40 of the Constitution recognised the right to strike, but determined that the law should govern the way in which it is exercised. The law in question was only adopted in 1990 (*legge* n° 146/1990). Prior to its adoption, however, the Court intervened in numerous cases in the sphere of the application and limits of the right to strike. In this regard, the Court, amongst others, had held that the strike in question, for political reasons, was legitimate (Case n° 290/1974), and had further specified that a strike could not jeopardise public services of primary importance and fundamental rights of citizens such as the right to medical assistance (Cases n° 31/1990, 125/1980, 4/1977 and 222/1976).

The judgments of the Constitutional Court on the subject of television broadcasting are particularly renowned. As such, in 1974, the Court was asked to decide on the constitutionality of the State monopoly in broadcasting. In Case n° 225/1974, the Court set forth seven minimal conditions which had to be fulfilled in order for a state monopoly to be considered legitimate. Such conditions were fully accepted by the legislator in the reform passed by the law

others, it has succeeded in laying down the general guidelines that the legislator afterwards followed;[29] in others again, the action of the Court has met with less fortune, and did not succeed in overcoming the resistance put up by the political power.[30]

VII. The Predominance of the Criteria of Equality and Reasonableness in the Shaping of the Italian Constitutional Jurisprudence

One of the principal characteristics of the jurisprudence of the Italian Constitutional Court, particularly on the issue of freedom, is found in the absolute predominance that has been given, with

---

n° 103/1974. Moreover, the principles of multiplicity of information sources, as well as the prohibition on oligopolistic organisations, sanctioned by the Court (Cases 148/1981 and 826/1988), led to the recent reform of television broadcasting (*legge.* n° 223/1990).

29 On the subject of family law, for example, the Court has often endorsed the principle of equality between spouses, and has made numerous statements, which, for instance, have eliminated the discrimination between husband and wife in the punishment of adultery (Cases 126/1968, 127/1968, 147/1969), the inequality between husband and wife on the issue of maintenance in the case of separation (Case n° 133/1970) and so on. The principle of equality between spouses has since been further endorsed and put into practice by the reform of family law (*legge* n° 151/1975).

30 As was the case, with regard to conditions imposed upon the right to property for unspecified periods of time, where the Constitutional Court held that such limits constituted a form of expropriation, which therefore required provision for indemnity (Cases n° 6/1966, 55/1968 and 260/1976). However, with regard to the extent of indemnity due in the case of expropriation, the Court nevertheless established that this did not have to correspond to the market value of the expropriated property, but had to constitute a serious level of compensation for the economic harm caused by such action (Cases n° 5/1980 and 223/1983). As yet, the indications given by the Constitutional Court have not been accepted through the reform of property law, adopted by a law setting forth the general principles in this field.

respect to the other principles of the Constitution, to the reference to the principles of equality and reasonableness (that come from Article 3 of the Constitution).[31]

In 1984 a writer who was interested in the problem pointed out that "in 1979, of a total of twenty-two judgments that had declared the unconstitutionality of the legal norms, nineteen had recourse to the general principle of equality; in 1980 of the twenty-three annulments that were made in the course of considering the preliminary questions raised by the judge at first instance ("*giudizio in via incidentale*"), seventeen were based on Article 3 paragraph 1, and eight exclusively so; in 1981 of a total of twenty-seven, seventeen judgments were about the same thing, but eleven judgments of acceptance were founded only on equal treatment; in 1982 the figures were once again identical to twenty-seven, seventeen and eleven; while in 1983 they amounted to twenty-four, fifteen and seven".[32]

Finally, taking the first six months of 1992 as our last reference point, the statistics show that - of the 18,500 judgments made by the Court since it came into being - 7,125 judgments refer to the principle of equality of Article 3, which represents 38.5% of the total. The reference to the principle of

---

[31] On the principles of equality and reasonableness in the constitutional case-law, see in general, among others, C. Lavagna, *Ragionevolezza e legittimita' costituzionale*, in AA.VV. *Studi in memoria di C. Esposito*; F. Modugno, *Legge (vizi della)* in *Enc. Dir.*, XXIII, Milano 1973; A.M. Sandulli, *Il principio di ragionevolezza nella giurisprudenza costituzionale*, in *Dir. e soc.* 1975; G. Zagrebelsky, G. Ferrara and A. Baldassarre, in AA.VV. *La Corte costituzionale tra norma giuridica e realta' sociale op.cit.*; L. Paladin, *Corte costituzionale e principio generale d'eguaglianza: aprile 1979- dicembre 1983*, in *Scritti sulla giurisprudenza costituzionale in onore di V. Crisafulli*, I, Padova 1985; A.S. Agrò, *Article 3* in *Commentario della Costituzione* edited by G. Branca, Bologna - Roma 1975; A. Cerri, *L'eguaglianza nella giurisprudenza costituzionale*, Milano 1976; A. Anzon, *Modi e tecniche del controllo di ragionevolezza*, in AA.VV. *La giustizia costituzionale ad una svolta*, Milano 1991.

[32] L. Paladin, *op. cit.* 606.

reasonableness appears in 226 of these judgments, registering a clear increase beginning in 1986: 16 in 1987, 21 in 1988, 16 again in 1989, 11 in 1990, 33 in 1991 and 18 in the first half of 1992.

We can therefore assert that the decision-making criteria progressively deduced by the Court on the basis of Article 3 of the Constitution, represent one of the essential points in the historical development of the control of constitutionality in Italy.

VIII. From Article 3 Paragraph 1 of the Constitution to the General Principle of Equality

Article 3, paragraph 1 of the Constitution declares that "all citizens have equal social standing and are equal before the law, without distinction of sex, race, language, religion, political opinion, or personal or social conditions"

Initially, this norm was interpreted restrictively as prohibiting the establishment of privileges by the means of special laws or derogations from the general norm. This formulation, which reflected the liberal idea of equality as the equal standing of all citizens before the law, asserted the general application of the juridical norms independently of their content. The reasoning of the Court in some judgments in 1957, followed the approach whereby "the evaluation of the relevance of the diversity of the situations in which legal subjects can be found and that are to be regulated cannot be other than reserved to the discretionary powers of the legislator.... Every comparison of the suitability of the differences of the legislation for the different situations to which the law referred would imply value-judgments of a political nature, or at least a control on the use of the discretionary powers of Parliament, which the Constitutional Court is not competent to exercise".[33] In substance, the Court excluded any type of control of the distinctions made by the law, apart from those that were expressly included within the ambit of Article 3 and that of

---

33 cf. Case n° 28/1957.

themselves could be considered constitutionally illegal.

However, an interpretation of this sort soon appeared to be excessively limited in two respects.

Firstly, it was clear that leaving the evaluation of the diversity of situations to the absolute freedom of the legislator practically emptied the principle of equality of any content. In a heterogeneous society, such as the present one, alongside the demands for equal judicial treatment of equal situations, there emerges, in fact, an increasing need for differentiation: the generality and abstraction of the law are not sufficient to guarantee equality.[34] It is not by accident that the majority of the laws concern certain categories of citizens, (the disabled, servicemen, craftsmen, tradesmen etc.): and even the criminal law, in which the need for equal judicial treatment is most felt, has to take all the particular circumstances of the crime into account.[35] It is undeniable that the belief that the law should give equal consideration to like situations, and different treatment to those which are to be distinguished, has led to a generalisation of the prohibition on discrimination beyond the grounds expressly sanctioned by Article 3 of the Constitution (sex, race, language, religion, political opinion and social and political conditions). In this respect, the principle, whereby the evaluation of different circumstances governing the relationships between individuals was subject to the supreme authority of the legislator, was soon abandoned.

A first sign of this transformation can already be noticed in Case n° 53/1958 where the Court, declaring the unconstitutionality of a law which equalised rents in respect of rural properties, affirmed that "...it is neither to carry out evaluations of a political nature nor to control the use of the legislator's discretionary power, if it is declared that the principle of equality is violated when the legislator subjects situations, that it itself considers and

---

34 cf. A. Cerri, *op. cit.* 11.

35 cf. P. Barile, *Diritti dell'uomo e libertà fondamentali*, Bologna 1984, 75.

declares to be different, to the same treatment".[36]

Secondly, it also became clear that, in certain cases, it may be necessary to make a distinction between categories, such as sex, race, language, etc., which according to the terms of Article 3 of the Constitution exclude the possibility of such a distinction.

In many cases it is the Constitution itself that authorises and imposes distinctions: such as, for example, those laws for the protection of linguistic minorities (Article 6), of religious creeds (Articles 7, 8, 19 and 20), and maternity rights for women workers (Article 37). Insofar as differentiation based on personal and social conditions is concerned, Article 3 paragraph 2 of the Constitution confers upon the Republic the task of removing obstacles of an economic or social nature that restrict in practice the freedom and equality of citizens and impede the full development of personality, thus demanding legislation that favours the advancement of the disadvantaged categories to a greater extent. As a consequence, in certain cases, it may be necessary to verify whether special aims can, from time to time, allow for the "presumption of unconstitutionality" of differentiation based on sex, race, language, religion, political opinion, or on social and personal conditions, to be overridden. In fact, in Case n° 56/1958, the Court had already asked the question of whether a specific reason could justify a law establishing a differentiation based on sex.[37] It thus came to abandon its policy of non-intervention in the evaluation of the differentiations and justifications made by the laws, that the Court had followed in its first judgments.

---

36 In the case in question, the unconstitutional law sought to equalise rents, whereas the pre-existing discipline provided for differentiation in rents, according to location, productivity of the land, as well as the characteristics of the property for rent., etc.

37 In this judgment, the Court rejected the unconstitutionality of a law which limited the participation of women on the juries in the Court of Assizes, maintaining that such discrimination was justified. In Cases n° 64/61 and 126/68, the Court found that there were reasonable grounds that could justify the differential treatment between husbands and wives in adultery cases.

IX. From the General Principle of Equality to Reasonableness as a Limit on the Legislator in the Evaluation of Equality/Inequality of Treatment

The criteria, whereby the options open to the legislator for approximating similar situations, and differentiating amongst those that differ, could be controlled, soon came to be identified under the term known as the principle of reasonableness. This was stated by the Court in Case n° 15/1968 where it was expressly recognised that "the principle of equality is violated when the law treats differently citizens who are in the same situation, *without reasonable grounds*". The principle progressively assumed a general significance, in terms of which the distinctions founded on sex, race etc. have been considered to be permissible where they are "reasonably justified". In short, Article 3 of the Constitution has ended up by implying the prohibition of "unreasonable" laws, that discriminate arbitrarily between legal subjects in comparable situations or make arbitrary assimilations between subjects in diverse situations.[38] In this way the rigid application of Article 28 of the law of 11th March 1953 has been overcome. This law was characteristic of the preceding period and had aimed at preventing every kind of control on the use of the discretionary power of the legislator.

On the other hand, the assessment of reasonableness does not imply an evaluation at the level of the justice or appropriateness of a certain rule, but rather an evaluation at the level of its coherence with respect to the rules that the legislator has used in other similar instances. More precisely it has been said that the judgement of equality implies three terms (a "tertiary" scheme): that is, it requires the identification of a term of comparison (the so-called "*tertium comparationis*"), that is a normative parameter as the yardstick by which it can be said that the differentiation or

---

[38] P. Barile, *op. cit.*, and L. Paladin *Diritto costituzionale*, Padova, 1991, 167.

classification in question is reasonable or arbitrary, supplied with or lacking a suitable justificatory base, and therefore that it conforms or does not conform with the general requirement of Article 3.[39]

In its most simple and coherent formulation the constitutional judgment of equality has as its object a special or exceptional law, insofar as this derogates from a general law on that subject.[40] In fact, according to the established case-law, in general terms, the question of constitutionality concerning the principle of equality can only arise in relation to a norm which derogates from the general norm. Given that the judgments on equality aim to restore the coherence of the judicial order, compliance with the legislative choices requires the referral of the exceptions to the general rule.[41] Nevertheless, it could also be the case that a special or

---

[39] For this argument, see essentially L. Paladin, *op. cit.* 609 et seq. In this respect, the Court affirmed that, in relation to respect for the principle of equality, "the contested legislation should be considered against another or other normative sources..., in order to establish whether the legislator had framed its provisions in such a way as would be unreasonable to consider them unconstitutional" (Case n° 10/1980). In particular, the Court requested that the directions, by which judges resolve the question of constitutionality, in the case of an alleged breach of the principle of equality, should indicate the "tertium comparationis", since failure to provide such indication could lead to the rebuttal of the question.

[40] L. Paladin *op. cit.*, 634.

[41] According to the case-law tradition of the Constitutional Court, the purpose of the decision on the question of equality is to "re-establish equilibrium in the legal order, by redimensioning more general norms, which are considered to be valid and are subject to unjustifiable derogation by more specific legislation" (Cases n° 2/1982, 46/1983, 6/1988, 582/1988 etc). It is not possible, as the Court has observed, to have recourse to the paradigm of the principle of equality when the ordinary rules of law, from which we intend to extract the "tertium comparationis", themselves derogate from the rule that can be inferred from the normative system, and that except at the cost of the aggravation, rather than the elimination of the defects of coherence (Case n° 769/1988).

exceptional norm comes to be taken as the *tertium comparationis*. In such cases, obviously the unjustifiable differentiation between the foreseen content of such a norm cannot be contested in relation to the more general norm (since it would fall into the above-mentioned category). The extension of the derogatory norm's application, either as an exceptional or special norm, can only be challenged when it does not regulate similar cases that should have been included in the provision. In this situation the Court maintains that if the legislator can predict exceptions to the general rule it cannot effect "unjustified discriminations in their content".[42] If, instead, it is not possible to distinguish which of two conflicting norms must express the general rule, the question is rejected.

Equality, after all, as is understood in constitutional case-law, can only be restored in one way, and that is by the restoration of the general rule unjustly derogated from by the special ones.[43] In the judgments on the application of the principle of equality, therefore, the Court does not impose its own choices on those of the legislator, but restores the coherence of the legal order.

---

[42] Case n° 43/1987. In the case in question, the Court found the norm, whereby directors of certain local health authorities (Unità Sanitarie Locali: USL) could be elected as local councillors, to be unconstitutional, on the basis that this would have been an unjustifiable departure from the law pointing to the ineligibility of directors of other USL (even if such ineligibility departs from the principle that all citizens are eligible to stand for election: Article 51 Constitution). The Court stated that the principle of eligibility as the rule and ineligibility as the exception was not at issue; nevertheless, the legislator could make "reasonable exceptions to the principle, but not unjustifiable discrimination in the application of one such exception".

[43] One of the many judgments in this sense, is Case n° 582/1988, whereby the Court excluded the possibility of extending the system of benefits granted to the employees of the Treasury to equivalent employees in the Ministry of Finance. The special system available to employees of the Treasury, in the opinion of the Court, constituted an exception to the general system in this respect, and as such, was justified by the consideration given, which fell within the discretion of the legislator.

X. From Reasonableness as an Element of Equality to Reasonableness as Rationality

However, on various occasions the control of reasonableness has been used outside the "tertiary" scheme that we have referred to as typical of the judgements on the question of equality. This occurs in cases, in which the control does not touch problems of equality/inequality of treatment, but involves evaluations of adequacy, relevance, consistency, proportionality or the internal coherence or intrinsic reasonableness of the law.[44] In some of these cases the intrinsic reasonableness of the law is called into question.[45] In others, instead of referring to the law under consideration as such (that is to say to its premises, its objectives

---

[44] A. Anzon, *op.cit.*, 32.

[45] Case n° 155/1990, which relates to antitrust legislation in printing, is indicative in this respect. Such legislation was initially established by the law n° 416/1981 which focused on the notion of dominant position for publishers, and provided the annulment of acts which lead to exceeding the upper limit established beyond which a dominant position is prohibited.

A case was brought on the basis of this legal construction, in which it was claimed that the major national publishing group had exceeded this upper limit prohibited by the law n° 416/1981, by buying shares in an important daily newspaper. Following the judgment of the Court of first instance (which found the claim of dominant position unsubstantiated), and whilst awaiting the appeal court's judgment, the law n° 67/1987 was passed. The new system modified the previous law n° 416/1981 in two respects: a) firstly, it provided stricter criteria for association agreements between publishers which sought to reach a dominant position, affirming that the new provision simply clarified the way the criteria set by the prior law had to be interpreted; b) secondly, it extended the upper threshold beyond which a dominant position was prohibited in connection with printing of daily newspapers from 20 to 30%, with retroactive effect.

The Constitutional Court censored the intrinsic unreasonableness of the law n° 67/1987, insofar as "on the one hand it sought to penalise certain situations, by recourse to interpretative powers established in the first part of the censored legislation, and, on the other hand, it favoured the same situations by effective retroactivity as provided in the second part of the same legislation".

and to the means-ends relation that emerges from its substantive content) the test of reasonableness comes to refer more generally to the coherence of the law with respect to the logic within which the system operates and into which it must fit.[46] In cases of this kind it has been noted that it is no longer the principle of equality that operates alone, so much as the principle of reasonableness, which can be violated even outside the situation where two norms are competing.[47] Moreover, the same Court has spoken of reasonableness and equality as two distinct principles, even if both are derived from Article 3 of the Constitution.[48]

There are numerous judgments in which the Court affirms the unreasonableness of a certain rule in relation to the objectives set by a particular precept of the Constitution or in relation to the aims pursued by the legislator. This follows closely, in fact, the technique by which the excess of administrative power is controlled, as the "diversion" from a certain aim. In this regard - and even excluding generally speaking the admissibility of a constitutional judgment of control of the excess of legislative power - the doctrine has for quite some time realigned the profile of unconstitutionality of laws, with regard to the absence of a logical correlation (of functionality) between the legislative means used with respect to the objectives to be pursued.[49] From this point of view, a law can reveal itself as constitutionally illegitimate

---

[46] Thus, for example, in Case n° 142/1982 the Court found differentiation in the tax system, between expenditure incurred abroad and that incurred within the national territory, to be unconstitutional, in that it was contrary to the principle of protection of individual health, as expressed by Article 32, with which the normative system must comply.

[47] A. Barbera, F. Cocozza, G. Corso, *Le situazione soggettive. Le liberta' dei singoli e delle formazioni sociali. Il principio di eguaglianza*, in *Manuale di diritto pubblico*, edited by G. Amato and A. Barbera, Bologna 1991, 274.

[48] cf., amongst others, Case n° 284 /1987.

[49] cf. A. Sandulli, *op. cit.*, 570 ss.

when it subsequently loses its original justificatory reason: this is described as "supervening unreasonability" or as a "legislative anachronism".

But even when the Court speaks of the "intrinsic unreasonableness" of the rule that is being reviewed, it has been observed that the judgment is not entirely entrusted to the wisdom of the constitutional judges. On the contrary it depends – for the most part – on the correspondence between the norms themselves and the aims of the legislator; therefore the enquiry conducted by the Court aims at the reconstruction of the intrinsic logic of the body of laws in question, rather than the privileging of evaluative criteria extraneous to the laws in force.[50] The criteria used in this control, therefore, closely follow the review of the abuse of power that has been elaborated in the area of administrative justice and in this is more in the sense of "manifest illogicality" than of the "manifest injustice". In other words, the possibility is excluded that the Court, by virtue of the fact that sometimes it has spoken of justice or injustice, has now come to judge the justice of the laws, substituting the arbitrary power of the judge for that of the legislator.[51] Reasonableness remains therefore, in every case, a criteria of control that is *internal* to the choices of the legislator.[52]

---

50 L. Paladin, *op. cit.*, 655.

51 P. Barile, *op. cit.*, 81.

52 With regard to case-law on the subject of equality, for example, the Court has often reiterated that it is not competent "to make decisions in areas which fall to the exclusive competence of the legislator", and to be able to only "realign unjustified derogations and arbitrary exceptions with pre-existing rules established by law or general principles unequivocally established by law" (Case n° 314/1983).

The legal criteria that have been developed in the case-law on the intrinsic reasonableness of law are discussed more fully in the next two sections of this essay.

XI. Reasonableness and the Balance Between Interests and Values

More and more often it occurs that the Court, when resolving the questions under its jurisdiction, carries out a "balancing test" ("*bilanciamento*") between the different interests that are relevant to the instances under examination. However, different types of balancing should be distinguished.

A first kind occurs, where Court limits itself to evaluating the balance between the different interests that was made by the legislator. Here the Court, in the application of the usual principle of reasonableness, only carries out a control on the balance drawn by others. In this way, for example, the Court has checked the balance between economic and environmental costs;[53] between the need for a more rapid conclusion to criminal trials and the interests of the accused in exercising their right to defence in order to prove their innocence;[54] between the interests of the state in repressing the trafficking of drugs and that of addicts to supply themselves with drugs for their personal use;[55] between the right of the citizen to health care and the organisational and financial assets of the public administration[56] and so on. In these cases, the formulation of certain and pre-established criteria, such as those which could establish a basis for the prevalence of one conflicting interest over others, is lacking. In this respect, with particular regard to constitutional case-law concerning the limits on the right of freedom of thought (but having regard to its possible extension to other cases requiring the balancing of conflicting interests), it has been stressed that the "balancing test" is ultimately applied on a case-to case basis, by evaluation of the way in which the

---

[53] Case n° 127/1990.

[54] Case n° 363/1991.

[55] Case n° 333/1991.

[56] Case n° 455/1990.

legislator has set off the conflicting interests on each occasion.[57]

A second type of balancing is carried out by the Court directly. This involves an interpretation of the meaning of the constitutional rules that must be applied in the judgment of constitutionality based on a test that balances between the various interests and values underlying the constitutional rules themselves. In this way, the Court superimposes its own balance over that of the legislator. The two types of judgment (and balancing) can however co-exist with each other. In this regard, in a recent judgment the Court has held that it is above all necessary to identify which are the interests of constitutional relevance that the legislator has given prevalence to in its discretionary weighing of the interests involved and then, the particular balance produced by the legislator in the reported case must be compared to the hierarchy of values involved in the legislative choice which is fixed in the constitutional norms.[58]

---

57 cf. L.Paladin, in *Quaderni costituzionali*, 1987, 11-12.

58 Case n° 467/1991. The question decided by the Court refers to the case of a conscripted soldier, who after being called for military service refused to perform it on the basis of a subsequent conversion to a religious faith.

The Court was called upon to determine the constitutional basis of different and more favourable treatment afforded by law, to those who refuse to perform military service on grounds of conscience prior to conscription, in relation to the (more rigorous) treatment of those who subsequently refuse to perform it. The provision of a different regulatory system, according to whether refusal to perform military service was expressed prior to or subsequently to being conscripted, was justified by the legislator on the basis that, in the second case, refusal as such would cause increased detriment to the organisational demands of military service, and hence more harm to the requisite performance of the obligation to defend the nation.

The Court considered the distinction adopted by the legislator as unreasonable. The Court held that, with respect to freedom to express ones moral or philosophical convictions (Article 21 Constitution) and freedom of religious expression (Article 19 Constitution), it "could not establish a reasonable criterion for discrimination, according to the moment in which the refusal was manifested. Such a moment, except where proof to the contrary, must be presumed to coincide with the maturity of a deep and compelling

But through the employment of a technique of this type the constitutional judgment of reasonableness has a tendency to transform itself from an "internal" control - that is turned towards the restoration of the intrinsic coherence of the legal order faced with defects in the relations between the juridical norms under consideration - into an "external" control - that leads the Court to superimpose its own evaluation of the interests at stake onto that determined by the legislator.[59] However, this control can allow the Court to, on the one hand, harmonise the different constitutional principles that can be raised with regard to certain legal instances and, on the other hand, to mitigate the abstraction of the constitutional process by encouraging a greater flexibility of judgment in relation to the particularities of the specific case before them.

The technique of balancing that is taking shape in Italy, calls to mind the proven experiences of other legal orders, in particular in Germany (*Guterabwegung*) and the United States (*balancing test*). But there remain, as always, significant differences with respect to these other countries. These are connected to two basic points: in the first place to the fact that as yet a hierarchy in the constitutional values has not been established (compared with what has happened in Germany); in the second place to the fact that the Italian Constitutional Court, as a matter of principle, is not called upon to resolve concrete controversies, but only "abstract" questions of constitutional legitimacy (by comparison to the US Supreme Court).

XII. Problems in the Control of Reasonableness

Even if it finds its rationale in the principle of equality

---

religious (or moral or philosophical) conviction".

[59] cf. R. Bin, *op. cit.*

established by Article 3 of Constitution, the principle of reasonableness by now constitutes a criterion of judgment that is assuming a more extensive and general value. Consequently this criterion is used by the Court as a standard of control which is not only connected to Article 3 of the Constitution but also with other rules such as, for instance, Article 97 (the principle of the proper working and impartiality of public offices) and Article 24 (the right to a legal defence). The so-called "political" function of control of reasonableness is becoming obvious, even in relation to its increasing application in constitutional judgments. Besides favouring an evolutive interpretation of the Constitution, this allows the Constitutional Court to give elasticity and concreteness to a judgment that, as mentioned before, continues be carried out with regard to normatively abstract instances. The Court, in fact, rather than making binding and irreversible declarations of principle on the content and means of application of the Constitutional rights can, through the use of this criterion, at least partly anchor its judgments to the concrete facts of the individual controversies and to the never ending changes in reality.

The indeterminacy of the Constitutional principles and their diverse combinations in relation to concrete instances therefore provides the Court with a wide scope for evaluation.

However, the greatest risk to the Court, when making judgments on the reasonableness of a law, is that, rather than being a judge of the legality of the law, it will transform itself into a judge of the merits, that is of the appropriateness of that law; substituting itself for the legislator in the evaluation of the political reasons that brought about the choice of a certain regulation. It cannot be doubted that, in many cases, there is a very thin line between legality and merit, with the consequent risk that the Court might encroach on choices that are, in principle, reserved to the legislator. And this brings the risk of an uncontrolled choice that is termed reasonableness, if the reasonableness should reveal itself in that which fifteen judges would consider to be reasonable, according to their free judgment.[60]

But, today, it is precisely in relation to this risk, that the requirement of defining precise limits on the power of the Court and criteria capable of guaranteeing the predictability of constitutional control tends to make itself felt more strongly. On this issue the dominant opinion holds the view that the review of constitutional legality should always remain attached to the limits of the Constitution. On this question the Court has said that even though a "judgment on the merits does not imply evaluations that are structurally different in terms of logic from the process of argument that is characteristic of the evaluation of [constitutional] validity that is implied by the control of legality,... in the latter [process] the rules or the interests that should be assumed as parameters of the judgment are those that are formally sanctioned in legal or constitutional norms".[61] In this regard, nevertheless, it is always the judicial opinion that makes the criteria of reasonableness visible and functional.[62] The consequence is that, the more the powers of the constitutional judge and the limits of their control of the law increase, the greater the need becomes for legal opinions that make the judgments transparent and convincing.

XIII. Predictions for the Future of the System of Constitutional Justice in Italy

What predictions can we make today for the future of the Italian system of constitutional justice?

The consideration of some of the trends that have been

---

60 A. Baldassarre, *op. cit.*, 127.

61 Case n° 1130/1988. In this respect, the Court affirmed that the judgment upholding the reasonableness of a law, which increased the contributions due to representative bodies of the Regional Council of Lombardy, did not imply interference with the evaluation of merit reserved to the discretion of the legislator.

62 C. Lavagna, *op. cit.*, 1588.

increasing in this period, both in the social fabric and in public institutions, leads to the prediction of an increasing influence in political life and in the control entrusted to the Constitutional Court. All the elements that have in the past encouraged the Constitutional Court to supply the deficiencies of the governmental and political processes, in fact, today have a tendency to show themselves in more accentuated, and in certain cases pathological, forms in the middle of a crisis that is involving the entire social and political order of the country, and that could – in a short time – lead to profound revisions in the constitutional system itself. Numerous competing factors have come together to create this trend. In particular there is, for example, the process of disintegration of the party system that has been at the head of national political life for more than 40 years. There are the increased conflicts between the institutions. And, finally there are the emerging new social and territorial fragmentations, that call the very principle of national unity into question.

In the same manner, the "expansion" of constitutional case-law could also be encouraged by the emergence of new areas of political conflict, that are currently taking shape inside the Italian system.

It is possible to point to three particular areas of potential conflicts. A first area is that which is appearing in relation to the necessity of identifying new boundaries for the Welfare State and adjusting the speed at which new "social rights" can be expanded – a problem which is caused by the crises of public spending and economic recession. In this field it currently seems clear that the Court – in view of the political campaign for large reductions in public spending that have been embarked upon by the latest governments – will increasingly be called upon to carry out the role of arbitration in social conflicts, constructing delicate balances between the principle of equality and the balancing of the public budget (in formal terms between Article 3 and Article 81 of the Constitution).

A second area of conflict will probably be that of constitutional reform, the study of which has recently begun in

Parliament. These reforms (which will involve all of the second part of the Constitution, regarding the structure and functions of the public administration), will definitely raise problems. These might be of a procedural nature, connected to the following of the special proceedings for constitutional revision provided for by Article 138 of the Constitution. Alternatively, these could be substantive issues, connected to the requirement of preserving what the Court has defined as the "supreme principles", the expressions of the essential core, that are considered to be inviolable elements of the original constitutional system.[63]

Finally, a third area that is open to new interventions by constitutional judgments, could emerge in relation to the future development of the process of European Integration. These developments – which are linked to the carrying out of the Treaty of Maastricht – will raise before the Constitutional Court the problem of identifying new relations between national and Community law in a way that is compatible with the Constitution. The Court will also have to search for a new balance between its own case-law and that of the Court of Justice of the European Community. Considering the increasing intrusion of community law into sectors traditionally covered by constitutional rules (those which are connected to civil and political freedoms and the constitution of the economy) it is easy to predict that the Italian system of constitutional justice will very soon also find itself engaged in the general redefinition of the "limitations of sovereignty" that Article 11 of the Constitution refers to as the necessary consequences of the Italian state joining international

---

[63] The Court affirmed in Case n° 1146/1988 that "the Italian Constitution contains certain absolute principles which cannot be subject to modifications as regards their fundamental content, neither by laws revising the constitution nor other constitutional laws". Equally untouchable are "principles expressly foreseen by the same Constitution, which impose absolute limits on the power of constitutional revision, as such, the form given to the Republic (Article 139), as well as principles, which, although not expressly mentioned amongst those which cannot be subject to the procedure for constitutional revision, belong to the core of supreme values which form the basis of the Italian Constitution".

organisations.

The intervention in these new areas of conflict cannot but also cause some reflection on the instruments and methods of the judgment of constitutionality. In this area, everything points to an ever wider use by the Italian Court of both the criteria of reasonableness (which in the end will most probably represents the real means by which the future developments of the welfare State will be regulated), and of the technique of balancing (which will probably lead to the raising of the problem, that up until now has been avoided by the Court, of the possible ranking of the values enshrined in the text of the Constitution).

But it is also probable that the increasingly political nature of constitutional review, that is apparent in Italy today, will end by encouraging, in the field of this control, the call for two further requirements, that have hitherto been left in abeyance: that of identifying particular "tests" on which the judgment of reasonableness can be hung, with the aim of making it predictable and controllable; and that of the introduction of the "dissenting opinion" as a means of making the process of the formation of a judgment and, as a consequence, its precise meaning, more transparent.

HUMAN RIGHTS AND JUDICIAL REVIEW IN GERMANY

Dieter Grimm*

I. HISTORICAL BACKGROUND

1. Germany received its first constitutions early in the 19th century. They were adopted in a number of German states, there being no unified Germany during that period of time. All of these 19th century constitutions were granted by sovereign princes, not adopted by the people, but in a number of cases the grant was preceded by an agreement between the prince and representative assemblies. Due to their origin, these constitutions were not democratic, although they were more or less liberal. Almost all of them had a catalogue of human rights guaranteeing personal freedom, equal protection of the laws, freedom of expression, freedom of property etc. None of the constitutions, however, provided for a constitutional court or judicial review. Rather, the representative assemblies were regarded as safeguards of human rights, as every abridgment of such rights was only justified if based on a law, and no law could be passed without parliamentary consent. On the other hand, parliament was not the exclusive legislator. Every law required the consent of the two houses of parliament and the prince. Thus, the main human rights problem of that time was not their application by the courts but their materialization through the legislature. The lower houses of the parliaments constantly initiated legislation in order to give effect to human rights, but most of these attempts failed in the upper houses or were rejected by the princes. The ordinary courts applied the law, but did not apply human rights. These were regarded as depending on legislative transformation, and wherever

* Justice, Federal Constitutional Court of Germany (since 1987), Professor of Law, University of Bielefeld (since 1979); Director, Center for Interdisciplinary Research, University of Bielefeld (1983-1988), Research Fellow, Max-Planck-Institut fuer europaeische Rechtsgeschichte, Frankfurt, (1968-1979).

D.M. Beatty (ed.), Human Rights and Judicial Review, 267-295.

such legislation was lacking the legal impact of human rights remained small. Politically, they served as a basis for all sorts of claims, and legally, they were interpreted as principles for shaping the social order rather than individual rights.

2. It was the Revolution of 1848 which brought forth the first constitution adopted by a constitutional assembly and designed for Germany as a whole. Its catalogue of human rights was much more elaborate than those in the earlier constitutions. It contained all of the liberal rights characteristic of constitutions of that period, but attempts by the left to add a number of social rights were rejected by the majority. The argument was that human rights were intended to limit government action in favour of individual freedom, but could not provide people with government assistance. Taught by the experience of the early constitutions, the new constitution established judicial review in order to give full effect to human rights. It is well known that the revolution of 1848 failed in Germany as it did elsewhere. The constitution did not come into force, and the catalogue of human rights which had been adopted prior to the constitution was abolished in 1851. However, the constitutions of the various German states more or less kept the human rights standard of the national constitution, but none of them established judicial review. The general opinion held that judicial review was incompatible with monarchical sovereignty which formed the basis of all German constitutions of that time. When, later on, Germany unity was achieved by Bismarckian Prussia, the constitution of the Empire did not contain a catalogue of human rights nor were the courts empowered with the right to judicial review. On the other hand, liberal legislation which was already starting to emerge in the sixties transformed many of the constitutional promises into law. This gave rise to a tendency of minimizing the legal impact of human rights. Their meaning was reduced to the formula that no government act restricting individual freedom or property was valid unless based on a law. But the formation of the law itself was not controlled by human rights. Thus curtailed, human rights were not distinguishable from the rule of law (Rechtsstaat) in general. The legal science

therefore concluded that human rights were a relic of a period where the rule of law had not been fully developed but that they had no legal importance beyond the rule of law.

3. When the Empire collapsed at the end of World War I, Germany received a democratic constitution adopted by a national assembly which was dominated by those political parties that had formed the opposition during the Empire. The Weimar constitution contained a catalogue of human rights including the classic liberal rights, but also a considerable number of social rights designed to improve the situation of workers, unemployed people, mothers, families, etc. The constitution provided for a constitutional court (Staatsgerichtshof), but it was limited in power to settle controversies between the Reich and its member states and to decide election cases. The court was not empowered with judicial review, since it was regarded undemocratic that judges controlled the popular will as expressed in the law. The question whether the ordinary courts had to apply laws which they regarded as unconstitutional was raised but not solved. Legal science continued to understand human rights in the same way as in the Empire. The classic liberal rights were subject to legislative limitation without exercising a binding effect on the legislature. Hence, their legal impact did not surpass the rule of law, whereas the so-called social rights were regarded to be mere political proclamations without any legal validity. It was up to the legislature to turn them into binding rights or not. In the course of the Weimar Republic, however, a younger generation of scholars began to interpret human rights as constitutional principles binding not only the executive but also the legislature and being enforceable by the courts. This discussion between positivists and materialists which is known as the methodological struggle (Methodenstreit) in the German science of public law was still undecided when the Weimar Republic failed, and the National Socialist government suspended all human rights, abolished the independence of judges and established a dictatorial rule.

II. BASIC APPROACH

1. Some of the questions left open by the Weimarien debate were expressly answered by the Basic Law adopted after World War II in 1949. It was the firm consensus of all political forces active in the constitutional assembly to prevent another failure of representative democracy in Germany and to establish effective safeguards against dictatorship and disregard of human rights. The constitution should therefore be the paramount law of the land and claim priority over any government act. In order to reach this goal, the Basic Law contains some important guarantees.

(1) The basic principles of the constitution - such as democracy, the rule of law, the principle of social state, federalism, respect of human dignity - may not be altered at all; not even by a constitutional amendment. With this provision in art.79(3) the Basic Law rejected the Weimarien theory that the power of amending the constitution is unlimited. No longer would it be possible that a democratic constitution could be abolished by using democratic forms as happened in 1933.

(2) According to art.1(1), human dignity is the unalterable foundation of the constitutional order. The state is not only obliged to respect, but also to protect human dignity. This is a reaction to the disdain of human dignity during the period of national socialism.

(3) All human rights guaranteed by the Basic Law have legally binding force. This provision in art.1(3) is also a reaction towards the attitude of the majority of Weimar constitutionalists to divide the catalogue of human rights into two parts: one with and one without legal effect.

(4) Moreover, the binding effect of all human rights is expressly extended to the legislature by art.1(3). Here we observe the Basic Law rejecting the assumption of the constitutionalists during the Empire and to a large extent also during the Weimar Republic that the legislature was free to restrict fundamental rights as it pleased. According to art.19(2) there is an ultimate limit to legislative measures: In no case may they touch the essential content of a human right.

(5) The Parliamentary Council which worked out the Basic Law reestablished the classic catalogue of liberal rights and added some new ones in the light of the experience made under the Nazi dictatorship, such as freedom of broadcasting, freedom of art etc. But it decided not to follow the Weimarien experiment with social rights. Instead, a general principle was included into the constitution according to which Germany is recognized as being a social state.

(6) Finally, the Parliamentary Council established a special institution designed to enforce the constitution against any other government authority. This institution is the Federal Constitutional Court endowed with ample powers, among them judicial review. The Basic Law, thereby, resolved the intensive debate that was waged during the Weimar period as to whether judicial review is a logical consequence of a constitution with legal and not only symbolic value (Kelsen), or whether it is detrimental to constitutionalism because it leads to a juridification of politics and a politicization of the judiciary (Carl Schmitt).

2. With regard to human rights, the Constitutional Court has two main competencies.

(1) It can review any law as to its conformity with the human rights contained in the Basic Law - either on request of the federal government, of the government of a land, or of one third of the members of parliament (abstrakte Normenkontrolle - art.93(1) no.2), or on request of any ordinary court which has to apply a law whose constitutionality it doubts (konkrete Normenkontrolle - art.100). In exceptional cases, a law can also be reviewed on the request of an individual whose fundamental rights are directly affected by that law and not just by its application.

(2) Upon individual complaint, the Court can review any act of a public authority as to its conformity with human rights (art.93(1) no.4a), provided that the complainant has exhausted all available means to find relief through the ordinary courts. In these cases the primary object of review is usually the decision of the lower court, but, if necessary, the original government act and the law on which the decisions are based may also be evaluated since

no act or court decision can be constitutional when the underlying law is unconstitutional.

3. While constitutional law thinking during the Empire was methodologically dominated by a strictly positivistic and formalistic approach and largely remained so during the Weimar Republic, the Constitutional Court from the beginning in 1951 took a clearly antipositivistic and material approach. This was partly due to the general antipositivist tendency in Germany after the Nazi dictatorship and the return to traditional values of individualism. It was also partly due to the experience of the late Weimar Republic when the formalistic approach toward constitutional law practised by the positivistic school had been unable to save the constitution from attacks dressed in constitutional forms. Democracy had been reduced to majority rule and was thus unable to prevent the abolition of democracy with democratic means. The rule of law had been reduced to mere legality, but could not ask whether the law itself was constitutional or not. Human rights had been reduced to the requirement that any restriction had to be based on a law, but they did not set any limit to legislation nor did they guide the interpretation of laws.

The Court's antipositivistic approach does not mean that the text of the constitution is neglected. On the contrary, the text is regarded as a starting point and the ultimate limit of interpretation, at the same time. Rather, the Court's antipositivism means that it is not prepared to follow the famous rule of the leading authority in constitutional law during the Empire, Paul Laband, who taught that grammar and logic are the only means of understanding and interpreting constitutional texts. The Court, instead, takes into account, on the one hand, the ideas expressed in constitutional provisions, and, on the other hand, the sector of social reality where a constitutional provision is to develop its normative force.

The fundamentals of the constitution, such as democracy, rule of law, social state, and human rights, were referred to as values and, after some critique as to the implications of a value philosophy, as principles. The constitutional order as a whole is, in sharp contrast to the relativism of the pre-war period, regarded as a value-oriented rather than value neutral.[1] The Basic Law is described as an order which recognizes the protection of individual freedom and human dignity as the ultimate goals of the law; its image of man is not the one of an autarchian, but of socially bound personality with obligations toward society.[2]

The value- or principle-orientation means that the value embodied in a constitutional provision, particularly in a human right, has to be maximized as much as possible.[3] This viewpoint has two main consequences. First, if a collision between two or more constitutionally guaranteed values occurs, the question is not to determine which one prevails but to find a solution which leaves the greatest possible effect to both of them (praktische Konkordanz). Even rights which are unconditionally guaranteed in the Basic Law such as freedom of conscience and freedom of the arts, therefore, allow some limitations if their exercise threatens other constitutionally acknowledged values.[4] Secondly, the best possible effect cannot be given to a human right without regard of the real situation which it meets. The meaning of human rights, in particular, cannot be determined regardless of changing situations. New threats to individual freedom require adaptations of the range of human rights. Thus, new menaces stemming from social development or from scientific and technical progress have generated new interpretations of human rights and in one case

---

[1] BVerfGE 2, 1 (12) *Socialist Reich Party*; 5, 85 (134 ff., 197 ff.) *Communist Party*; 6, 32 (40 f.) *Elfes*; 7, 198 (205) (Lüth).

[2] BVerfGE 4, 7 (15f.) *Investment Aid*; 12, 45 (51) *Conscientious Objector*; 65, 1 (41) *Census Act*.

[3] BVerfGE 39, 1 (38) *Abortion I*; 57, 70 (99) *Hessen University Law*.

[4] BVerfGE 28, 243 (261) *Dissident Soldier*; 30, 173 (193) *Mephisto*.

almost a new right.[5]

In choosing between two or more possible interpretations of a constitutional provision the Court proceeds by determining their real consequences and comparing them to the purpose of the right at stake. Preference is given to the interpretation whose consequences are closer to the constitutional goal.[6] This is a consequence of the idea that the understanding of the constitution must change when the circumstances to which it is applied have substantially changed. Otherwise, the interpretation would miss the goal pursued by the constitutional provision. The limits of interpretation are the text and the goal of the human right. Their modification is reserved to constitutional amendments, whereas giving utmost effect to a constitutional goal under changing circumstances is a matter of interpretation. The Court, therefore, feels entitled not only to interpret constitutional rules and apply them to individual cases, but also to develop the constitution within the boundaries just mentioned. Constitutional development thus becomes a matter of amendment and interpretation as well.

III. THE METHOD APPLIED

1. In application of these methods, the Court has added three important effects to the text of human rights.

First, it has broadened the scope of human rights protection. The Basic Law starts with a guarantee of human dignity as the

---

[5] Protection against electronic data processing (Recht auf informationelle Selbstbestimmung), BVerfGE 65, 1 (41 ff.) *Census Act*. For other examples see BVerfGE 49, 89 (140 ff.); 53, 30 (57 ff.) - atomic energy; 56, 54 (73 ff.) - airport noise; 53, 257 (290 f.); 69, 272 (300) extension of property right to positions which, in modern societies, fulfil the function of traditional property.

[6] BVerfGE 7, 377 (413 ff.) *Pharmacy*; 10, 118 (121); 35, 202 (226 ff., 238 ff.) *Lebach*; 43, 130 (136) *Political Defamation*; 44, 353 (373 f.); 46, 160 (165) *Schleyer Kidnapping*; 61, 1 (7) *Campaign Slur*; 65, 1 (43) *Census Act*; 77, 346 (354 f.) *Newspaper Distributor*; 85, 23 (31 f.) *Questions*; 86, 28 (38 f.).

guiding principle of the whole constitution and obliges the state to respect and protect human dignity. This provision in art. 1 is followed by a catalogue of human rights. They cover areas of individual activities, social relations and various institutions which tend to be threatened by governments according to historical experience. In Article 2, the Basic Law guarantees everybody's right to free development of his personality. The Court, in a 1958 case, interpreted this right not as a special freedom like the following rights and guarantees but as general freedom protecting any human activity not covered by a special guarantee in the constitution.[7] In the result, the Court established a complete system of human right protection and judicial review. Whenever a government activity touches an act or behaviour of individuals not mentioned in some special constitutional guarantee, the Court can review it under art.2(1).

Second, the Court intensified the protective force of human rights by developing the principle of proportionality. This was a far-reaching break with the older doctrine. During the Empire and the Weimar Republic, the prevailing doctrine had come to the conclusion that because human rights were subject to legal restrictions, they could not be superior to the law. Human rights existed only within the boundaries of the law and thus had no importance for the formation of the law itself. The Constitutional Court concluded from art. 1 that human rights were superior to the law. Laws could restrict human rights, but only in order to make conflicting rights compatible or to protect the rights of other persons or important community interests. The Court then ruled that any restriction of human rights not only needs a constitutionally valid reason but also has to be proportional to the rank and importance of the right at stake.[8]

---

[7] BVerfGE 6, 32 (36 f.) *Elfes*; 80, 137 (152 f.) *Riding in the Wood*; and dissenting opinion, p. 164 ff.

[8] BVerfGE 19, 342 (348 ff.); 30, 292 (315) *Mineral Oil Stock Pile*; 61, 126 (134).

The proportionality test is applied in three steps. The first question is whether a law or other government act limiting the exercise of a human right is capable of reaching its goal. The second question is whether it is indispensable to reach its goal. The third question is whether an adequate relationship exists between the human right limited by law, on the one hand, and the purpose which the restriction serves, on the other (adequacy or proportionality in a narrower sense). Operating at an earlier stage than the essential content limit in art.19(2), the proportionality principle has rendered the former almost insignificant.

In addition to reading the Basic Law as providing a comprehensive system of human rights protection and manifesting a principle of proportionality, the Court has also recognized human rights as being something more than negative entitlements which enable the individual to defend himself against government intrusions of his sphere of freedom. The basic idea is a rediscovery. The Court understands human rights not only as subjective rights but at the same time as objective principles as well.[9] This was their meaning when they were first adopted in Europe in the late 18th and early 19th century. In view of a legal and social order determined by absolutism and feudalism, they would have blocked the necessary reforms and strengthened the old order if understood as individual defenses against government actions. Therefore, they laid down the principles according to which government had to establish a liberal society, and only when this reform was completed could they serve as individual rights against governments trying to restore the old order or to unduly restrict individual freedoms.

In their capacity as objectives, human rights penetrate the whole legal and social order. While, in their capacity as subjective rights, they oblige the state to refrain from certain action, in their capacity as objective principles, they oblige the state to take certain action in order to protect human rights or to give real effect to them. These two dimensions of human rights

---

[9] The leading case is the Lüth decision, BVerfGE 7, 198 (204 ff.).

are not necessarily congruent. There may be duties of the government without corresponding individual rights. Nevertheless, these duties are legally binding and their fulfilment can be ordered by the Court in the proper case. Moreover, the Court has tended to include more and more of the objective elements into the subjective right and thus enlarge the standing of individual applicants.

In the course of more than forty years of jurisprudence, the Court has drawn several conclusions from the premise that human rights are also objective principles.

First the Court decided that any law restricting the exercise of a human right must be interpreted in the light of that right.[10] This decision, which was handed down in 1958, constituted a fundamental break with the tradition. Prior to this ruling, the only constitutional question addressed by the Court was whether a law limiting the exercise of a human right was itself constitutional. The interpretation of such a law did not raise constitutional questions. That was a matter for the ordinary courts and their understanding of the legal question involved. Now a statute touching a human right must be interpreted and applied in a constitutional manner. This requires, within the context of statutory interpretation, once again a balancing of the human right at stake and the purpose of its limitation.

This principle is especially relevant in the area of private law.[11] Traditionally, private law was regarded as being outside the range of human rights which were considered to be a part of public law, regulating exclusively the relationship between the individual and the state. The new doctrine brings the whole legal order under the influence of human rights. This implies that all decisions of the ordinary courts are subject to constitutional review, provided that the law they interpret and apply touches a human right. The difference becomes clear by a comparison with

---

10 BVerfGE 7, 198 (206, 208 f.).

11 BVerfGE 7, 198 (204 ff.).

the Austrian system. The Austrian Constitutional Court limits its review to acts of the legislature. It cannot review decisions of other courts. The result is that the interpretation and application of ordinary laws remains unaffected by the constitution, even if it results in a limitation of a human right.

Another corollary which the Court has drawn from the idea that human rights are also objective principles is that governments may be obliged to supply an individual or a class of individuals with the means necessary to make use of a right. This is particularly true in fields where the state takes care of social security and the cultural identity of the citizens. Here, the original concept of freedom from the state is insufficient and must be accompanied by a concept of participation in public institutions or goods. This is a consequence of the shift from a purely formal to a substantial notion of constitutionally protected freedom. Formally conceived, freedom means the absence of government interference. The individual's possibility of making use of his freedom is outside the range of constitutional law. In a substantial understanding, freedom includes the possibility of using the freedom. The Court first took this position in a case where it had to review state laws which limited the access to medical schools with the result that many applicants formally qualified to attend the school were denied admission.[12]

Since there are many ways to fulfil this obligation, and since the constitution does not prescribe the use of a specific means, the government's duty is normally not accompanied by an individual's right. In some extraordinary cases, however, the duty can mutate into an individual claim. This is the case when, without government assistance, a human right would be completely worthless for an individual. It can also be the case when the state itself subjects the exercise of a right to requirements which can normally not be met without public assistance. The constitutional guarantee to establish private schools in art.7(4) is a case in point. The constitution recognizes such institutions on the condition that

---

12 BVerfGE 33, 303 (330 ff.) *Numerus Clausus*.

their standards are equal to those of the state schools, that the teachers' position is legally and economically safe, and that the school does not promote a separation of pupils according to the wealth of their parents. In its interpretation of this provision the Court relied on the fact that it has become extremely difficult for private persons to meet all these requirements to justify its conclusion that the state is obliged to support private schools.[13] However, in cases of this sort, the Court applies a sort of reverse principle of proportionality. The individual is entitled to request only what he can reasonably expect from society, taking into account the multitude of other obligations the government must satisfy.[14] Thus, in cases like in the medical school case, where the fulfilment of the duty would have required the expenditure of enormous amounts of money the Court refrained from obliging the government to spend this money, and ruled, instead, that in the long run it should take steps to ameliorate the situation.

A third conclusion which the Court has drawn from the objective character of human rights is a duty of legislatures to protect human rights against threats from private individuals or groups. This principle was developed in the first abortion case decided in 1986.[15] In a major reform of its criminal law, the legislature had decided to leave an abortion unpunished if performed within the first three months of the pregnancy. The Court ruled that the right to life in art. 2(2) of the Basic Law not only forbids the state to destroy life itself but, in addition, obliges the state to protect human life against violations by others. The addressee of this constitutional duty is the legislature which has to pass laws securing protection of the human right. In a second abortion case in 1993, the Court added that the protection has to be a sufficient one in view of the rank and importance of the

---

13 BVerfGE 75, 40 (62 ff.).

14 BVerfGE 33, 303 (333).

15 BVerfGE 39, 1(42).

human right at stake. Where limitations of a human right can go too far (Uebermassverbot), a protection can fall short from its goal (Untermassverbot).[16] The approach of the German Court stands in sharp contrast with the more traditional reasoning followed by the Austrian Court when it was asked to review a very similar law. According to the Austrian Court no constitutional question was involved since the state did not kill foetuses itself, but only abstained from punishing abortions.

Although the abortion case was the first occasion in which the Court recognized the legislature's duty to take active steps to protect human rights against threats stemming from third parties (Schutzpflicht), it is now clear that this decision did not constitute the typical case where this duty is relevant. The abortion case concerned a legislative act abolishing a protection which had existed for a long time. The typical case for application of the Schutzpflicht is a case where new technical, economical or social developments create new dangers for a human right. This is true, for instance, with problems of protection of the environment, protection of human life and health against the use of atomic energy, genetics, protection of freedom of personal development against the possibilities of automatic data processing, protection against excessive noise etc. If a human right is seriously affected by such developments, the Court has said that the legislature is constitutionally obliged to take measures securing the right menaced.[17]

This is true even in the field of contractual relations. Private autonomy, conceived of as the right to determine by contract what the law is inter partes, presupposes a certain balance of power among the contracting parties. If the balance is grossly disturbed,

---

16 BVerfGE 88, 203 (281 ff.).

17 BVerfGE 46, 160/164 *Schleyer Kidnapping*; 49, 89 (130 ff., 140 ff.) *Kalkar*; 53, 30 (57 ff.) *Mülheim-Kaerlich*; 56, 54 (73 ff.) *Airport Noise*; 79, 174 (201 f.) *Traffic Noise*; 85, 386 (400 f.) *Telephone Misuse*.

contracts tend to bring forth distorted results. In cases where this leads to heavy impairments of one party's fundamental rights the legislature is obliged to take protective measures. In the absence of such laws the ordinary courts are obliged to take human rights into account as far as possible within the framework of statutory interpretation when they construe and enforce contracts.[18]

The last conclusion, drawn from the objective dimension of human rights may be described as the protection of human rights by procedure and organization. The reason behind this development is the growing number of cases where it is impossible to protect a constitutionally guaranteed freedom by substantive statutory provisions. This may occur when the field of a certain state activity is so complex or the knowledge so small that it is impossible to regulate the activity by the application of statutory rules. If the activity is likely to affect human rights, some compensation for the missing substantial protection is necessary. Where the administrative decision cannot be sufficiently determined by law, the Court has ruled that the process of decision making must be regulated in a way that forces the administration to give attention to those human rights which are possibly affected.[19] This occurs as well where a human right, like the asylum right in art. 16(2) or a legal position derived from a human right, can be exercised only if an appropriate procedure is provided.[20] This requires procedural safeguards. The legislature, therefore, is under a constitutional duty to pass such laws.

The same is true where human rights are exercised in social

---

18 BVerfGE 81, 242 (255) *Salesman*.

19 BVerfGE 53, 30 (65) *Mülheim-Kaerlich*, and dissenting opinion p. 72 ff.

20 BVerfGE 56, 216 (235) *Asylum*; 63, 131 (143); 65, 76 (94); 73, 280 (294 ff.) *Notary Public*.

institutions, be it public institutions like schools or universities,[21] or private institutions like enterprises,[22] mass media etc. Freedom in these cases can become real only when the institutions are themselves freely organized. Broadcasting is a good example. The Court understands freedom of the media as a freedom which serves a certain purpose, namely free formation of opinions, private as well as public. Free formation of opinion requires unrestricted information about all relevant events and ideas. The media whose function it is to provide this information must therefore be free themselves. Freedom with respect to fulfilling their social function does not only mean freedom from the state but also freedom from social forces. This sort of freedom cannot be achieved by pure market regulation. The fundamental right, therefore, requires an organization of the broadcasting system which is likely to guarantee the fulfilment of the function of the media.

The attitude of the German Court becomes quite clear if compared with the jurisprudence of the U.S. Supreme Court in the same field. The Supreme Court, like the German Court, assumes that freedom of broadcasting is not guaranteed in the interest of the broadcaster, but in the interest of the listening an viewing public. Its purpose is to produce an informed public capable of conducting its own affairs. Hence, the medium has to function consistently with the ends and purposes of the constitution. It is the right of viewers and listeners, not the right of the broadcasters which is paramount.[23] The Supreme Court concludes from these premises that government is entitled to regulate broadcasting. However, it is not prepared to require government to impose controls upon

---

21 BVerfGE 35, 79 (114 ff.) *Group University*; 55, 37 (58 ff.) *University Professors*.

22 BVerfGE 50, 290 *Co-determination*.

23 Red Lion Broadcasting Co. v. FCC, 395 U.S. 367 (389 ff.).

private broadcasters.[24] By contrast, the German Court reasons that, because of the purposes art. 5(1) is meant to serve, government is obliged to take action in order to ensure those ends are reached. Referring to this principle, the Court has reviewed a number of broadcasting statutes and declared numerous provisions as being incompatible with art. 5(1) of the Basic Law because they did not furnish enough safeguards for the freedom of broadcasting.[25]

As mentioned above, all these dimensions were developed subsequently from the idea that human rights are not only individual rights but objective principles as well. In this capacity they do not oblige government to refrain from certain actions but force government to take action in order to secure or effectuate individual liberties against societal risks or dangers. Therefore, it seems appropriate to subsume all these effects under the notion of a protective duty (Schutzpflicht). This duty can be called the second side of the coin of human rights; the first one being the defense against state actions. The state is constitutionally obliged to fulfil this duty. Non-action is a violation of the duty. If the state does not comply with the duty, the Court can state this and oblige government to take appropriate measures.

The protective duty may indicate the general direction of its fulfilment. But the Court will not dictate a specific manner which alone satisfies the requirement of a human right. The various rights bind the state as to whether it acts or not. But the state, and in particular the legislature, has a wide latitude how to fulfil a constitutional duty. In the absence of specific requirements in the Basic Law, the Court can only oblige the state to initiate some action which is capable of protecting a human right, but it cannot

---

24 Columbia Broadcasting System v. Democratic National Committee, 412 U.S. 94 (117 ff.).

25 BVerfGE 12, 205 (259 ff.); 57, 295 (323 ff.); 73, 118 (152 ff.); 74, 297 (322 ff.); 83, 238 (295 ff.); decision of February 22, 1994.

determine what the content and detail of that measure will be. The specific means that will be used to discharge its positive duty to act is left to the politicians to decide. This has been confirmed by the Court again and again.

So far we have been focusing our attention on questions concerning the freedom and liberty of the individual and the duties to which these concepts give rise. Now we must say something about the other great pillar of modern constitutions; equality. The Basic Law contains a general equal protection clause and some special equality clauses such as prohibition of discrimination because of race, gender, religion, etc. The special equality clauses are construed strictly. This is impossible with the general clause. The application of the equal protection clause always requires a comparison between facts or cases which are equal in some respects and unequal in others. Complete equality would be identity. The question is whether the equal or the unequal factors are regarded as relevant for a certain treatment. This decision is principally up to the legislature. The Constitution, as construed by the Court, requires sound reasons for unequal treatment and a balance between the degree of inequality and the purpose which the unequal treatment serves. This requirement is stricter the more a law touches the exercise of human rights or the less it allows a person to avoid the unequal treatment.[26]

As far as gender is concerned, the Basic Law not only contains an antidiscrimination clause in art. 3(3), but also a special guarantee of gender equality in art. 3(2) whose inclusion was the result of massive complaints by women who were unsatisfied with the mere antidiscrimination clause and asked for special guarantees. For a long time the Court said these two clauses were identical in meaning and that art. 3(2) was just a repetition of art. 3(3). In more recent decisions, however, the Court has said that it is unlikely that two different provisions in the original text have

---

26 BVerfGE 88, 87 (96 f.) *Transsexuals*, as last decision in a long line beginning with BVErfGE 1, 14 (52) *South-West-State*.

the same meaning. It has, therefore, construed art. 3(2) as a temporary exception from the strict prohibition to discriminate in art. 3(3). According to the Court, art. 3(2) establishes not only formal but also material equality among men and women.[27] Since women still suffer many disadvantages in society, the Court has interpreted art. 3(2) as allowing special privileges to be given to women as long as the factual inequality exists. As soon as a state of equality is attained the clause may become obsolete, and only the antidiscrimination clause of art. 3(3) will remain.

2. All these developments have practical consequences in the jurisprudence of the Court.

A. There are numerous grounds on which the Court has concluded that no violation of human rights has occurred.

The first possibility is that the complainant or his behaviour is not protected by the human right whose protection is sought. Some human rights are attributed only to Germans and not to aliens, e.g. the right to assembly. The same is true with regard to corporations. According to art. 19(3) national corporations can claim those human rights which, by their nature, are not only applicable to individuals. Corporations under foreign law are generally excluded from the protection of human rights. The same is true for national corporations under public law, since human rights are designed to protect the individual against the state, not state agencies against other public authorities.[28] An exception is only made for such public corporations which enjoy autonomy in their field and exercise a fundamental right. This has been acknowledged with regard to universities and public broadcasting stations.[29]

Every single human right is designed to protect a certain

---

27 BVerfGE 85, 191 (206 ff.) *Nightwork of Women*; decision of October 19, 1993.

28 BVerfGE 21, 362 (369 ff.).

29 BVerfGE 15, 256 (262); 31, 314 (322).

sphere of life or certain classes of actions. It is an important task of the Court to determine the range (Schutzbereich) of each human right. In free speech cases, for example, the Court held that a deliberate lie is not protected by art. 5(1).[30] Neither is the exercise of economic pressure protected by free speech guaranty because it exceeds the use of argument.[31]

A second possible ground on which a constitutional case may be dismissed is the lack of sufficient state action. Either the state did not act at all or its action cannot be characterized as a limit on a human right (Eingriff). For human rights in their capacity as defenses against the state, intrusion (Eingriff) is a central notion. Only when there is an "Eingriff" into a human right, is the question posed whether this "Eingriff" violated the constitution or not. Since the constitution allows intrusions under certain conditions, not every intrusion violates the constitution. But lack of an intrusion excludes a violation. Originally, a narrow notion of "Eingriff" prevailed. A state action was characterized as "Eingriff" when it was a legal act directed against an individual or group of individuals and intended to restrict a constitutionally protected liberty. This definition reflected the situation of the liberal state which, in principal, left society alone and acted only in order to prevent clear and present dangers. The means of fulfilling this task was an "Eingriff" into the private sphere as described above. This narrow notion, however, was not responsive to the situation of the modern welfare state with its expanding activities to guarantee social security, stimulate economic development, protect society against all sorts of risks etc. If human rights protection were limited to intrusions in the classical meaning, it would leave the individual unprotected against the modern activities of the state. Accordingly, today, the Court understands "Eingriff" to mean every action of a public authority which makes the exercise of a human right impossible or

---

30 BVerfGE 61, 1 (8) *Campaign Slur.*

31 BVerfGE 25, 256 (264 f.) *Blinkfüer.*

extremely difficult. On the other hand it must be the right which is hampered. Mere chances, based on favourable conditions, are still not protected; nor do minor inconveniences or annoyances qualify as intrusions. In the near future, the Court will have to decide whether information or warnings given to the public by the state, e.g. the information that certain religious groups are dangerous for the development of juveniles, constitute an "Eingriff".

As mentioned before, not every "Eingriff" into a human right is a violation of that right. As a matter of fact, most human rights contain a clause giving the legislature the right to limit its use. Sometimes, the constitution contents itself with requiring a legal basis (viz. that it be prescribed by law) for such restrictions. Other times, the law is subject to special requirements. In addition, the Court has developed the principle of proportionality, as described above. It is applied to statutes touching a human right and to acts applying such statutes, be it by the executive or by the judiciary. Consequently, the Court concludes that no violation of a human right has occurred (1) when the "Eingriff" into the right had a legal basis, (prescribed by law)(2) when the law was properly adopted, (3) when it did respect the constitutional requirements for restrictions, and (4) when it was not unproportional. Nor will the Court find a violation of a human right when the act applying such a law took the human right into account and is, for its part, in accordance with the principle of proportionality.

When confronted with a law which is unconstitutional only if construed in a certain way the Court will refrain from declaring it void but instead require an interpretation which is compatible with the constitution.[32] This will not be done, however, when the interpretation that is required to conform with the constitution is in clear contradiction with the legislative intent.[33]

---

32 BVerfGE 2, 266 (282); 64, 229 (241).

33 BVerfGE 8, 28 (34).

In cases where it is alleged that the state has failed to discharge its positive duty to initiate protective measures (Schutzpflicht), the complaint will be dismissed when the right does not contain sufficient grounds for the claim at stake or when the government has already fulfilled the duty derived from that right. No individual can claim a particular law should be passed unless the constitution puts the government under a specific obligation to legislate and the appellant is favoured by that provision.

B. When we shift our attention from cases in which no violation of human rights has occurred, to those in which a law is found to be constitutionally infirm, (1) it is necessary to distinguish between the formal and the substantive dimension of whatever law is being reviewed.

Formal Requirements

Being a federal state, Germany has divided the legislative power among the federation and its member states. The first question, therefore, is whether the legislative body which passed the law was competent to do so. The second question is whether all procedural requirements were observed. If a government decree (Verordnung) is subject to judicial review an additional question is whether the government was duly empowered by parliament and whether it has observed the limits drawn by the constitution in art. 80 for decrees.

Substantive Requirements

The Basic Law formulates some general requirements for laws limiting human rights and some special requirements concerning particular human rights. Furthermore as we have seen,, some additional requirements are grounded in the jurisprudence of the Court.

First, a law restricting a human right has to be a general law. Laws concerning single cases are prohibited according to art. 19(1). In addition, this provision of the Basic Law stipulates that the law must name the human right which is subject to restriction.

In the words of Art. 19(2), no law may touch "the essential content" of a human right. Retroactive penal laws are completely forbidden according to art. 103(2).

Most human rights in the Basic Law contain specific requirements as to their restriction. The normal case is a formula like the one in art. 2(2): "These rights may only be encroached upon pursuant to a law." A number of human rights provisions add special requirements, specifying certain purposes ("only to avert an imminent danger to the existence or the free democratic order" - art. 11), or limiting the legislative power to certain types of cases (e.g., in the right to free assembly - art. 8, to open air meetings). Where there is no express permission to limit a human right as is the case in art. 4 (freedom of religion, conscience etc.), or art. 5(3) (freedom of art and science), the Court has ruled that only limitations which reconcile these human rights with other constitutional rights of the same rank and importance are allowed.[34] Non-compliance with one of these requirements constitutes a violation of the human right involved and normally leads to the invalidation of the law.

The most important requirement that has been developed in the jurisprudence by the Court is the principle of proportionality. As far as human rights, in their capacity as defenses against the state are concerned, a law is unconstitutional when it contains a useless, unnecessary or inappropriate restriction. The first is true when the law is unable to reach its aim, the second when milder means are available to reach the same effect, the third when the legislature has not achieved an adequate balance between the human right which is restricted and the legal value protected by that restriction.

Some other principles have been deduced from the rule of law, including the prohibition of retroactive laws outside criminal

---

34 BVerfGE 28, 243 (251) *Dissident Soldier*; 30, 173 (193) *Mephisto*.

law,[35] and the principle of sufficient precision of laws.[36]

The legislature has, within certain boundaries laid down in art. 80, the right to delegate its legislative power to the executive. The Court, however, concluded from the principle of democracy that every "essential" question has to be decided by parliament itself.[37] Questions are regarded as being essential mainly when the exercise of a human right is affected by the regulation. Thus, a number of government acts were declared unconstitutional because they had no sufficient legal basis.

As far as human rights, in their capacity as imposing legislative duties to act are concerned, a law can be declared unconstitutional if it does not sufficiently protect a human right, either in terms of substance or in terms of procedure. The same is true with laws organizing public or private institutions.

The intensity of control varies, however, according to the human right involved and also according to the kind of laws reviewed. Laws restricting personal freedom or political rights are controlled more intensively than laws regulating the economy and thus touching economic freedoms.[38] Within a single right, the Court often distinguishes between a more private and a more social sphere, e.g. with regard to free development of personality (art. 2(1)), inviolability of home (art. 13), and freedom of property (art. 14). In addition, in cases of laws whose future effect is uncertain

---

35 BVerfGE 13, 261 (272) *Corporate Income Tax*; 23, 12 (32); 88, 384 (403) *GDR Construction Credit.*

36 BVerfGE 49, 89 (133 f.) *Kalkar.*

37 BVerfGE 33, 1 (10 f.) *Prisoners' Human Rights*; 47, 46 (78 ff.) *Sex Education*; 49, 89 (126 ff.) *Kalkar*; 57, 295 (320 f.) *Third Broadcasting Decision*; 58, 257 (268 ff.) *School Dismissal*; 76, 1 (75) *Aliens' Families*; 77, 170 (230 f.) *Chemical Weapons*; 83, 130 (151 f.) *Mutzenbacher.*

38 BVerfGE 4, 7 (17 f.) *Investment Aid*; 7, 377 (400) *Pharmacy*; 50, 290 (339 ff.) *Co-determination.*

because of lack of reliable knowledge and the necessity of prognostic assumptions, the Court has developed a gradual system of control.[39] In a number of cases dealing with economic regulation the Court only asks whether the assumptions of the legislature were evidently wrong.[40] In other cases, which bear on personal liberties or involve potential risks for human rights, the Court will examine whether the legislature's assumptions were seriously formed and plausibly founded.[41] In a third group of cases,where the law has an immediate effect upon personal rights such as dignity, life, health, speech, the Court exercises an intensive control as to the contents of a law.[42] If the prognostic assumption turns out to be wrong later on, the legislature is under a constitutional duty to correct the laws.[43] But the Court does not substitute parliamentary assumptions with its own views. Neither does the Court examine whether the legislature found the best, the most efficient, most expedient or the most just way to solve a problem.

The legal consequences of the finding that a law is unconstitutional vary. The normal result is the annulment of the law (§ 78 Law on the Federal Constitutional Court). However, the Court has recognized some exceptions to this rule. In cases of violation of the equality clause, the legislature usually has two

---

39 BVerfGE 50, 290 (333).

40 BVerfGE 36, 1 (17) *Inter-German Basic Treaty*; 37, 1 (20); 40, 196 (223).

41 BVerfGE 25, 1 (12 f., 17) *Mill Act*; 30, 250 (263); 39, 210 (225 f.) *Mill Structure Act*; 49, 89 (140 ff.) *Kalkar*.

42 BVerfGE 7, 377 (415) *Pharmacy*; 17, 269 (276 f.); 39, 1 (46, 41 ff.) *Abortion I*; 45, 187 (238) *Life Imprisonment*; 82, 272 (280 f.) *Constrained Democrat*; 85, 1 (13 f., 17 f.) *Bayer Stockholders*.

43 BVerfGE 25, 1 (12 f.) *Mill Act*; 49, 89 (130 ff.) *Kalkar*; 50, 290 (335, 377f.) *Co-determination*.

possibilities to cure the mistake. It may either include the neglected group of persons into the benefit attributed by the law, or abolish the benefit for all. In these circumstances, therefore, the Court does not annul the law but leaves it to the legislature to choose the solution it prefers.[44] However, with rare exceptions the law may not be applied in the meantime. In addition, when the Court is of the view that the detriment to the constitution would be greater if the law were invalidated immediately than if it were upheld temporarily, it will allow the legislature a period of time in which to pass a new law. The Court has followed this approach, for example, in a case in which it found parts of the Income Tax Act to be infirm.[45] The Court also refrains from annulling a law when its unconstitutionality is the result of social change which has only recently become apparent.[46] In these circumstances, rather than abolish the law the Court will oblige the legislature to repair it in due time. It will also rule whether the law may or may not be applied in the meantime. In extremely rare cases, the Court has itself enacted a transitory rule.[47]

(2) The application of a - constitutional - statute by administrative agencies or courts may violate the constitution when it does not take sufficient account of the human right affected by the statute. This, of course, creates the problem where to draw the line between (a) the construction and application of ordinary laws which is the matter of the ordinary courts, and (b) genuine constitutional matters. The Court applies a formula which is

---

44 BVerfGE 22, 349 (359) *Legal Aid*; 84, 168 (186 f.); 85, 191 (211 f.) *Nightwork of Women*.

45 BVerfGE 8, 1 (19 f.) *Civil Servants' Salary*; 33, 303 (347) *Numerus Clausus*; 83, 130 (154) *Mutzenbacher*.

46 BVerfGE 34, 9 (25 f.); 53, 257 (304) *Tax Splitting*; 61, 319 (352).

47 BVerfGE 39, 1 (68) *Abortion I*; 84, 9 (22 ff.) *Martial Name*; 88, 203 (336 ff.) *Abortion II*.

rather vague. According to that formula, it will not review the fact finding and the procedure of the ordinary courts unless a violation of a procedural human right is alleged, and it will only look to see whether a complete or fundamental misunderstanding of a human right has occurred.[48] In other cases, the opinion of the ordinary courts governs. When the Court finds a violation of a human right, it is not allowed to decide the case itself but has to pass it back to the ordinary courts which are obliged to follow the opinion of the Constitutional Court as far as human rights are concerned.

C. In 1993, 5,440 cases were brought to the Court. The number of cases has constantly risen over the years: in 1951 478 cases were brought, in 1961 1,056, in 1971 1,542, in 1981 3,098, in 1991 4,077. From the beginning in 1951 until the end of 1993, about 96,000 cases have been brought and about 93,500 have been decided. Among the annual cases, more than 95% are individual complaints. Among a total of about 90,000 individual complaints which have been decided over the years, about 2,450 were successful, which is less than 3%. Most of the individual complaints are handled in a simplified procedure by three judges. About fifty individual complaints per year are decided by the whole panel. All other procedures have to be decided by a panel. From 1951 to 1992, 269 laws have been declared unconstitutional, 175 federal laws and 94 state laws. In most cases, only parts of the law were declared to be unconstitutional; in 34 cases the entire law was declared unconstitutional. In 1992, 14 laws were brought directly to the Court, out of which 5 were found incompatible with the Basic Law.

IV. EVALUATION

Is the Federal Constitutional Court an activist court or does it exercise judicial self-restraint?

The answer requires some differentiation.

(1) The German Court has ample powers. It can take

---

[48] BVerfGE 18, 85 (92 ff.).

jurisdiction on 18 different grounds.[49] Two of these, however, have never become practical (impeachment of the Federal President and impeachment of judges). Others have played a relatively minor role (forfeiture of basic rights; prohibition of political parties). But other routes to the Court have been widely used. It seems to be characteristic for the political process in Germany that not only individual citizens, but also the losers in parliament or in inter-organ or federal disputes will petition the court when important questions are at stake. Thus, one would hardly find a major political decision which was not contested before the Court, starting from German integration into the Western alliance soon after the foundation of the Federal Republic, over the internal reforms and the reconciliation with the East in the seventies, to unification with East Germany in 1990 and the foundation of the European Union in 1993. Cases of this kind, of necessity, create the impression of a rather activist and politically influential constitutional court.

(2) The Court is not active, however, in the sense that it easily deviates from the boundaries drawn by the constitution or that, instead of reasoning legally, it prefers political argumentation. The Court tries to keep a methodological standard of interpretation that guarantees controllable results and to respect earlier precedents although there is no rule of stare decisis in Germany. It has repeatedly stressed that the constitution is but a framework and general directive for politics and leaves ample room for political choice and policy changes according to election results. There have been occasions, however, in the famous Civil Servant Loyalty case, for example, where the Court did exceed its powers and used pending cases to decide questions which were not raised by them, thus reversing the sequence of political decision and judicial control.[50] Quite often, the Court also appeals to the government to take action in order to protect human rights, and

---

49 cf. & 13 Law on the Federal Constitutional Court.

50 For an example see BVerfGE 39, 334 *Civil Servants' Loyalty*.

from time to time, it combines these appeals or the annulment of a law with recommendations as to how a law may be designed so that it will meet the constitutional test. None of these recommendations is legally binding, but, given a rather juridified political culture in Germany, they have acquired some binding force in fact.

(3) The Court has certainly been active in terms of unfolding and developing the constitution. It has elaborated a theory of human rights which exceeds the jurisprudence of most other countries with judicial review. Firstly, the notion that there is a protective duty (Schutzpflicht) implicit in the concept of human rights has given extensive importance to the constitution. In addition, the principle of proportionality, particularly its third stage - the proper balancing of conflicting constitutional values - has also substantially contributed to this effect. It is true that the Court has used these tools in different ways. It controls state action strictly where personal and political liberties are encroached upon or where fundamental requirements of equality are neglected. By contrast, it restrains itself where questions of policy making or the spending power are concerned. Nevertheless, the Court brings a good deal of political and juridical decisions under control of the constitution and, consequently submits them to judicial review. There can be no doubt that, in the end, this leads to a loss of parliamentary power and a gain of court power, yet in the name of human rights. It is more the sort of freedom guaranteed by human rights than the sort of freedom guaranteed by democratic participation which prevails in this system.

HUMAN RIGHTS AND JUDICIAL REVIEW: THE EUROPEAN COURT OF HUMAN RIGHTS

Rudolf Bernhardt*

Introduction

There are certain similarities, but also considerable differences between national courts deciding human rights matters and an international human rights court. Similarities: National and international catalogues of human rights guarantees contain similar or even identical provisions, and the courts have to see whether and how far State organs, including the legislature, have respected these guarantees. Differences: Competences and composition of national and international courts vary considerably, the background of the judges is quite different, they come from legal systems with distinctive traditions. While "judicial review" on the national level means that courts can either declare that an unconstitutional law is invalid erga omnes or at least that the law is not to be applied in the concrete case, an international human rights court can only state that a law and/or its application are incompatible with the relevant Convention; such a statement does not have immediate consequences for the validity and applicability of the law in the internal legal order.

In order to see the similarities as well as the differences more clearly, this essay will, at first, briefly describe the basic structure of the European system for the protection of human rights. Thereafter, we will highlight special features of this system. Finally, some theoretical and practical conclusions will be drawn.

History and Basic Structure of the European System for the Protection of Human Rights

Grave and large-scale violations of basic human rights and incredible atrocities were committed during the Second World War, especially under the responsibility of the German Nazi

D.M. Beatty (ed.), Human Rights and Judicial Review, 297-319.

government inside and beyond the territory of the German Reich. At the end of the war, it was quite clear that the protection of human rights could no longer be left to the discretion of the government of each State, not only aliens but also the citizens living in their own country needed some international protection. Steps in this direction were undertaken on the universal as well as the regional level.

In December 1948, the General Assembly of the United Nations Organization adopted the famous Universal Declaration of Human Rights, which was, however, not a legally binding document. Other declarations and binding treaty obligations were later adopted on the universal level, e.g. the Convention against Racial Discrimination and the two United Nations Human Rights Covenants on Economic, Social and Cultural Rights and on Civil and Political Rights which were adopted in 1966 and came into force ten years later.[1] As far as these and other conventions provide for a control machinery, the machinery consists either of a reporting system under which States have to submit periodic reports which are scrutinized by a more or less independent body, or, exceptionally, of limited petition rights of individuals. These control bodies can express their views and criticize human rights violations, but they do not have the competence to render binding decisions. This is still the prevailing situation on the universal

---

*Professor of Law at Frankfurt Comparative Public Law and Public International Law, Heidelberg, 1970-1993 (no emeritus). Professor of Law at Heidelberg University, since 1970. Dr.jur. honoris cause, Meijii University of Tokyo, 1990. Honorary member of the American Society of International Law, 1990. Judge at the European Court of Human Rights, since 1981. Vice-President of the Court, since 1992.

[1] Documents of the 1993 World Conference on Human Rights speak of "six core United Nations treaties" on human rights; in addition to the three Conventions mentioned above, the following Conventions belong to this core: The Convention on the Elimination of All Forms of Discrimination against Women; the Convention against Torture and Other Cruel, Inhuman or Degrading Treatment or Punishment; the Convention on the Rights of the Child. See U.N. Doc. A/CONF. 157/TBB/4, 16 June 1993.

level.

In Western Europe, the Council of Europe created a more progressive or innovative system for the regional protection of human rights. The European Convention on Human Rights, adopted in 1950 and in force since 1953, was modelled after the Universal Declaration of 1948, but it not only formulated a human rights catalogue, it provided, in addition, for a rather complicated control system. Two new organs were invented, the European Commission of Human Rights and the European Court of Human Rights. (Similar organs were later introduced by the American Convention on Human Rights for the Western hemisphere.)

The European control system provides the following procedures: Inter-State applications[2] can be brought before the European Commission by "any High Contracting Party" (Article 24 of the Convention). The Commission "shall draw up a Report on the facts and state its opinion as to whether the facts found disclose a breach by the State concerned with its obligations under the Convention" (Article 31). Thereafter, "the Committee of Ministers [of the Council of Europe] shall decide ... whether there has been a violation of the Convention" (Article 32). Thus, and as a rule, a political organ has to take a legally binding decision.

The European Convention of Human Rights permits, in addition to the procedure just described, petitions from individuals "claiming to be the victim of a violation by one of the High Contracting parties of the rights set forth in this Convention" (Article 25). But individual applications require express and formal recognition of this right by the State concerned. Finally, Article 46 provides that the European Court of Human Rights can take a final decision, instead of the Committee of Ministers, if a State has accepted the jurisdiction of the Court. No application can go directly to the Court, it is always the Commission which must at first find out whether an application is admissible and whether a friendly settlement can be reached. If such a settlement has not

---

[2] Inter-State applications are in practice very rare, but they have been useful in certain circumstances. At present, no such applications seem to be pending.

been possible and if the Commission has submitted its report on the merits of the case, the Commission itself or an interested State can bring this case to the Court[3] - always provided that the State party to the dispute has recognized the Court's jurisdiction.

The Commission started its activity in 1954, the Court came into existence in early 1959. Many States were at first reluctant to accept individual petitions under Article 25 and to recognize the jurisdiction of the Court according to Article 46. Nevertheless, over the years the Commission received, annually, a growing number of individual applications, more than 90% of them were declared inadmissible; no remedies against such inadmissibility decisions are given. If the Commission declares that an application is admissible, and if it has - after the failure to reach a friendly settlement - submitted its report on the merits, the final and binding decision has to be taken either by the Committee of Ministers or by the Court. In reality, during the first 15 years of its existence, the Court received only 11 cases, but the situation has totally changed since the late 1970s. The Commission now registers annually between 1500 and 2000 individual applications, and the Court has adopted 72 judgments in 1991 and 81 judgments in 1992.

The reasons for this development cannot be explained in detail here and only a few remarks are possible. In early 1993, all 26 member States of the Council of Europe had ratified the European Convention on Human Rights, and all of them had recognized the right of the Commission to receive individual applications and the jurisdiction of the Court. In the meantime, more States from central and eastern Europe have either already become members of the Council of Europe[4] or formally applied for membership.[5]

---

[3] The 9th Additional Protocol provides that the individual concerned can also bring his/her case to the Court, but this Protocol is not yet in force.

[4] Six States have been admitted in 1993 (Estland, Lithuania, Slovenia, Czech Republic, Slovakia, Romenia), bringing the number of member States of the Council to 32.

It is the practice of the Council to admit States only if they have clearly indicated their intention to adopt, after a certain period of internal reform, the European system for the protection of human rights. There is now a good chance that the European Convention on Human Rights will become more and more a "Human Rights Constitution" for all Europe. Some dangers are inherent in this development and may be relevant for the problems discussed in this book. An effective human rights system may require some homogeneity in the legal and social structure of the participating States.

The European Court of Human Rights normally decides in Chambers with nine full members, the President of the Court and the national judge are ex officio-members of the Chamber, the other members are appointed by lot for each case. Important cases can and some must be sent by the Chamber to the Plenary Court; this possibility has often been used in the past, but with more than twenty five and possibly up to forty judges, the Plenary Court may become unable to work adequately.[6]

Each member State of the Council of Europe has the right to have a judge in the Court. Each State has to submit a list with three names. The Parliamentary Assembly of the Council of Europe elects one of these three nominated persons, as a rule the first on the list, but exceptions to this rule occur. The candidates "must either possess the qualifications required for appointment to high judicial office or be jurisconsults of recognized competence" (Article 39 § 3 of the Convention). No former experience as a judge on the national level is required; in practice, judges of high national courts, professors of law and holders of various other positions in their home country (advocates, government officials,

---

[5] Among them Russia and other successor States of the former Soviet Union.

[6] The present discussion on a reform of the whole system cannot be described here. One proposal envisages, instead of the present two-level system with Commission and Court, a single human rights court with full-time judges.

In October 1993, the Court changed the Rules insofar as a Grand Chamber with 19 judges now can decide cases instead of the Plenary Court.

etc.) have become members of the European Court. Only a limited number of the members of the Court has special experience in the area of international law. In fact, each member of the Court has worked and often continues to work primarily in a national legal order, all of these orders have special traditions and structures, and this has some influence on the arguments and the approach to legal problems under the European Convention. It must be added that, as far as can be seen, there are no different "schools" in the Court. Judges from different parts of Europe and trained in different legal systems often reach the same result, or judges coming from the same region may reach different results and use different arguments in concrete cases.

The European Convention on Human Rights as a Treaty and as a Human Rights "Constitution"

The European Convention is a treaty under international law, it has been elaborated, concluded and ratified according to the practice and rules valid for treaties, and it can be denounced[7] by any of the "High Contracting Parties". This is one side of the coin.

The substance of the Convention (the provisions containing the material human rights guarantees) is similar to a constitutional human rights catalogue or a national human rights bill. The guarantees are often phrased in general and broad terms. Thirteen Articles of the Convention (Articles 2 to 14) contain the substantial guarantees, together with a few additional protocols which have been added over the decades.

Both the treaty character and the "constitutional" aspect of the Convention should be seen together, but in the course of time the constitutional aspect has become predominant. The Convention remains a treaty, with all the difficulties of amending the text now

---

[7] Article 65 of the Convention. Until now, only once a State has denounced the Convention (Greece in the 1960s under military régime; when Greece became democratic again, it rejoined the European human rights community.)

binding for nearly thirty States. There is no real enforcement machinery in the sense that violations of the Convention can be corrected and punished by the use of force, as is normally the case under national law. It remains legally possible for States parties to the Convention to denounce it, or at least to no longer recognize the right of individual petitions and the jurisdiction of the European Court. Public opinion would probably, at present, oppose and exclude such steps, since no European State could give the impression that it neglects human rights. But conditions can change, and the existing rules of international law may be used again for changing or abolishing treaty commitments. It is to be hoped that such changes will not occur, but the legal framework for unilateral withdrawal exists.

It must further be seen that the effective application of the Convention and the smooth working of the supervisory machinery presuppose and require a spirit of cooperation and a considerable homogeneity among the participating States. This does not mean that the legal, political, economic and social conditions are more or less uniform in Europe, quite the contrary: there are and there will remain great differences between the situation e.g. in Finland, in Spain, in Iceland, in Italy or in Greece. But in the area of human rights covered by the Convention guarantees member States must either already respect common standards or must be willing to change the national rules as far as required by the Convention and the case-law developed by the Court and the other Convention organs. That this spirit of cooperation at present really exists is underlined by different factors: the States have not only always renewed their acceptance of the competences of the European Commission and Court of Human Rights, but they have until now always respected the decisions of the Court; in many cases national legislation has been changed or new laws have been enacted in order to satisfy the European requirements as determined by the

European Court.[8]

It has been said before that over the years the character of the Convention as a "Human Rights Constitution" has become more important than the treaty character; this can be shown by several developments, some of which will later be described in more detail. In the first place, in the great majority of cases decided by the European Court, violations of the most fundamental human rights are no longer at stake. Most cases involve encroachments of civil liberties which occur in all States which in general respect the rule of law. Detention of suspected persons for more than four days without the control of a judge or other legal officer, reimbursement of expenses for an interpreter in criminal proceedings, prohibitions to build houses in certain areas, access to official files and similar matters with which the Strasbourg organs are often concerned may be of great importance to the individual concerned, but they do not necessarily belong to the core of human rights. The European Court often has to deal with cases which, in general, are adequately decided by national courts including Supreme or Constitutional courts. But the European Court now develops to a certain extent uniform European standards. The "constitutional" character of the Convention also becomes apparent if we look at the principles of interpretation. In classical international law, treaties have been interpreted by looking into the travaux préparatoires or by a restrictive interpretation of the obligations of the State; quite different principles have been adopted for the interpretation of the Convention (see infra). Developments in modern societies are taken into account and the Convention is regarded as a "living instrument"; this also underlines the "constitutional" character of the Convention.

---

[8] The Registry of the Court publishes regularly a "Survey of Activities" of the Court which contains also a section on "Effects of Judgments or Cases", see pp. 50 ss. of the Survey for the years 1959-1991.

The Court's General Approach to the Convention and Important Trends in the Case-law

1. One must always remember some basic facts. The European Convention on Human Rights is the only text which governs the activity and the judgments of the Court. It is a text with broadly phrased provisions which needs interpretation. Activities (and omissions) of State organs - including the legislature and national courts - are the objects of international judicial control. The European Court has to decide whether a certain behaviour of State organs is compatible with the Convention or not.

The binding interpretation and application of the Convention is entrusted to a body which consists of judges that come from different States, "no two judges may be nationals of the same State". The judges must be jurists, but they have different backgrounds, experiences and professions. In each case, at least thirteen judges are involved - nine full members of the Chamber and four substitutes. Whenever a Chamber relinquishes jurisdiction in favour of the Plenary Court, all judges might sit and decide in a concrete case; until now in some plenary decisions more than twenty judges have taken part.

The number of the judges and the diversity of professions and experiences among them (and also regular changes in the composition of the Court) make it impossible for the Court to develop a coherent and generally scholarly doctrine on the protection of human rights under the Convention. Some judges may adhere to natural law opinions, others not. Some judges may underline the necessity of general principles and guidelines for the case-law, others prefer a case-to-case approach and an adequate solution for each case without any general principles. All this is also present in national courts, but, for the reasons already mentioned, an international court is in this respect in a special and especially difficult situation. If, according to the judgment of competent observers, the European Court and its jurisprudence have gained a good reputation, this is mainly attributable to the quality of the bench and its decisions and not to any general doctrines.

Nevertheless, we will describe some principles which have been developed and recognized by the European Court in the course of its activity.

2. In spite of its pragmatic, case by case approach and the endeavour to find an adequate and just solution for each concrete controversy, some general guidelines and principles can be found in the jurisprudence of the Court. The first to be mentioned here has been reported and underlined in the *Söring* judgment[9] in these words:

> "... the object and purpose of the Convention as an instrument for the protection of individual human beings require that its provisions be interpreted and applied so as to make its safeguards practical and effective."

This is a kind of teleological interpretation; the object and purpose of the Convention being the protection of the individual, the interpretation of its provisions must see that the Convention guarantees become effective. This excludes a narrow interpretation in favour of State sovereignty and the freedom of State organs whenever effective protection necessitates restrictions on State power. On a similar line of reasoning, the Court has several times stated that the provisions in the Convention (mainly the second paragraphs of Articles 8-11) permitting restrictions of the individual freedoms must be interpreted narrowly. In dubio pro libertate seems to be a recognized principle of interpretation applied to the Convention. But it should not be forgotten that the principle does not always give clear guidelines and that in some cases not only the freedom of the applicant, but also the rights of other individuals are involved, like in cases of public defamations or where the freedom of religion or belief is used to indoctrinate other persons. Here as elsewhere, abstract principles and rules do not always help to solve concrete cases and controversies.

---

[9] The judgments are quoted according to the official publications of the Court: Publications of the European Court of Human Rights, Series A, No.161, p.34.

Nevertheless, in conflicts between State regulation and sovereignty on the one side and individual freedom on the other, the maxim in dubio pro libertate plays a role under the European Convention and according to the case-law of the European Court.

Should constitutional and conventional texts be given an historical or a contemporaneous interpretation? This is a question which is much discussed in constitutional law as well as in international law. Should the American Constitution be interpreted primarily according to the intentions and views of the founding fathers in the last quarter of the 18th century? Should the European Convention be interpreted in line with the prevailing ideas and social conditions in 1949/1950, or are present-day conditions at the end of the 20th century more important than the travaux préparatoires and the state of the societies in the middle of this century?

The answer of the European Court to this question is entirely clear, in spite of occasional objections of some governments that they or their predecessors did not intend this or that restriction. The Convention is, according to the clear jurisprudence of the Strasbourg organs, a living instrument and must be interpreted by taking into account present-day conditions. This has become important in many areas. The legal and social position of unmarried mothers and their children has drastically changed since 1950, the same holds true for homosexual relations and in many other fields. Since the *Marckx* judgment[10] of 1979, the European Court has many times declared that the Convention must be interpreted and applied in conformity with contemporaneous conditions and convictions. This can hardly be otherwise for several reasons. A human rights text would become widely ineffective if individuals could enjoy only those rights and freedoms which were already granted to their parents and grandparents, irrespective of modern developments. It must also be seen that many States have later adhered to the Convention without any influence in the drafting period - why should they be

---

[10] Series A n° 31.

bound by the ideas of the drafters and not by the actual text as interpreted and applied in recent practice? The clear and unequivocal acceptance of the principle of contemporaneous interpretation by the European Court is again a guideline and does not provide easy answers in concrete cases.

Should the Court wait until new conditions are clearly accepted in the society before adopting a new interpretation, or should it be in the forefront of modern developments? This old controversy, well-known in national law, between a conservative approach on the one side and judicial activism of judges on the other is not without importance in the context of the European Convention and the Convention organs. The author of this essay does not think that judicial activism is adequate for an international convention binding more than 30 States, but, as said before, the interpretation of the Convention must take account of modern conditions and developments. It is again necessary to find some middle-road, and this has been tried by the European Court.

3. The notion "margin of appreciation", often invoked by the Court, requires some explanation. An international human rights court faces a problem which is normally not known to a national court. How far can or must the international court investigate the factual and legal situation on the national level? The problem became apparent in the very first case before the European Court of Human Rights, in the *Lawless* case.[11] The Irish government had invoked the emergency clause in Article 15 of the European Convention. This clause permits "in time of war and other public emergency threatening the life of the nation ... measures derogating from its [the High Contracting Party's] obligations ... to the extent strictly required by the exigences of the situation ..." If the national authorities are convinced that a public emergency exists and that certain measures are strictly necessary, can an international body come to a different result, and on which basis? Comparable questions arise in connection with other provisions of

[11] Series A n° 3 (Judgment of 1 July 1961 on the merits).

the Convention. The second paragraphs of Articles 8-11 permit certain restrictions of the freedoms which are "necessary in a democratic society". Who should decide whether a certain restriction is necessary and therefore permitted?

The doctrine developed in the case-law of the European Court is easier to explain in abstract terms than to apply in concrete cases. The doctrine says: National authorities have a margin of appreciation in evaluating the situation and in deciding on the necessary measures, but it is up to the international organs to control whether the conventional limits of the national margin of appreciation have been respected. In practice this has meant: national Governments are allowed to determine the actual situation and the measures to be taken, but always under international control. The doctrine is in essence widely accepted, but its correct application in actual cases may be controversial. One example of this is the *Markt Intern* judgment mentioned below. Nine members of the Court were of the opinion that the national courts in permitting the disputed restrictions imposed on the freedom of commercial speech, had violated Article 10 of the Convention, while the other nine judges (including the President with his casting vote) underlined the necessity to give States a wide margin of appreciation in this area. Occasionally, the whole doctrine has been challenged, but it is the view of the author of this essay, absolutely necessary for a proper cooperation and an adequate distribution of competences between national authorities and the international bodies. The latter are neither equipped to make detailed investigations inside the States nor are they competent to evaluate all the political and social conditions on the national level. But the international organs must ensure, on the basis of the information given by the national authorities including the courts, that the human rights guarantees in the Convention are respected.

While, the so-called margin of appreciation has many different aspects, all of them concern the proper distribution of competences and supervisory functions between national authorities on the one side and the European institutions on the other side. When the second paragraphs of Articles 8 to 11 of the European Convention permit only those restrictions on individual freedoms which are "necessary in a democratic society", the Convention seems to refer to common European standards. Here again, we face difficult problems, and in a good number of judgments the majority and the minority of judges have taken different positions concerning the margin of appreciation in the concrete circumstances. A general guideline may be found in the existence or non-existence of common European standards. Common standard does not mean uniformity throughout all member-States of the Council of Europe. What is decisive is whether one can find similar approaches to and similar solutions for a social problem in the majority of European States and in the different national societies.

In the Marckx case, quoted above, the European Court found that according to European standards it could no longer be accepted that an unmarried mother and her child were legally in a much weaker position than the members of other families. Other judgments can be quoted where the Court found that, in view of the non-existence of common European standards, States enjoy a wider margin of appreciation. In the Handyside judgment of 7 December 1976[12], the Court expressed the view that:

> "...it is not possible to find in the domestic law of the various Contracting States a uniform European conception of morals. The view taken by their respective laws of the requirements of morals varies from time to time and from place to place... By reason of their direct and continuous contact with the vital forces of their countries, State authorities are in principle in a better position than the international judge to give an opinion on the exact content of these requirements..."

In the Muller judgment of 24 Mary 1988[13], States measures against "obscene" paintings were considered to remain inside the national margin of appreciation in spite of the fact that the same

[12] Series A. No.24.

[13] Series A. no.25.

paintings could be exhibited without difficulties in other countries or even in different parts of the same country. Similar problems arise in connection with so-called transsexuals. In the Rees judgment of 17 October 1986[14], the European Court declared:

> "Several States have, through legislation or by means of legal interpretation or by administrative practice, given transsexuals the option of changing their personal status to fit their newly-gained identity. ...In other States, such an option does not - or does not yet - exist. It would therefore be true to say that there is at present little common ground between the Contracting States in this area and that, generally speaking, the law appears to be in a transitional stage. Accordingly, this is an area which the Contracting Parties enjoy a wide margin of appreciation."

These considerations and quotations show that the margin of appreciation is closely connected with the existence of common European standards. But it must also be admitted that opinions are often divided whether such standards exist or not. The doctrine seems to be widely accepted, but its application in concrete circumstances often poses problems.

4. In order to illustrate the case-by-case approach practiced by the Court, a few plenary decisions may be quoted and briefly explained. We take three plenary decisions where the judgment was supported by a great majority or even all of the participating judges, and three other decisions where the Court was split and only a small majority supported the result reached. These decisions are not representative of the practice of the Court in general in the sense that they permit general insights. Rather they demonstrate the pragmatic approach and the effort of the Court to reach adequate and just results according to the peculiarities of each case.

---

[14] Series A no.106. See also the judgments in the Cossey case (Series A no.184) and in the B. v. France case (Series A no.232).

In the *Young, James and Webster* case,[15] decided in 1981, the freedom of association, guaranteed in Article 11 of the Convention, was at issue. Three employees of British Railway were dismissed, after several years of employment, the only reason being that they refused to join a trade union; closed shop agreements having been legalized by the United Kingdom parliament. The European Court found, by 18 to 3 votes, a breach of the Convention. The decision and its reasoning were confined to the concrete circumstances of the applicants being dismissed after several years of employment solely for their refusal to join the union. In the course of its decision a majority of the judges also found that the negative freedom of association, — the right not to join an association, — is protected by the Convention.

In the *Lingens* case,[16] decided in 1986, the Plenary Court, sitting with 18 judges, found unanimously a violation of Article 10, guaranteeing freedom of expression. The journalist Lingens had published articles attacking the (former) Austrian Chancellor Kreisky, and an Austrian court found Lingens guilty of defamation. In the opinion of the European Court, the views expressed by Lingens must be seen together with the concrete circumstances, namely with prior negative remarks of Kreisky in a political controversy. The specific circumstances justified, according to the European Court, a sharp reply by Lingens. The Court ruled that such strong reactions must be permitted in an open and democratic society which is based on freedom of expression.

A third example is taken from a quite different context. A young person of German nationality was arrested in the United Kingdom, and his extradition to the United States had been granted. Once in the United States, the accused faced the possibility of being sentenced to death for capital murder and, connected therewith, several years of confinement on "death row". In its *Söring*

---

[15] Series A, N° 44.

[16] Series A n° 103.

judgment,[17] rendered in 1989, the European Court - again in plenary session with 18 judges present - decided unanimously that the extradition of Söring to the United States would violate the prohibition of torture and inhuman treatment set out in Article 3 of the Convention. Once again, without discussing in detail the merits of the case, the Court's decision was based on the concrete circumstances which surrounded the petitioner's extradition.

In other plenary decisions, where the Court was split, and a significant minority of judges dissented, one can see a similar emphasis in the reasoning of the Court on the facts of a particular case. In the *Sunday Times* judgment[18] of 1978, the Court held by eleven votes to nine that there had been a breach of Article 10 (freedom of expression). British courts, including the House of Lords, had found that a certain publication, connected with an ongoing lawsuit, would constitute contempt of court and should be prohibited. The European Court considered that in the concrete circumstances of this case the Convention's guarantee of freedom of expression was of primary importance and it refused to follow the national judiciary which had taken the opposite position.

In the *Markt Intern* case,[19] decided in 1989, the European Court found by nine votes to nine with the casting vote of the President, that Article 10 of the Convention had not been violated. (The European Commission had expressed, with twelve votes to one, the opposite opinion.) German courts had granted an injunction against the publication of an article in a commercial context. In this case, the European Court based its result on the margin of appreciation to be given to the national authorities.

Our last example is taken from the *Cruz Varas* judgment,[20] rendered in 1991. Leaving aside the substantive questions of that

---

[17] Series A n° 161.

[18] Series A n° 30.

[19] Series A n° 165.

[20] Series A n° 201.

decision (it concerned the expulsion of a Chilean citizen from Sweden to Chile), only an important procedural problem should be mentioned. A majority of ten judges found against nine dissenting judges that interim measures of protection indicated by the European Commission were not binding for the State concerned since the Convention did not provide for binding orders even in the case of an imminent expulsion and the danger of inhuman treatment in the target State.

5. It may be mentioned, finally that, before the European Court of Human Rights, facts are controversial only in exceptional cases. In general, the facts of a case have already been clarified by the national courts; if doubts remain, the European Commission undertakes whatever investigation is necessary. The European Court is not entirely excluded from taking evidence on its own; but this competence has not played any significant role in practice. The European Court resembles a national court of cassation which is responsible only for determining the law on the basis of the facts found by the lower courts; but in view of the scarcity of strict procedural rules, the European Court may, exceptionally, make further enquiries.

Concluding Remarks: Questions and Answers under the European Human Rights System

1. The European Convention on Human Rights was drafted and adopted at a time when the gross violations of human rights which occurred before and during the Second World War were in vivid memory. It is curious then that the Convention did not play a greater role in the years immediately after its adoption and coming into force. One explanation for this fact is that the democratic States of Western Europe (Western Europe more in a political than in a geographic sense) had in the meantime organized their internal order in a manner that human rights and civil liberties were widely respected and protected. A number of these States were even convinced that international control was neither necessary nor

compatible with their understanding of sovereignty. It is astonishing how this situation changed during the last 15-20 years. More and more States not only ratified the Convention, but they also accepted the right of individuals to lodge petitions to the European Commission, and they accepted the jurisdiction of the European Court of Human Rights. Both institutions had to handle more and more cases, although only a few of them have been concerned with alleged violations of fundamental rights in a strict sense. The great majority of cases have concerned civil liberty matters which occur in democratic States in which the rule of law is undisputed. The organs instituted by the European Convention are now developing European standards for these civil liberties. This seems to be accepted by the organs as well as the societies of the participating States. Decisions of the European organs are not infrequently criticized, but the system as such is not drawn into doubt. A certain homogeneity in the human rights area is on the one hand, an essential condition for an effective functioning system; the activities of the European organs, on the other hand, contribute to the creation of this homogeneity.

The events in Europe since 1989 now constitute a new challenge for the human rights system and protection under the 1950 Convention. Nearly all former socialist States in central and eastern Europe have applied for membership in the Council of Europe and, connected therewith, for admission to the European Convention of Human Rights. They are willing to accept the standards reached under that Convention. It is not easy to predict the influence these newly democratic States will exercise on the further development of the Convention guarantees and institutional machinery. But this is a question which is closely connected with the political and economic developments in Europe in general.

2. The European Court of Human Rights has to decide whether concrete and specific measures for which State organs are responsible and which encroach on rights and freedoms of individuals are compatible with the Convention. There does not exist any abstract control of norms and legislative acts, but, in

connection with concrete acts or omissions, the behaviour of all State organs can be scrutinized.

It is obvious that acts of the executive and of administrative agencies of any kind fall under the control of the organs instituted by the European Convention. Measures of the police, of the public prosecutor, of offices and social workers responsible for the protection of children, of traffic control agencies, etc. can be challenged before the European institutions.

It is also beyond doubt that all national courts are under European supervision. Judgments and other acts of national courts can violate the European Convention of Human Rights. In this respect, two kinds of violations can be distinguished, substantive and procedural deficiencies. The content of a judgment of a national court can be incompatible with the Convention; this was the case when the Austrian courts condemned the journalist Lingens for defamation although his statements were covered, in the opinion of the European Court, by the freedom of expression. Procedural deficiencies, however, play a much greater role before the organs in Strasbourg. Impartiality of the judges, the exigences of fair trial, the necessity of oral hearings, the length of the procedure in national courts - these and other guarantees contained in Article 6 (and also in criminal matters in Article 5) of the Convention have been invoked in Strasbourg in hundreds of cases. No national court is excluded from this European control, even a constitutional court can be found in breach of the Convention.[21]

What is probably even more remarkable is the European control of national legislation. It has already been mentioned that no abstract control of legislative acts takes place, but this does not mean that legislation escapes international supervision. There are now many cases and judgments in which the European judges have found that State legislation is incompatible with the Convention. The easiest cases occur where only a certain interpretation and

---

[21] See the recent *Ruiz-Mateos* judgment of 23 June 1993 where the European Court found that a procedure before the Spanish Constitutional Court violated Article 6 of the Convention.

application of the law by a national court is found in breach of the Convention. If the text of the law permits another interpretation which is compatible with the Convention, the international obligation does not require that the legislation must be formally amended. But the very existence of a national law may violate the Convention; this has been found by the European Court in cases where legislation declared homosexual acts to be punishable and the applicants were under constant danger of public prosecution.[22] When the European Court found that Belgian legislation treated the unmarried mother and her child in a manner incompatible with their right to family life (Article 8 of the Convention), the breach of the Convention consisted in concreto in the treatment of the two persons concerned, but it was obvious that the legislation in general had to be amended. A State can also be found in breach of the Convention because no adequate legislation exists. This was the case in a very peculiar situation - the Netherlands criminal law did not protect a handicapped young girl against sexual misuse;[23] positive obligations of States to protect individuals are to a certain extent recognized in the case-law of the European Court. As far as the second paragraphs of Articles 8-11 of the Convention permit restrictions on Convention rights, these restrictions must be "prescribed by law". When a State practiced telephone tapping in a moderate manner, but without adequate legal basis, as was the case in the *Malone* and in other judgments,[24] the European Court found a violation of the Convention.

It cannot even be excluded that a provision in a State constitution may be incompatible with the Convention. The Irish constitution

---

[22] See the *Dudgeon* judgment of 22 October 1981, Series A n° 45, *Norris* judgment of 26 October 1988, Series A n° 142, and the *Modinos* judgment of 22 April 1993, to be published in Series A n° 259.

[23] Case of X and Y v. the Netherlands, judgment of 26 March 1985, Series A n° 91.

[24] *Malone* judgment of 2 August 1984, Series A n° 82; see also the *Huvig* and *Kruslin* judgments of 24 April 1990, Series A n° 176.

prohibits any divorce, with the consequence that married citizens are not permitted to marry again after the formally still existing marriage has factually broken down. Although the European Court did not find a violation of Article 12 of the Convention,[25] its competence to exercise its control was not disputed. The prohibition of abortion contained in the Irish Constitution - and, at least to a certain extent, also found in other constitutions -, can at least theoretically collide with Convention rights.[26]

The last examples demonstrate that there are hardly any State acts or omissions which escape international control under the European Rights Convention. But the examples also show that the European organs must take into account a great diversity of national traditions and legal rules among the State parties to the Convention. An international régime of this kind may necessitate, in order to function smoothly and effectively, some judicial self-restraint of the international actors. But it can also be stated that acts of the democratically elected legislator are subject to international control. This now seems to be generally recognized by the member States of the Council of Europe.

3. The European Convention on Human Rights and the organs created by the Convention are protecting the classical human rights, many of which have a long history, dating back to the Magna Carta of 1215 and even to ancient Greek and Roman philosophical foundations. The present discussion of these rights, on the universal as well as on the regional level, show that the old freedoms still have their importance and that international protection is required. But one must also recognize the limits of this protection. Some modern problems can probably be solved with the present texts and institutions; this is shown by some

---

[25] *Johnston* judgment of 18 December 1986, Series A n° 112.

[26] *The Open Door* judgment of 29 October 1992, Series A n° 246, was not concerned with the prohibition of abortion as such, but with the prohibition of information about clinics abroad.

decisions of the European Court of Human Rights. For instance, can young aliens under certain conditions claim a right to remain in the country where their family is living?[27] It is also beyond doubt that members of a minority can invoke the Convention rights in order to challenge interferences into their religious and private sphere. But there are many other problems which can hardly be solved by the human rights institutions. This holds true for genuine social rights and even more for the so-called human rights of the third generation - the "right" to a clean and healthy environment, to peace, development, etc. Such problems can hardly be solved by traditional means of judicial control, and they clearly fall outside the competence of institutions like the European Court of Human Rights.

4. At present, an intensive discussion is taking place among the member States for a reform of the human rights institutions under the European Convention. So far, no one has advocated weakening or abolishing the system. Rather, the intention is instead to make this system more effective and less time-consuming. There seems to be widespread agreement that the European Convention and the international machinery for the protection of human rights have been successful. Human rights and judicial review have gained, in addition to the rules applicable exclusively inside States, an international dimension. The international dimension and control imply that national sovereignty is reduced or limited, but this now seems to be generally accepted for the human rights guaranteed by the European Convention.

---

[27] See the *Moustaquim* judgment of 18 February 1991, Series A n° 193, and also the *Beldjoudi* judgment of 26 March 1992, Series A n° 234.

THE LAST GENERATION: WHEN RIGHTS LOSE THEIR MEANING

David Beatty*

1. INTRODUCTION

We began this collection of essays by observing that in the history of protecting basic human rights, by entrenching them in international covenants and in the constitutional framework of nation states, we are living at something of a watershed. In one direction, it is now just over two hundred years since the American Supreme Court was given the power to invalidate laws which violate the US Bill of Rights, and soon it will be fifty years since the second great wave of constitutional bills of rights swept across the world following the second world war. In the other direction, we are witnessing, in the countries of eastern Europe, the former Soviet Union and in various parts of the developing world a third, and what must certainly be the most dramatic profession of faith in the process of judicial review and constitutional bills of rights which the world has known.

This convergence of historical landmarks and epochal proliferation of the idea of relying on courts and a process of constitutional review to define the limits and check the excesses of modern governments, presents a natural opportunity to reflect on the question of what constitutional bills of rights are all about and what they are going to mean for the societies which have just, or are just about to embrace them. By studying what is now a very rich and extensive jurisprudence of constitutional review we can, I believe, anticipate many of the decisions judges in these newly-emerging states are likely to face. Unlike their predecessors, judges now have precedents they can draw on from around the world on practically every constitutional issue they will be asked to decide.

Comparing the analytical methods used by the courts with the most extensive experience of constitutional review also allows us to consider the claims of two groups of legal scholars who hold sharply divergent views about what to make of the sudden

D.M. Beatty (ed.), Human Rights and Judicial Review, 321-361.

resurgence and revival of interest in constitutionalism, and in particular on the desirability of empowering the third branch of government to act as a check on the other two. For some time now it has been the case that two sets of views, at opposite ends of the spectrum, have claimed centre stage in the discussions about the idea of protecting basic human rights by means of constitutional guarantees. On one side stand human rights activists who not only embrace the constitutional entrenchment of basic human rights but who call for the recognition of second and even third generation guarantees.[1] 'Red' (social, economic, cultural or 'group') and 'green' (environmental, development, peace) rights, they say, should be added to the traditional list of 'blue' (political and civil) liberties which were the focus of the American Bill of Rights and, for the most part, the constitutional documents written at the end of World War II as well.

Against the enthusiastic endorsement of the human rights activists, a second, more sober group of analysts, who cut across the whole right-left divide of the political spectrum, have sounded a note of caution and even scepticism about the attempt to integrate bills of rights and a process of judicial review into a democratic

* Faculty of Law, University of Toronto

1 See, e.g. U. Baxi 'From Human Rights to the Right to be Human' (1986) 13 *Ind International Q* 185; 'Taking Suffering Seriously' in R. Dhavan, R. Sudarshan & S. Khurished (eds) *Judges and the Judicial Power* 1985 Sweet & Maxwell, London; F. Michaelman 'Welfare Rights in a Constitutional Democracy' (1979) *Washington University Law Quarterly* 659; A. Osuka 'Welfare Rights' (1990) 53(2) *Law & Contemporary Problems* 13; A. Rycroft 'The Protection of Socio-economic Rights' in H. Corder (ed) *Essays on Law & Social Practice* 1988 Juta, Cape Town; E. Sparer 'Fundamental Human Rights, Legal Entitlements and the Social Struggle ...' (1984) 36 *Stanford Law Review* 509; R.L. Siegel 'Socioeconomic Human Rights: Past and Future' (1985) 7 *Human Rights Quarterly* 255; C. Stark 'Europe's Fundamental Rights in their Newest Garb' (1982) 3 *Human Rights L.J.* 103.

system of government.[2] Arguing that the process by which judges determine whether a law is constitutional or not is highly subjective, radically indeterminate, and frequently generates very regressive results, the critics - or sceptics - take the position that reforming the structures and processes of the elected branches of government is a better way of ensuring the establishment of just societies than enhancing the power of the courts. On their analysis, the substantial freedom and discretion judges have in evaluating the validity of any law against a constitutional bill of rights condemns the process of judicial review as a very undemocratic retrenchment in our understanding of how nation states should be organized and governed.

At first blush it might seem that, as a practical matter, the current popularity of constitutional bills of rights around the world makes the views and the arguments of the sceptics largely academic. Whatever the rhetorical power of their warnings against 'the legalisation of politics', they have had little if any impact in countries gaining their freedom from arbitrary and dictatorial regimes. In the same way that the countries which were able to shed their legacies of colonialism and fascism at the end of the second world war opted, more or less enthusiastically, for systems of constitutional review, the idea of constitutional bills of rights has been thought by all of the people of eastern Europe, the former Soviet Union, southern Africa, etc., as providing a critical bulwark against their totalitarian and racist pasts.

In fact, not only have these new constitutional regimes rejected the sceptical story the critics are wont to tell, many of

---

2 See, e.g. R. Bork, *The Tempting of America, The Political Seduction of the Law*, Free Press, 1990, N.Y.; P. Brest 'The Fundamental Rights Controversy: The Essential Contradictions of Normative Constitutional Scholarship' (1981) 90 *Yale Law Journal* 1063; A. Hutchinson 'Charter Litigation and Social Change' in R. Sharpe *Charter Litigation* Butterworths 1987 Toronto; M. Mandel *The Charter of Rights and the Legalization of Politics* 1989 Thompson & Wall, Toronto; M. Tushnet *Red, White and Blue: A Critical Analysis of Constitutional Law* (1988), Harvard University Press, Cambridge, Mass.

them purport to make an even stronger commitment to the idea of constitutionalism and bills of rights than was the case at the end of the second world war. In these countries, the pleas of human rights activists to constitutionalize second and third generation rights have had some success. In addition to entrenching the traditional guarantees of equality, life, liberty and security of the person and the fundamental freedoms of expression, religion, association etc, many of the constitutions that are now being written insist that Governments must also show some respect for people's cultural and economic well-being. Rights to basic levels of health, education, economic welfare, a clean environment etc, find their place with increasing frequency alongside the traditional first generation of rights.[3]

In this essay I want to use the debate between the sceptics and the human rights activists to help us examine the concept of rights and in particular rights of the second and third generations. I want to test the claims of both groups against the experience we have gained over the last fifty years in the practice of judicial review. As we shall see, the record of the courts cautions against the temptation of thinking that the debate between human rights activists and those who are sceptical about the integrity of law and the process of judicial review has been largely settled and that those favouring the extension and further evolution of human rights have carried the day. At the conclusion of the essay, in fact, I will argue that exactly the opposite is true and that it is the doubts voiced by the sceptics and critics which should set the agenda for future scholarship and research.

The agenda of reform recommended by human rights activists, turns out to be badly overdrawn. Even though they have clearly prevailed in the war of the words, the way the courts have reacted to calls to recognize a new generation of rights suggests the victory is likely to have little, if any, practical effect

---

3 See, e.g., the new constitutions in Hungary, the Czech and Slovak Republics, Portugal, South Africa and Namibia in A.P. Blaustein & G.H. Flanz *Constitutions of the Countries of the World*, Oceana Publications.

on the ground. It turns out that, unlike the sceptics, human rights activists can take very little encouragement for their vision of new vistas of rights from a comparative study of how courts have protected people's most important social and economic needs so far.

In fact, the truth is even harsher than that. When one compares how the major courts have responded to claims to enforce second and third generation rights, it is clear that guaranteeing people a right to 'wholesome and cultured living'[4] in a constitution will at best be a meaningless, empty gesture. The words will be treated as surplus text and for all practical purposes ignored. At worst, they will act as a source of doctrinal obfuscation and popular disillusionment that bills of rights are no different than anything that is touched by the law in saying things they don't really mean.[5] The lesson of looking back and analysing the jurisprudence that the judges have written so far is that the protection of people's social, economic and cultural well-being is neither dependant on nor furthered by their explicit recognition in the text of the constitution. In the most basic and theoretical terms, these cases actually challenge the belief of human rights activists that human rights are an evolutionary or generational idea.

One might say the overriding ambition of this essay is a call to students of human rights law to return to more traditional forms of legal scholarship and research. It is intended to encourage those who believe we can and should improve our record of protecting human rights to take seriously the reluctance of the courts to take on new and unprecedented responsibilities. My hope is that by studying how courts have analyzed claims asserting an enormous range of economic and cultural rights, human rights

---

4 This is a phrase used in article 25 of the Japanese Constitution.

5 This will be an especially serious cost for those who believe that constitutions serve inspirational and hortatory goals as well as creating legally enforceable rights.

activists will be persuaded to abandon their faith in the entrenchment of a new generation of guarantees and to focus their attention on the difficulties and deficiencies which the critics say impair the integrity of the whole idea of constitutional review.

In the first part of this essay I want to dispel the myth that protecting people's social and economic interests requires a new generation of rights. To encourage human rights activists to see the potential of the first generation guarantees I catalogue the ways in which courts have already been able to protect people's social, economic and cultural interests using, for the most part, the language characteristic of the traditional texts. There is, it should be said, nothing new in all this. Human rights activists are aware of this jurisprudence which makes the idea of drawing bright lines between generations of rights unhelpful, if not misleading. First generation bills of rights can, it turns out, provide as much protection for the social and economic spheres of peoples' lives as they have for their political and civil liberties.

The focus of the second part of the essay shifts from the cases in which the courts have protected various social and economic rights to those in which they have not. In drawing limits on how far they will exercise their powers of review and impose limits on what Governments can do, we will see that, like the sceptics, the courts think that it is critical to adhere very strictly to the principle of the separation of powers between themselves and the other two branches of government. Unless and until the human rights activist can identify a sufficiently compelling reason to abandon what both courts and critics regard as one of the most basic pillars in the liberal democratic form of government, second and third generation guarantees are not likely to play a very important role in the future protection of human rights.

The essay concludes by asking human rights activists to consider the possibility that, even staying within the conventional parameters of judicial review, the courts could protect peoples' basic social and economic interests more consistently and faithfully than they have in the past. Building on the cases in which the courts have already provided significant protection for the economic and cultural spheres of peoples' lives, human rights activists are encouraged to sharpen their skills of legal analysis to discover whether, with the traditional tools, there isn't more the courts could do.

II. THE RIGHTS PEOPLE HAVE

With so many calls for the recognition of new generations of constitutional guarantees, it is easy to forget that courts have already been able to extend a significant amount of protection both around and within the social and economic spheres of peoples' lives. The rhetoric of 'rainbows of rights' suggests a distinction between economic and group rights on the one hand and traditional political and civil guarantees on the other, which a study of how constitutional review has been practised around the world shows does not exist. The fact of the matter is that, working with the principles of review which underlie the basic first generation guarantees, courts all over the world have been able to protect a wide range of social, economic and cultural interests and activities. Even the oldest and the sparsest bills of rights have been enough for the courts to protect the linguistic, cultural and political rights of numerous groups and to guarantee basic rights in education, employment and material well being to the population at large.

In the field of education, the entitlements recognized by the courts have generally been of two kinds. First, individuals have been guaranteed a basic equality of opportunity to take advantage of whatever educational facilities a state may provide. According to the German Constitutional Court, for example, in designing admissions policies to educational institutions Governments must, as a matter of principle, make use of all of their educational and training capacities and allocate the resulting opportunities on objective criteria which give each applicant a fair chance of success.[6] In *Brown v Board of Education* and its progeny, the

---

6 *Numerus Clausus* case 33 *BVerfGE* 303, parts of which have been translated into English and appear in Donald P. Kommers *The Constitutional Jurisprudence of the Federal Republic of Germany* 1989

American Supreme Court advanced the cause of equal opportunity by ruling unconstitutional educational programmes which were blatantly racist.[7] Simultaneously both the US Supreme Court and its counterpart in Delhi, have given the constitutional green light to numerous affirmative action programmes which were designed to offset some of the disadvantages and handicaps which prevent people from being able to compete for many positions in any meaningful sense.[8]

In addition to being attentive to the ambitions of individuals to acquire whatever educational qualifications are necessary to allow them to pursue the careers of their choice, courts have also been sensitive to the parallel interest many groups have in retaining control over how their members are educated. For example, in a landmark decision, the American Supreme Court has recognized the right of the Amish people to educate their own children outside of the system of compulsory state schools.[9] Both the Canadian and Indian Supreme Courts have issued similar judgments in which they have required regional Governments to recognize the right of minority groups to retain as much direction and control of their children's education as possible.[10]

In the area of work and employment, the protection afforded by courts has been even more pervasive. Unreasonable

---

Duke Univ Press, p.295.

7 *See: Brown v Board of Education of Topeka* 347 U.S. 483 (1954). See also *Plyer v Doe* 457 U.S. 202 (1982) striking down a Texas law denying children of illegal aliens access to public schools.

8 See, e.g. *Balaji v Mysore* A.I.R. (1963) S.C. 649; *Regents of University of California v Bakke*, 438 U.S. 265 (1978).

9 *Wisconsin v Yoder* 406 U.S. 205 (1972). See also *Meyer v Nebraska* 262 U.S. 390 (1922).

10 *Mahe v Alberta* (1990) 68 D.L.R. (4th) 69; *In re Kerala Education Bill* A.I.R. 1958 SC 956.

restrictions on the freedom of people to work at trades and occupations for which they are qualified have been struck down all over the world. Pharmacists in Japan,[11] retailers (and pharmacists) in Germany,[12] butchers, hawkers and promoters of games of skill in India,[13] optometrists and public servants in the United States,[14] and lawyers in Canada[15] all have benefitted from rulings by the highest courts in their countries removing impediments to these vocations and trades which failed basic tests of reasonableness and fairness.[16]

In addition to ensuring that access to sought after employment

---

11 *Sumiyoshi v Hiroshima* 29 Minshu 572 (April 30 1975), translated and reproduced in part in Murphy & Tanenhaus , *Comparative Constitutional Law*, St. Martin's Press, N.Y., and discussed in Hiroshi Itoh 'Judicial Review and Judicial Activism in Japan' (1990) 53(1) *Law & Contemp Problems* 169, 175; Matsuo Nakamura 'Freedom of Economic Activities and the Right to Property' (1990) 53(2) *Law & Contemp Problems* 1,6.

12 *Pharmacy* case (1958) 7 *BVerfGE* 377; *Taxi* case (1960) 11 *BVerfGE* 168; *Retail Trade* case (1965) 19 *BVerfGE* 330 reproduced in part and discussed in D Kommers *The Constitutional Jurisprudence of the Federal Republic of Germany supra* note 6 at 285, 293.

13 *Mohammed Hanif Quareshi v Bihar* A.I.R. 1958 S.C. 731; *Bombay Hawkers Union v Bombay* A.I.R. 1985 S.C. 1206; *R.M.D. Chamarbaugwalla v India* A.I.R. 1957 S.C. 628, cf. *Municipal Corp. Ahmedabad v. Jan Mohammed*, A.I.R. 1986 S.C. 1205

14 *Gibson v Berryhill* 411 U.S. 564 (1973); *Hampton v Mow Sun Wong* 426 U.S. 88 (1976); *In re Griffiths* (1973) 413 U.S. 717.

15 *Andrews v Law Society of B.C.* (1989) 56 D.L.R. (4th) 1; *Black v Law Society of Alberta* (1989) 58 D.L.R. (4th) 317. See also *R v Thibault* [1988] 1 S.C.R. 1033.

16 For a reference to similar decisions in Italy see E Cheli 'La Constitution Face en Progres Economique et Social: Le Cas de l'Italie', in *Italian Reports* 3rd World Congress, International Association of Constitutional Law, Warsaw 1991.

opportunities is not blocked by unjustifiable restrictions, the courts have insisted that the laws which regulate relations at the work place must also satisfy basic standards of reasonableness and proportionality. Across a wide range of issues and employment contexts they have exercised their powers in ways to support people's employment security and employability. In some cases the judges have ruled that proper procedures must be followed when important occupational interests are altered in ways prejudicial to the worker.[17] In others, the courts have used one or other of the traditional guarantees to provide people a measure of employment security[18] or to enhance their employment prospects more generally.[19] And, paralleling their support of affirmative action policies in the field of education, both the Indian and American Supreme Courts have handed down major decisions giving the constitutional seal of approval to employment equity programmes designed to promote the employability of disadvantaged individuals and groups.[20]

---

17 See, e.g., *Konig v. Federal Republic of Germany* (1978), 2 E.H.R.R. 170; *Le Compte, Van Leuvan et De Meyere v Belgium* (1981) *E.H.R.R.* 1; *Disciplinary Court* case (1964) 18 *BVerfGE* 241; *Perry v Sniderman* (1972) 408 U.S. 593; *Cleveland Board of Education v Loudermill* (1958) 470 U.S. 532.

18 *Young, James & Webster v UK* (1981) 3 *E.H.R.R.* 37; *Gaming House* case (1978) 1 *International L.L.R.* 289; *Cleveland Board of Education v Lafleur* (1974) 414 U.S. 632; See also decision of the Corte Costituzionale No 97, 1987 noted in L M Diez-Picazo & M-C Ponthoreau 'The Constitutional Protection of Social Rights: Some Comparative Remarks', European University Institut Working Paper, Law 91/20, p 13.

19 See, e.g. *Slaight Communications v Davidson* (1989) 59 D.L.R. (4th) 416; *Lebach* case (1973) 35 *BVerfGE* 202, translated in part in Kommers *The Constitutional Jurisprudence of the FRG supra* note 6, p.414.

20 See, e.g. *Kumar v Karnataka* A.I.R. 1985 SC 1495; *Thomas v Kerala* A.I.R. 1976 SC 490; *United Steelworkers v Weber* (1979) 443 U.S. 193; *Fullilove v Klutznick* (1980) 448 U.S. 448; and *Johnson v Transportation*

The courts have also used the "first generation" guarantee of formal equality to ensure that laws fixing salary and pension scales respect basic norms of fairness and proportionality.[21] On other occasions they have turned to the traditional guarantee of freedom of expression to protect the right of workers in the private sector to publicize their views and their services in the community,[22] and the right of public servants to engage in a wide range of public and political activities.[23]

Although much of the courts' work in the area of economic relations has involved striking down laws which offend the basic principle of equal opportunity, it has not always been of this kind. In some cases, the attention of the courts has been focused on the constitutionality of broad statutory schemes designed to promote the welfare of employees as a group. In many of these cases the role of the courts has been a supportive one - upholding the constitutionality of collective bargaining and employment standards legislation which tried to protect and improve the lot of working

---

Agency (1987) 107 S.Ct. 1442. See also *Metro Broadcasting v. F.C.C.* (1990) 110 S.Ct. 2997.

21 *Daily Rated Casual Labour v India* (1988) 1 S.C.C. 122; *Randhir Singh v Union of India* A.I.R. 1982 S.C. 879; *Retired Officials* case 8 *BVerfGE* 1, 20. See also 6 *BVerfGE* 257, 264 noted in Hans Rupp, 'Judicial Review in the Federal Republic of Germany' 9 *Am J Comp L* 29; *City of Los Angeles v Manhart* (1978) 435 U.S. 702; *Frontiero v Richardson* (1973) 411 U.S. 677.

22 *Barthold v Germany* (1985) 7 E.H.R.R. 383; *Rockett v Royal College of Dental Surgeons*, [1990] 2 S.C.R. 232; *Virginia Board of Pharmacy v Virginia Consumer Council* (1976) 425 U.S. 748.

23 *Osborne v Canada*, [1991] 2 S.C.R. 69; *Kameshwar Prasad v Bihar* A.I.R. 1962 S.C. 1166. See also the decision No. 46, 1958 GC 569 discussed in Malcolm Evans 'The Italian Constitutional Court' (1968) 17 *ICLQ* 602, 626 striking down a general law prohibiting all strikes in the public service.

people.[24] Even when they recognized that laws of this kind directly interfered with important rights of liberty,[25] property,[26] and even religious freedom,[27] the courts confirmed their constitutional integrity by pointing to even more basic interests and constitutional guarantees which they served.

On other occasions, the courts have used their powers of review in a positive way and have required the elected branches of government to revise and even extend laws regulating employment relations and economic security to meet traditional guarantees of equality, human dignity and due process of law. In the same way they have protected people's right to carry on a business or vocation,[28] the courts have also insisted that fair procedures, including hearings, be established to administer social welfare programmes. The European Court of Human Rights and the American Supreme Court, for example, have recognized traditional due process rights of this kind for those in receipt of various forms

---

24 See, e.g. *Belgian Police* case, E.C.H.R. Series A No. 19 27/10/75; *Swedish Engine Drivers* case, E.C.H.R. Series No. 20, 6/2/76; *Co-determination* case (1979) 50 *BVerfGE* 290 in D Kommers *The Constitutional Jurisprudence of the FRG supra* note 6, p.278; *NLRB v Jones & Laughlin Steel* (1937) 301 U.S. 1; *West Coast Hotel v Parrish* (1937) 300 U.S. 379; *C.B. Boarding & Lodging* v. *State of Mysore* A.I.R. 1970 S.C. 2042.

25 See *NLRB v Jones & Laughlin Steel* and *West Coast Hotel v Parrish ibid.*

26 See, e.g. *Co-Determination* case *supra* note 24; *Workers' Chambers* case (1978) 1 I.L.L.R. 27.

27 See, e.g. *Christian Medical College Hospital Employees Union v Christian Medical College* A.I.R. 1988 S.C. 37.

28 *Supra* note 17.

of financial assistance from the State.[29]

Beyond these procedural guarantees, the courts have also handed down judgments which have required lawmakers to make basic programmes of social assistance more widely available. The Italian, German and American courts have been most active in protecting the economic welfare of those who are relatively disadvantaged and powerless in this way.[30] For example, the American Court has held unconstitutional legislative provisions which denied basic income assistance and welfare services to women,[31] members of various religious communities[32] or on the basis of general eligibility criteria that were arbitrary and discriminatory in some other way.[33] For its part, the Supreme

---

29 See, e.g. *Feldbrugge v Netherlands* E.C.H.R. 1986 Ser A No. 99; *Deumelund v Germany* E.C.H.R. 1989 Ser A No. 100; *Goldberg v Kelley* (1972) 405 U.S. 134; *Sniadach v Family Finance Co* (1969) 395 U.S. 337.

30 See, generally: David P. Currie 'Lochner Abroad: Substantive Due Process and Equal Protection in the Federal Republic of Germany' (1989) *Sup Ct Rev* 333; Giuseppe de Vergottini 'The Constitution in front of economic and social progress' 1991 *Int Assn of Constitutional Law* supra note 16; F Michaelman 'On Protecting the Poor through the 14th Amendment' (1969) 83 *Harv L Rev* 7. For an example of a decision of the Canadian Court protecting the economic well-being of older workers, see *Tétreault-Gadoury* v. *Canada* (1991), 81 D.L.R. (4th) 358.

31 See, e.g. *Turner v Dept of Employment Security* (1975) 423 U.S. 44; *Califano v Westcott* (1979) 442 U.S. 682. See also *Frontiero v Richardson* (1972) 411 U.S. 677.

32 See, e.g. *Sherbert v Verner* (1963) 374 U.S. 398; *Thomas v Review Board* (1981) 450 U.S. 707; *Hobbie v Unemployment Appeals Commission* 107 Sup CT 1046 (1987).

33 See, e.g. *Dept of Agriculture v Murray* (1973) 413 U.S. 508; *Dept of Agriculture v Moreno* (1973) 413 U.S. 528; *New Jersey Welfare Rights Organisation v Cahill* (1973) 411 U.S. 619. See also *Graham v Richardson* (1971) 403 U.S. 365.

Court of India has issued rulings calling on the State to reeducate and rehabilitate people who have been freed from relationships of bonded labour[34] and to ensure that its health care facilities meet basic standards of human decency.[35]

It is not difficult then to compile a list of cases in which the courts have been able to protect a wide variety of interests and activities which are central to people's personal welfare and physical well-being. The catalogue is not exhaustive but it is, I trust, of sufficient length to dispel the belief that to protect a person's basic economic interests it is necessary to create a whole new generation of rights. Rights in the field of education, employment, financial security and even health care are an important part of the protection which the traditional guarantees have been able to provide.

The same story can be told about group rights. Comparing how constitutional review has been practised around the world shows that a wide variety of interests which are critical to the identity and character of various ethnic, linguistic, religious and community groups have also been protected by constitutions born of the first generation. Like economic rights, it turns out, there is no need to create a new conceptual category to recognize the most important social, cultural, spiritual etc interests and aspirations of groups.

The courts have helped numerous groups of people preserve the most essential attributes and ideas of their communities from attack from the outside in essentially the same way they have enhanced people's economic security and material well-being. Broadly, two strategies have been employed. In some cases the rulings of the courts facilitate groups being able to control their

---

34 See, e.g. *Bandhua Mukti Murcha v India* A.I.R. 1984 S.C. 802; *Neeraja Chaudhary v State MP* A.I.R. 1984 S.C. 1099.

35 *Vikram Deo Singh Tomar v Bihar* A.I.R. 1988 S.C. 1782. See also *Rakesh Chandra Narayan v Bihar* A.I.R. 1989 SC 348, where the court appointed its own management committee to ensure that the proper quality of care was provided.

own destinies, to define their own identities and to control the central aspects of the communities within which they live. In others, the courts have acted to protect relatively powerless groups from blatant discrimination and/or arbitrary treatment by the State.

Examples of both kinds of protection abound. We have already noticed how, at various times, the Supreme Courts of Canada, India and the United States have held that linguistic and religious minorities must be allowed to control as much of the education of their children as possible.[36] For its part, the German Constitutional Court, like the American Supreme Court, has insisted that religious communities be given a very large space within which their own ideas and beliefs can prevail.[37] Indeed, in several instances the instinct of the courts to protect the autonomy of these groups, to define the central features of their communities, has been so strong that they have been allowed to override the basic labour rights of the people they employ.[38]

In addition to preserving a measure of freedom for people to organize their most primal relationships free from interference by the state, the courts have also issued judgments which have helped groups promote their interests more effectively in the larger societies in which they live. In a series of decisions concerning the constitutionality of party finance and campaign expenditure laws, for example, the German Constitutional Court has

---

36 See the cases cited in notes 9 and 10. See also *Smt. Damyanti v India* A.I.R. 1971 SC 966.

37 Compare D Kommers *The Constitutional Jurisprudence of the Federal Republic of Germany*, *supra* note 6 ch 9; and L Tribe *American Constitutional Law* Foundation Press, 2ed, ch 14:16. For a parallel initiative of the Indian Supreme Court, see Commr. *H.R.E. v. Swamiair* A.I.R. 1954 S.C. 282.

38 See, e.g. *St Xavier College* A.I.R. 1974 S.C. 1389; *Catholic Hospital Abortion* case (1983) 70 *BVerfGE* 138 reported in English in (1987) 5 *ILLR* 112; *Corporation of Presiding Bishop of the Church of Jesus Christ of Latter Day Saints* v. *Amos* 483 U.S. 327 (1987).

substantially improved the likelihood of small and otherwise marginal groups having their voices heard.[39] Other groups have benefitted from rulings which have allowed legislators varying degrees of latitude in apportioning voters between electoral districts. The substantial tolerance some courts have shown in permitting departures from a strict one person, one vote, rule has guaranteed that some groups will have an influence in the political process beyond what their numbers strictly warrant.[40]

Ensuring that groups are able to control the decisions which affect the most important religious, educational, linguistic, cultural, etc., aspects of their lives, and to participate effectively in setting the rules in the larger communities in which they live, are two ways the courts have been able to provide some protection for people's most important social and community relationships. One might call this a judicial predisposition to a right of communal or group autonomy. The other instrument courts have used to protect groups vulnerable to being treated arbitrarily by the state is the principle of equality or non-discrimination. As we have already seen, across a wide range of economic, educational and linguistic interests and activities, the courts have repeatedly

---

39 See, e.g. *The Party Finance* case (1966) 20 *BVerfGE* 56 reported in English in T.C. Becker *Comparative Judicial Politics* Rand McNally; *Campaign Contribution* case (1968) 24 *BVerfGE* 300, 342, 363; and see generally D Kommers *The Constitutional Jurisprudence of the FRG* ch 5 *supra* note 6. Cf *Bullock v Carter* (1972) 405 U.S. 134; *Buckley Valeo* (1974) 424 U.S. 1.

40 Compare: *Ref re Electoral Boundary Commission Act* (1991) 81 D.L.R. (4th) 16; *Reynolds v Sims* (1964) 377 U.S. 533; *Gaffney v Cummings* (1973) 412 U.S. 735; *Thornburg v Gingles* (1986) 106 S.Ct. 2752; *Koshiyama v Tokyo Metropolitan Election Comm* (1964) 18 Minshu 270; *Kwijawa v Chiba Prefecture Election Comm v Koshiyama* (1983) 37 Minshu 1243; *Apportionment* case (1963) 15 *BVerfGE* 130 excerpted in part in D Kommers The Constitutional Jurisprudence of the FRG supra note 6 p 192. See generally L Tribe American Constitutional Law ch 13:8 supra note 37; Hiroyuki Hata 'Malapportionment of Representation in the National Diet' (1990) 53 (2) *Law & Contemp Probs* 157.

struck down crude attempts to prejudice particular groups by denying them opportunities and benefits which are available to others. Simultaneously, they have validated policy initiatives which provide compensation and/or special programmes for particularly disadvantaged groups in order to ensure that the constitutional ideal of equal opportunity is made as meaningful as possible.

In the areas of employment and education, we have already seen how courts have made use of the anti-discrimination principle to protect the interests and identities of many different groups. The decisions rendered by the Supreme Courts of Canada and the United States, protecting employment or entrepreneurial interests of various immigrant,[41] alien,[42] religious,[43] gender,[44] and linguistic[45] groups and by the Indian and American Courts supporting affirmative action programmes for the most disadvantaged,[46] provide classic examples of how first generation constitutional bills of rights have protected the material well-being of the members of numerous groups from acts of insensitivity, if not hostility, by the state.

In the field of education one finds the same courts promoting the interests of various linguistic and ethnic groups using the same principle of formal equality. Here again one sees the American Court being quite impatient with lawmakers who enact policies

---

41 See, e.g. *Yick Wo v Hopkins* (1886) 118 U.S. 356.

42 Compare *Andrews v Law Society of B-C supra* note 15; *In re Griffiths* (1973) 413 U.S. 717; and *Hampton v Mow Sun Wong supra* note 14.

43 See the cases cited in note 32 *supra*.

44 See, e.g. *Cleveland Board of Education v Lafleur* (1974) 414 U.S. 632. See also the cases referred to in note 31 *supra*.

45 See, e.g. *Ford v Quebec* (1988) 54 D.L.R. (4th) 577.

46 See the cases cited in note 20 *supra*.

which blatantly discriminate against people's freedom to decide what kind of education their children will have on the basis of their membership in some group.[47] And, as we have already noted, both the American and Indian Supreme Courts have endorsed the constitutional validity of affirmative action programmes and policies designed to redress the inequalities and disadvantages faced by members of various minority groups and to allow them to compete fairly for the most sought after educational opportunities.[48]

There is not, I suspect, much to be gained by continuing to catalogue the ways in which courts have been attentive to the needs and aspirations of various groups. That traditional bills of rights can protect important interests and ideas of numerous groups in the same way it can promote people's economic or material welfare is a jurisprudential fact, evident to anyone who studies how courts have exercised their powers of constitutional review. A comparative study of how the courts have applied the analytical framework which underlies the old-fashioned, first generation rights over the last fifty years shows that there is no need for any new conceptual apparatus or generations of rights in order to protect the economic and cultural spheres of people's lives.

Rather than adding to the list of economic and group rights that have been recognized by the courts, our time will be better spent if we pause to notice a couple of things about the decisions we have identified so far.[49] Examining these cases a little more carefully will shed some light both on what the future is likely to hold in those countries which are just beginning to explore the nuances of charters of rights as well as on the larger theoretical

---

47 See the cases cited in notes 7 and 9 *supra*.

48 See the cases cited in note 8 *supra*.

49 Although it lies outside the scope of this essay, it should be noted that the law of federalism provides a second source of constitutional principles which are available to accommodate and protect the identities and aspirations of relatively large ethnic, cultural, religious etc groups.

debate between the sceptics and the human rights activists.. Collectively , there are a number of features of these cases which are quite remarkable and warrant some additional comment.

Next to its breadth, perhaps the most striking feature about the jurisprudence that has been written in the area of economic and group rights is its depth. The contribution of the courts in protecting people's most basic sociological and economic interests is as impressive for its quality as its quantity. As we have seen in many of the judgments we have referred to, the involvement of the courts has gone well beyond issuing abstract declarations about what rights people have. Not infrequently, the courts have ordered Governments and legislatures to take positive action, including the enactment of legislation, to remedy the violation of people's constitutional guarantees. Indeed, they have done this even when they knew it would involve considerable cost to the state.

Practically all of the major courts with the most extensive experience with constitutional bills of rights have issued judgments of this kind.[50] We have already noticed how both the German and Indian Courts have insisted that Governments must carry out the programmes they have initiated to the full reach of their declared ambition. In its celebrated *Numerus Clausus* decision, for example, the German Constitutional Court required the educational authorities to ensure that their institutional capacities were fully utilized before imposing numerical quotas on admissions.[51] As well, it has insisted that the payments provided in various welfare, income-protection and election financing schemes be made available to a wider range of beneficiaries than

---

50 It is ironic that the Japanese Supreme Court is one of the few courts which has not issued a judgment of this kind, even though the Japanese Constitution includes a provision which, on its face, expressly guarantees everyone a minimum standard of 'wholesome and cultured living'.

51 *Supra* note 6.

the Governments responsible for those laws had desired.[52] For its part, the Supreme Court of India has issued landmark decisions requiring reluctant state governments to establish rehabilitative programmes to assist those freed from relationships of bonded labour and to substantially improve the material conditions of certain hospitals and health care facilities under their jurisdiction.[53] As well, it might be noted, both of these courts have held that the state has a positive duty to protect people and the environment against hazards of various kinds.[54]

The Italian, Canadian and American courts all have rendered parallel decisions which have required the relevant government authorities to initiate or extend legislative or administrative programmes that would have had significant resource implications for the state. In the minds of some commentators, the Italian Court may be the most active defender of social and economic rights of all. The financial implications of the so-called 'sentenze-addittives' are one of the most controversial features of the constitutional jurisprudence written by the Italian Court. In one celebrated case the Court required Government to provide handicapped students immediate access to all secondary and

---

52 See generally, David P Currie 'Lochner abroad ...' *supra* note 30; D Kommers *The Constitutional Jurisprudence of the Federal Republic of Germany* ch 5, *supra* note 6.

53 See the cases referred to in notes 34 and 35 *supra.*

54 See, e.g. *Mehta v Union of India* A.I.R. 1987 S.C. 1086; See also *Rural Litigation* v. *State of U.P.* A.I.R. 1985 S.C. 652; *Aircraft Noise Control* case (1981) 56 *BVerfGE* 54; *Mülheim Kärlich* case (1979) 53 *BVerfGE* 62; *Kalkar* case (1978) 49 *BVerfGE* 89. See also *Chemical Weapons* case (1987) 77 *BVerfGE* 170, portions of which are translated and discussed in D Kommers *The Constitutional Jurisprudence of the Federal Republic of Germany supra* note 6, and see *Powell & Rayner* v. *U.K.*, E.C.H.R., February 21, 1990, Series A #172.

post-secondary educational institutions.[55]

Traditional ideals of equality and due process have also been the basis on which the Canadian and American Supreme Courts have required positive action on the part of the state to rectify violations of people's constitutional rights. The jurisprudence ordering the desegregation of American schools is unquestionably the most celebrated example of judges involving themselves directly in the protection of social and economic rights.[56] As well, as we have seen, the American Court, like its German and Italian counterparts, has also insisted that social assistance programmes be redesigned to make their benefits more widely available and their administrative structures adhere more closely to the ideals of 'due process of law'.[57] For its part, the Canadian Court has insisted that educational programmes established for minority language students be funded on the same per capita basis as that on which the majority's programmes are costed[58] and, following the example of the Americans, has required the state to invest heavily in its legal and judicial system in order that its 'first generation' legal rights are guaranteed.[59]

All of these cases, in which the courts have ruled that the other two branches of government have a duty to take some positive action to redress a violation of someone's constitutional rights, make it clear that the judges do not perceive their role of protecting people's economic and cultural rights as being purely or even primarily a passive one. The courts can and have required

---

55 See L Diez-Picazo & M-C Ponthoreau 'The Constitutional Protection of Social Rights' *supra* note 18 p 12; E Cheli 'La Constitution Face au Progres Economique et Social' *supra* note 16.

56 See L Tribe American Constitutional Law ch 16:18-19 *supra* note 37.

57 See the cases referred to in notes 29-33 *supra.*

58 *Mahe v Alberta supra* note 10.

59 *R. v. Askov* [1990] 2 S.C.R. 1199.

Governments to pass laws or take initiatives even when large sums of money were at stake. When the courts are convinced that someone's constitutional rights have been violated, they have not been afraid to remedy it, whatever the cost.

This strength in the courts' resolve in protecting the economic and cultural spheres of people's lives is one of the most striking features of the constitutional jurisprudence the courts have written so far. What is less obvious but just as remarkable is the fact that in virtually all of these cases the method of reasoning and framework of analysis used by the courts is basically the same as they employ when they are protecting people's political and civil rights. Even in the cases in which the courts enforce constitutional guarantees positively and require governments to act, it is principles of formal equality - of rationality (necessity) and proportionality (consistency) - which do most, if not all, of the work. Notwithstanding the very different styles in which constitutions have been written, it turns out that the analytical tools employed by the courts are exactly the same.

In many of the cases which resulted in a finding that someone's economic or sociological interests had been trampled by the state, in the court's mind the violation occurred because the challenged law had been drafted either too broadly or too narrowly, given the purposes it was meant to achieve. The means or the particular policy instrument chosen by the Government was not well suited - not proportional - to its ends. In other cases, it was a principle of balance or consistency at work. Laws which interfered with the economic and cultural domains of people's lives would be struck down when the public interest they were meant to promote was not regarded as being weighty enough to justify the substantial restrictions which they imposed.

One can point to cases, touching virtually every one of the interests and activities we catalogued at the beginning of this essay, in which the court's analysis of the means by which a Government went about regulating some aspect of people's social and economic lives, was decisive in its finding that the challenged law was constitutionally flawed. Whenever judges have struck down laws which denied certain individuals or groups the right to engage in particular vocations[60] or to enjoy the benefits of various schemes of income support,[61] more often than not it was this principle which was at work. Invariably, in the first groups of cases, the courts felt the barriers preventing people from pursuing the careers of their choice were much broader and more restrictive than they needed to be. Conversely, the criteria limiting the availability of social assistance were condemned because they made the law radically under-inclusive and in conflict with the basic objectives the programmes were meant to promote.

The courts have also relied on the principle of rationality or necessity when they have struck down laws which threatened workers' security in their employment[62] or their ability to express themselves either politically[63] or commercially.[64] It has also been central to their insistence that affirmative action programmes be targeted at the individuals and groups which suffer the disadvantage the law seeks to alleviate.[65] As well, it underlies and explains those cases in which courts invalidated laws which limited people's freedom to express themselves and educate their children in the languages of their choice.[66]

In all of these cases the judges' attention was focused on the means by which those elected to government pursued their political

---

60 See the cases referred to in notes 11-15 *supra.*

61 See notes 30-33 *supra.*

62 See, e.g. the cases referred to in note 18 *supra.*

63 See, e.g. *Osborne v Canada supra* note 23.

64 See, e.g. the cases referred to in note 22 *supra.*

65 See, e.g. *Deepak Sibal v Punjab University* A.I.R. 1989 SC 903; *Balaji v Mysore supra* note 8; *Regents of the University of California v Bakke* 438 U.S. 265 (1978). cf L. Tribe Constitutional Choices Chapt. 14.

66 See, e.g. *Ford v Quebec supra* note 45; *Meyer v Nebraska supra* note 9.

programmes. Rarely do judges examine or challenge the objectives or public interest which a challenged law seeks to promote. When, for example, affirmative action programmes are found to be constitutionally defective generally it is not because of the goals or values they pursue. Rather, it is because the classification or criteria (the means) used by the law to identify its beneficiaries are not drawn with sufficient precision and care.[67] Similarly, the quarrel courts have sometimes had with language and education laws which limit the freedom of minority groups to speak their own languages and to educate their children in a manner which is consistent with their ethnic, cultural or religious traditions, has never been with the broad communitarian interests (such as a well educated and responsible citizenry or a 'visage linguistique') which laws of this kind are designed to promote. Rather, in these cases as well, the courts' findings of unconstitutionality are invariably grounded in the belief that alternative policies were available to the Governments involved; policies which would have allowed them not only to realize their own agendas but which would also have respected the right of minority groups to control those interests and activities which are most fundamental to the identity and character of their communities.[68]

Although the principle of rationality or alternative means has been the primary instrument the courts have used to protect people's social and economic rights, it is not the only principle that has been at their disposal. Occasionally, even when it is accepted that a limitation on people's economic and social freedom is necessary in terms of the objectives which a Government is pursuing, the courts have still found laws to be constitutionally defective where the public interest they promoted was viewed as being not weighty enough to justify the restrictions which they

---

67 See note 65 *supra*.

68 See, e.g., *Wisconsin v. Yoder, Meyer v. Nebraska, supra* note 9; *Mahe v. Alberta, Re Kerala Education Bill, supra* note 10.

contained. When courts have perceived a radical imbalance between the public interest promoted by a law and the constraint it imposes on the social and economic spheres of people's lives, they have not hesitated to exercise their powers of review and declare the law to be unconstitutional.

That, for example, was what the German Constitutional Court did when it evaluated a law which restricted the number of people who could be admitted to the pharmacy profession in order to protect the standard of living of those who were already in business.[69] This balancing, or cost/benefit method of analysis, has also been used by the US Supreme Court in striking down provisions which denied eligibility or restricted the rights of different individuals and groups to various welfare and employee benefit schemes, essentially in the interest of administrative cost and efficiency.[70] Indeed, the German Constitutional Court and the Supreme Court of India have both followed a balancing or utilitarian method of reasoning to hold that there may be some matters and values which are so central to religious or ethnic communities that Governments can not interfere with or limit them, even when the purpose of the law is to protect workers from arbitrary and unfair treatment.[71]

Comparing how courts have evaluated laws regulating the social and economic well being of communities around the world shows that, regardless of what words are used to describe the rights which a constitution guarantees, a court's analysis of the validity of a challenged law will be grounded on one or both of these basic measures of rationality and proportionality. Here, as

---

69 See *Pharmacy* case *supra* note 12.

70 See, e.g. *Goldberg v Kelly* (1970) 397 U.S. 254; *Califano v Goldfarb* (1977) 430 U.S. 199. See also *Frontiero v Richardson supra* note 31; cf *Singh v Min. of Employment and Immigration* (1985) 17 D.L.R. (4th) 422.

71 Compare *St Xavier College* A.I.R. 1974 SC 1389 and *Catholic Hospital Abortion* case *supra* note 38.

with the more traditional political and civil rights, the primary concern of the courts is to ensure that the politicians and their officials live up to their constitutional and international duties to act rationally and reasonably when they activate the lawmaking powers of the state. The cases show the courts hold Governments to the same standards of lawmaking in fashioning their social and economic programmes as in any other area of public policy. This jurisprudence confirms that constitutional review and the role of the courts is much more about ensuring that everyone who exercises any power of the state respects basic measures of justice and equality than it is about cataloguing and enforcing very discrete and particular entitlements called rights. Understanding how important the principles of rationality and proportionality are to the work of the courts also explains, as we shall now see, why, notwithstanding all of the protection they have been able to provide, all of the courts think that there are limits to the amount of justice they can dispense.

III. RIGHTS THAT CAN NEVER BE

We have now spent some time examining the ways in which and the method by which courts all over the world have exercised their powers of constitutional review to protect the ethnicity and economic wellbeing of numerous individuals and groups. My purpose has been to counter the idea that the material and social spheres of people's lives belong to a newer generation of rights. Studying how courts all over the world have worked with "first generation" bills of rights shows that the same principles and method of analysis are applied when the courts accept the validity of people's cultural and financial claims as they do when they enforce the more traditional political and civil guarantees.

As important an insight as this undoubtedly is, it is not the only lesson which a comparative study can teach. There is in fact a deeper truth to discover. Studying how the courts have responded to people's petitions to recognize their social and economic claims shows not only what kinds of interests and activities judges are inclined to protect, it also identifies those they will not.

A comparative study of how the courts have responded when they have been asked to direct their Governments to respect and provide for people's most basic social, economic and cultural needs, shows that there are limits no judge will cross. In terms of the relief which the courts can provide, the principles of rationality (necessity) and proportionality (consistency) exhaust their authority. If neither of these principles can satisfy a petitioner's claim, there is, for all practical purposes, nothing more a court can or will do. On virtually every occasion when the courts have been asked to do more than this, the record shows that they will balk.

In conceptual terms, studying how traditional bills of rights have been used to protect people's economic and group rights clarifies what it means to say that there can only be one generation of rights. Not only is it a mistake to think that the economic and cultural rights people have can only be protected by a new order of constitutional guarantees, it turns out that it is a very basic conceptual error - what philosophers would call a 'category mistake' - to even think in such generational, evolutionary terms. In the real world of constitutional law, the principles of rationality and proportionality not only allow the courts to provide substantial protection to the most basic economic and cultural aspirations which people may have, they define the limits of what we can legitimately expect the judges to do.

In terms of the everyday world of politics and policy formulation, it is easy to identify the line from which the courts have consistently recoiled. In functional terms the line is drawn around the power to fix a community's political priorities and to control the fisc or the purse. The fact is that no matter how much encouragement the words of a constitution may seem to provide, no court has ever stood up to the other two, elected branches of government and told them that the actual amounts or levels of financial or cultural support they have provided are inadequate as a matter of constitutional law. Except in cases when a finding of discrimination or unequal treatment has been made out, whenever claimants have asked a court to second guess the amount of money a Government has decided to spend on particular social or cultural programmes, they have, without exception, gone away empty-handed.[72]

In legal parlance, the courts have consistently and without exception held that claims of this kind - which ask them to establish basic levels of economic and cultural well-being beyond those fixed by the elected representatives of the people - are 'non-justiciable'. In lay terms, all of the courts recognize that the elected branches of government have the ultimate authority to decide how much of a community's resources will be spent educating, housing and healing its people and how much will be set aside to alleviate the suffering of those facing conditions of poverty and extreme privation. Even when a constitution explicitly guarantees people a sweeping right to a minimum standard of 'wholesome and cultural living' or provides very specific entitlements to social assistance, pensions and health care programmes, as in Japan and Italy, the courts have acknowledged that legislators possess the final discretion to settle, as a matter of hard currency, what meaning these constitutional entitlements will have.[73] Even the Supreme Court of India, which has been especially vocal in urging governments to be responsive to the plight of those forced to live at the margins of human existence, has stopped short of ordering the central or one of the regional

---

72 See, e.g. *Asahi v Japan* (1967) 21(5) Minshu 1043, translated in part in H Itoh & L Beer *The Constitutional Case Law of Japan 1961-70* Univ of Washington Press (1978) and *Hiroki v Governor of Hyogo Prefecture* (1982) 36(7) Minshu 1235; *Widows Child Welfare* case (1951) 1 *BVerfGE* 97. See also *Belgian Language* case ECHR Series A 23 July 1968 at pp 31-32; *Asif Hameed v Jammu & Kashmir* A.I.R. 1989 S.C. 1899, esp at paras 17, 21-23.

73 *Asahi v Japan* ibid; and see L M Diez Picazo & M-C Ponthoreau 'The Constitutional Protection of Social Rights' *supra* note 18 at pp 11-12.

Governments to provide work or higher levels of social assistance.[74]

The steadfast refusal of the judiciary to assume responsibility for the budget and the fiscal priorities of the state is not difficult to understand. It is based on the idea, central to all liberal democratic theories of government, that the functions and powers of each of the three branches of government should be kept separate and distinct. Policy formulation and administration are the principal tasks of the legislature and executive. Election to these branches of government is based, in the most general sense, on platforms which showcase preferred packages of social policies and political priorities. The election of Governments carries with it a mandate to raise whatever resources are necessary to implement the programmes which the people preferred.

Judges, on the other hand, are not elected - except only in the most indirect and attenuated sense - because of their political or social philosophies. Their task is to enforce, not revise the law, which includes the constitution of course. From the decisions they have made about people's economic and group rights, we have seen that the role of the third branch of government is to guarantee that all laws and official action taken in the name of the state must meet what are, in effect two very basic measure of distributive justice or formal equality. For the most part, the principles of rationality and proportionality impose duties on how those elected to govern must "act" in translating their political platforms into law; not on what the content of their policies and programmes should be.

To borrow a phrase Ronald Dworkin has popularized, one could say the role of the court is to ensure that those who are entrusted with the powers of the state show equal concern and respect for those whose lives they can affect. The principle of rationality guarantees everyone a measure of equal respect by

---

[74] See e.g. *Kishen Pattnayak v Orissa* (*Food Petitions* case) A.I.R. 1989 SC 677; *Municipal Corp of Delhi v Gurham Kaur* A.I.R. 1989 SC 38; *Olga Tellis v Bombay* SC 13.

ruling unconstitutional laws which restrict their freedom unnecessarily or gratuitously. The principle of proportionality ensures Governments will show the same concern for everyone's life by insisting that there is some consistency in how burdens and benefits which are contained in the law are distributed.

So long as the courts restrict their role to the impartial application of these broad precepts of equality and personal autonomy, they can with good reason be called 'the least dangerous branch'[75] of government. Indeed, the duties and obligations which these principles impose on the 'will of the people' and on the powers of the other two, elected branches of government are not only consistent with, they actually promote the same values and ideals which underlie democracy and popular sovereignty as well. By contrast, it would constitute a serious setback for the forces of democracy and the sovereignty of the people if judges ever did assume that, in addition to being guardians of the constitution, they held ultimate power over the purse. The juxtaposition of such sweeping powers in the branch of government least representative of and accountable to the people would be to signal a regression to the kind of oligarchic institutions which distinguished (and ultimately discredited) colonial ideas of 'responsible' government.

Now at this point, if not before, human rights activists will undoubtedly want to assert a (constitutional?) right of intervention and reply. Many will have had enormous difficulty with an account which accepts - indeed endorses - the courts' refusal to recognize what they regard to be the essence of the new generations of rights. They will say the protection of human rights will be only partial and incomplete until the courts take up the task of ensuring that Governments guarantee every person a

---

[75] The phrase, introduced into the constitutional discourse of the United States by Alexander Hamilton in his contribution to the *Federalist Papers*, was invoked by Alexander Bickel in the title of his highly-acclaimed book *The Least Dangerous Branch: The Supreme Court at the Bar of Politics* 1962 Yale Univ Press.

satisfactory level of physical and spiritual well-being. For them, talk of economic and group rights would be a charade if it did not guarantee substantial social and economic entitlements.

To the separation of powers argument advanced by the courts, they will reply that the jurisprudence shows that the line which is supposed to divide the judiciary from the other two branches of government is crossed all the time. Human rights activists are well aware of the jurisprudence we have reviewed and they often make the point that the courts routinely issue judgments which require Governments to take specific legislative initiatives which can involve very substantial costs for the state. To support their claim, reference is often made to those cases in which courts have ordered the state to provide free legal aid[76] or appoint more judges[77] to satisfy the guarantees, common to all constitutions, that everyone has a right to be tried fairly and fairly expeditiously. As well, they commonly cite those judgments, which we have already noted, in which the courts have extended the benefits of various social assistance programmes to individuals and groups which the Governments who designed them meant to exclude.[78]

Human rights activists argue that judgments such as these undermine the force of the separation of powers argument. They will say that if it is appropriate for the courts to order Governments to guarantee a basic level of legal and social services in cases such as these, there can be nothing wrong also insisting that politicians respect whatever minimum standards of housing,

---

76 See, e.g. *Hussainara Khatoon v. Bihar* A.I.R. 1979 S.C. 1369, 1380-81; *Gideon v Wainright* (1963) 372 U.S. 335; *Miranda v Arizona* (1966) 384 U.S. 436; *Social Court* case (1959) 9 *BVerfGE* 124, translated into English in M Cappelletti & W Cohen *Comparative Constitutional Law* 1979 Bobbs-Merrill; *Airey v Ireland* ECHR 1979 Series A No 32; See also *Comparative Constitutional Law* p 428 where a number of decisions of the Italian Constitutional Court are noted.

77 *Askov supra* note 59.

78 See the cases referred to in notes 21 and 30-33 *supra*.

health care, education, income etc are pre-conditions for enjoying a 'wholesome and cultured' life. Without guarantees of this kind, they will say, ideas of formal equality and personal freedom can be used to legitimate living conditions of extreme inequality and deprivation.

Both in spirit and as a matter of empirical observation, the case of the human rights activist pulls hard on most people's sympathies. The cause of the dispossessed and the disadvantaged is a compelling one and the fact is, as we have seen for ourselves, on many occasions judges have been very strong and direct in their dealings with the elected branches of government and have insisted that initiatives be taken and social programmes extended at considerable cost to the state.

But however appealing the claim of the human rights activists may first appear, neither the justice of their cause nor the past jurisprudence of the courts warrants assigning the third branch of government ultimate power over the purse. It is never a sufficient answer to say that the ends justify the means, and on closer examination it turns out that there is nothing in the way the courts have protected economic and group rights so far which can be used as precedent for judges taking over the job of fixing the levels of social welfare and cultural well-being which must be guaranteed in any particular community.

In fact, as we have seen, the courts have never challenged the sovereignty of the people to maintain control of the purse. To the contrary, they have consistently recognized and adhered to the principle of separation of powers between themselves and the other two, elected branches of government. They have never disputed the levels at which any programme of social welfare have been set. Instead, there has been a universal recognition that denying the legislative branch the authority to say just how 'wholesome and cultured' life in each community will be would constitute a massive compromise of the principle of democratic rule.

The decisions to which human rights activists point in support of their case do not really involve the judiciary laying claim to the power of the purse. In fact, they are of a quite different kind.

For the most part they follow logically from a straightforward application of the principle of formal equality. Rather than take issue with the level of assistance a programme may guarantee, the courts have simply required legislatures and Governments to make whatever services they do provide available to everyone in a non-discriminatory way. There is no attempt to tell the elected representatives of the people how rich such programmes have to be. Rather than question the practical goals and objectives (the levels of assistance) the people and their representatives set for themselves, in these cases the focus of the courts is strictly on the means - the criteria of distribution - that are chosen to identify who the beneficiaries of these programmes will be.

Even the cases in which the effect of the court's decision has meant that Governments had to spend considerable sums of money on legal aid schemes or in the construction and staffing of more courts, the idea of equality has done much of the work. Essentially, the reasoning of the courts in cases of this kind has been that Governments should set up legal aid schemes in those proceedings when one of the parties (including the state in criminal trials) will have counsel to represent them.[79] Even the decision of the Supreme Court of Canada, ordering one of its regional Governments to provide more facilities and staff for the courts so that people could have their cases decided within a reasonable time, was based on a gross inequality in how those charged with similar offences in different parts of the country were brought to trial.[80]

Those judgments in which courts have ordered a state to pay a person's legal costs are like those in which the judges have insisted that there must be some social, economic, environmental etc programme or policy in place but have stopped short of asking whether in substance and in detail what has been done is good

---

79 See the cases referred to in note 76 *supra*.

80 *Askov supra* note 59.

enough.[81] In all of these cases the courts have recognized that Governments may have different options, with different price tags, available to them to ensure that the legal process is equal and fair, and they have respected the sovereignty of the people and their elected representatives to choose the policy that best suits their needs.[82] Indeed, the Constitutional Court of Italy, regarded by some as the most active court in the field of social and economic rights, upheld the constitutionality of a system of legal aid which provided no compensation for the lawyers involved in part on the ground that questions concerning the adequacy of social programmes like the provision of legal aid do not raise issues within the domain of constitutional law.[83]

---

81 'Programmatic' decisions of this kind are part of the constitutional jurisprudence all over the world. In its decisions imposing a duty on the State to protect people's environmental interests or to rehabilitate prisoners, for example, the German Court gives the elected branches of government virtually unfettered control in deciding what the details of those programmes should be: see D Kommers *The Constitutional Jurisprudence of the Federal Republic of Germany* and the cases referred to in note 54 *supra*. The European Court of Human Rights has adopted a similar approach on the provision of minority language education: see, e.g. *Belgian Education Language* case *supra* note 71, as has the Japanese Supreme Court on the question of electoral reform: see, e.g. H Hata 'Malapportionment of Representation' supra note 40. This approach is also well known in Italian Constitutional Law: see, e.g. L M Diez Picazo & M-C Porthoreau 'The Constitutional Protection of Social Rights' *supra* note 18, and it has even governed the decisions of the Supreme Court of India in assigning responsibility for fixing the operative criteria in affirmative action programmes: see, e.g. *Kumar v Karnataka supra* note 20; See also *Neeraja Chaudhary v State of M.P.* A.I.R. 1984 S.C. 1090 (duty to rehabilitate persons freed from bonded labour).

82 See, e.g. *Airey v Ireland supra* note 76.

83 See Decision Corte Costituzionale Dec 22/64 [1964] 9 Giur Cost 1163, noted in Cappelletti & Cohen *Comparative Constitutional Law supra* note 76, p 428. And see generally E. Cheli and F. Donati, "Methods and Criteria of Judgment on the Question of Rights to Freedom", chpt 6 in

IV. WHAT PEOPLE HAVE A RIGHT TO EXPECT

So human rights activists have no answer to the judges who insist on respecting a separation of powers between themselves and the other two, elected branches of government. There is, in fact, no precedent for the judiciary fixing the priorities and levels of state support for people's most basic economic and interpersonal needs. The judiciary has been steadfast in refusing all invitations to assume power over the fisc, and it is difficult to imagine what circumstances could justify changing its view. To recognize a right to go to court to require Governments to improve the levels of economic and cultural well-being in their communities would mean the end of peoples' sovereignty to define their own political priorities and community values.

In the absence of any satisfactory accounting for the principle of separation of powers and democratic rule, human rights activists act blindly, if not irresponsibly, in continuing to agitate for the entrenchment and judicial definition of minimum standards of social and economic well-being. They encourage people to engage in what will only be fruitless and wasteful litigation, and ultimately to lose respect for the constitution as an inspirational charter of what their community's standards of justice should be. Unless and until they can reconcile such constitutional guarantees with the principle of democratic rule, human rights activists must only look to the courts to promote the ends of justice with the two basic principles of equality - of rationality and consistency - which have guided their work for the past two hundred years.

That human rights activists must lower their sights in what they can legitimately expect of the courts does not mean that they must close their eyes. Disappointment need not lead to despair. Even if their prescription of how people can improve the level of social justice in their communities is wide of the mark, their instinct that courts can do better than they have in the past must surely be right. However highly one rates the performance of the courts in the enforcement of constitutional bills of rights, on this

---

this volume.

point everyone - critics and activists alike - should agree.

The fact is that there is much work the human rights activist can do to enhance the protection of people's social and economic rights without obliterating the line which separates the jurisdiction of the courts from the other two branches of government. Rather than encourage the courts to take over tasks that fall within the jurisdiction of the elected branches of government, human rights activists can help courts use their traditional powers of review even more effectively than they have so far. This is a role familiar to legal analysts and one they have performed with distinction in the past.

Some of the most effective writing in the area of constitutional law in the United States, for example, has focused on the decisions of the American Supreme Court during the so-called 'Lochner era' when members of that Court imposed significant limitations on the ability of the Congress and state legislatures to attend to the needs of the relatively powerless and disadvantaged.[84] The consensus of the overwhelming majority of writers who have analyzed those cases is that the Court acted quite improperly in so drastically limiting the kind of labour and social policies which popularly-elected Governments could pursue.[85]

Today, of course, the concern of the human rights activist is quite different from what bothered most people about Lochner and its progeny. Their worry is not that the courts are interfering too much, but that they may not be protecting people's social and economic rights vigorously enough. Those who are familiar with the cases know that they do provide considerable support for the sceptics' criticism that the judiciary has been much more diffident

---

84 For an analysis of the Court's decisions in the Lochner era and many of the commentaries: L Tribe *American Constitutional Law* ch 8 *supra* note 37.

85 For a dissenting view, see B. Siegan *Economic Liberties and the Constitution*, University of Chicago Press, 1980.

deciding when it will protect people's constitutional rights than the catalogue of cases in the preceding sections might suggest. The fact is that for virtually every case we identified in which a court did provide some protection for someone's economic or group rights, one can point to a parallel decision in which another court did not.

The decisions the US Supreme Court handed down during the Lochner era are unquestionably the most notorious cases in which the courts have exercised their powers of review in ways which prejudiced rather than protected people's basic economic and social needs. But they are far from being the only cases of this kind. It would be an easy matter for the critics and sceptics to catalogue a list of cases to counter those we noted in Part Two. It is a matter of record that the rights of linguistic[86] and religious[87] minorities to control the education of their children have not always prevailed. Nor have opposition groups and political minorities been successful in every challenge they have made to election laws which were prejudicial to their interests.[88] Arbitrary and discriminatory barriers to employment have not been removed in every case, and not every unjustified dismissal has been remedied.[89] The expectation of those who live on some

---

86 See, e.g. *Belgian Education Language* case *supra* note 72.

87 See, e.g. *R v Jones* (1986) 31 D.L.R. (4th) 569; *Re Education Act* (1988) 40 D.L.R. (4th) 17; cf *San Antonio Independent School District v Rodrigues* (1973) 411 U.S. 1.

88 See, e.g. *Mathieu Mohen v Belgium* (1987) 10 E.H.R.R. 1; *MacKay v Manitoba* (1989) 51 D.L.R. (4th) 385; and see generally Masahiro Usaki 'Restrictions on Political Campaigns in Japan' (1990) 53(2) *Law & Comtemp Probs* 133.

89 See, e.g. *Konigsberg v State Bar of California* (1961) 366 US 36; *Washington v. Davis* (1976) 426 U.S. 429; *Williamson v Lee Optical Co* (1955) 348 U.S. 483; *Koizumi v Japan (Gypsy Taxi* case) 17 Keishu 12, translated in part in Itoh & Beer *Constitutional Case Law of Japan supra* note 72 p 80; *Mitsubishi Jushi Corp* case (1973) 27 Minshu 1536;

form of income assistance or benefit from affirmative action policies that they will receive the protection of a constitutional bill of rights has ended in disappointment as often as not.[90] Even public servants have had a very uneven record persuading the courts to allow them to participate in the full range of political activities.[91]

The large number of cases in which those seeking protection for their economic and cultural needs have been turned back by the courts is certainly grist for the sceptics' mill. But they also provide a rich jurisprudence for the human rights activist as well. The length of the queue of disappointed litigants provides a benchmark of just how much the courts' record might be improved. Every time it can be shown that the doctrinal analysis followed by a court is wanting in some way, human rights activists expand the protection which the courts and bills of rights should provide.

When human rights activists familiarize themselves with all of the cases in which courts have not exercised their powers of review to protect an economic or cultural interest of some person or another, they should be encouraged that they will be able to help the judiciary be more rigorous in protecting rights of this kind. In most of these cases they will find that the reasoning and doctrinal analysis that is used by the courts when they turn

---

Balakotaiah v India A.I.R. 1958 S.C. 232; *Kosiek v Germany* E.C.H.R. 1986 Series A No 105; *Civil Servant Loyalty* case (1975) 39 *BVerfGE* 334, partially translated in English in D Kommers *The Constitutional Jurisprudence of the Federal Republic of Germany supra* note 6 p 232.

90 See, e.g. *Dandridge v Williams* (1970) 397 U.S. 471; *Mathews v Elridge* (1974) 424 U.S. 319; *Wygant v Jackson Board of Education* (1986) 106 S.C. 1842.

91 See, e.g. U.S. *Civil Service Commission v Letter Carriers* (1973) 413 U.S. 548; *Kosiek v Germany supra* note 89; *Civil Servant Loyalty* case *supra* note 89; and see generally M Usaki 'Restrictions on Political Campaigns in Japan' *supra* note 88.

claimants away empty-handed is quite similar. In many cases, building on a separation of powers argument, the courts have said that in the areas of economic and cultural policy judges should apply the principles of rationality and proportionality cautiously and with considerable deference because policy formulation in these areas involves the compromise of competing interests, and in these sorts of matters the elected representatives of the people have a comparative advantage and special expertise. At other times, based on similar thinking, the courts have only used the principle of consistency or reasonableness and their review has been partial and incomplete.[92] In extreme cases some courts have even said that the constitution only protects against direct, intentional limitations on people's ability to control the social and economic aspects of their lives which has effectively meant no review at all.[93] In almost all of the cases in which a court has not exercised its powers of review to protect the economic or

---

92 See e.g. *National Union of Belgian Police* April 12/75 Series A #19; *Belgian Language Education* July 23/68 Series A; *CoDetermination* Case (1979) 50 BVerfGE290; *Numerous Clausus* Case (1972) 33 BVerfGE303; translated and reported in part in Donald P. Kommers, *The Constitutional Jurisprudence of the Federal Republic of Germany*, Duke University Press 1989 Durham. *McKinney v University of Guelph* (1990) 76 D.L.R.4th 545; *West Coast Hotel v Parrish* 300 U.S. 379 (1937); *Williamson v Lee Optical* 348 U.S. 483 (1955); *Dandridge v Williams* 397 U.S. 471 (1970); *San Antonio v Rodriguez* 411 U.S. 1 (1973); *Shimizu v Japan* (Fukuoka Bathouse) 9 Keishu 89; *T. Surozomo v Japan* (All Japan Agriculture Forestry Workers' Union-Zennorin) 27 Keishu 1973: discussed in T. Kamata "Adjudication and the Governing Process: Political Questions and Legislative Discretion" (1990) 53(1) Law and Contemp. Probs 181; *Glass Chatons Importers v India* A.I.R. 1961 S.C. 1514; *Kumari Chitra Gosh v India* A.I.R. 1970 S.C. 35.

93 See e.g. State of J & K v Ghulam Rasool A.I.R. 1961 S.C. 1301; Washington v Davis 426 U.S. 229 (1976); Japan v Osawa (Sarafutsu Case) 28 Keishu 393 (1974) discussed in Laurence W. Beer "Freedom of Expression: The Continuing Revolution" (1990) 52(2) Law and Contemporary Press 39, 49-52.

cultural interests of some individual or group, it was one of these ideas or ways of reasoning which was at work.

Each of these doctrinal moves has received some attention from legal scholars around the world. Questions have already been raised whether any of these analytical 'spins' really can justify the courts taking a more cautious and conservative approach to defending human rights in the social and economic spheres of people's lives.[94] However, much broader and more comprehensive studies remain to be done. The fact that the courts have employed very similar analytical devices and modes of reasoning when they think about what kinds of economic and cultural interests they will protect, provides still more evidence that it is much more a matter of legal doctrine and judicial reasoning than constitutional text which determines what "rights" people will have.

Encouraging legal analysts to concentrate on the cases and the method of reasoning favoured by the courts may be thought by some not to be very fashionable these days. In many parts of the world legal scholars have moved into related fields of philosophical, literary, economic, historical, sociological etc inquiry. However, as attractive as these broader forms of policy analysis undoubtedly are, the rewards of returning to traditional analysis of legal doctrine, at least in the area of constitutional law and the protection of human rights, should be just as alluring.

The most immediate and tangible gains, of course, would be in strengthening the protection which constitutional bills of rights can provide in the economic and social spheres of people's lives. The ultimate goal should be a uniform standard of rigorous scrutiny for all legal rules and regulations, unless a compelling state interest could be identified which justified less searching

---

94 See, e.g. R. McCloskey 'Economic Due Process and the Supreme Court: an Exhumation and Reburial' (1962) *Sup Ct Rev* 34; Mutsuo Nakamura 'Freedom of Economic Activities and the Right to Property' *supra* note 11; D. Beatty 'Labouring Outside the Charter' (1991) 29 *Osgoode Hall LJ* 839; M. Galanter *Competing Equalities*, 1984 Oxford University Press.

forms of review. Beyond this, careful analysis of how the major courts around the world have restricted their powers of review also offers the prospect of promoting greater harmony within the legal community itself. If the wildest dreams of human rights activists were to come true, and if courts did apply the principles of rationality and proportionality as widely and as vigorously as it is possible to do, the differences between them and their more sceptical colleagues about the integrity of bills of rights would be substantially muted, if not completely resolved. If the courts were persuaded to abandon whatever doctrinal and analytical moves comparative analysis showed to be flawed, it would be expected that the cries of subjectivity and indeterminacy would gradually fall away. A jurisprudence freed of all doctrinal imperfections should make it easier for the sceptics to understand why, all over the world, people continue to put their faith in constitutional bills of rights and the courts and the ideal of the rule of law.

International Studies in Human Rights

1. B. G. Ramcharan (ed.): *International Law and Fact-finding in the Field of Human Rights*. 1982 ISBN 90-247-3042-2
2. B. G. Ramcharan: *Humanitarian Good Offices in International Law*. The Good Offices of the United Nations Secretary-General in the Field of Human Rights. 1983 ISBN 90-247-2805-3
3. B. G. Ramcharan (ed.): *The Right to Life in International Law*. 1985 ISBN 90-247-3074-0
4. P. Alston and K. Tomaševski (eds.): *The Right to Food*. 1984 ISBN 90-247-3087-2
5. A. Bloed and P. van Dijk (eds.): *Essays on Human Rights in the Helsinki Process*. 1985 ISBN 90-247-3211-5
6. K. Törnudd: *Finland and the International Norms of Human Rights*. 1986 ISBN 90-247-3257-3
7. H. Thoolen and B. Verstappen: *Human Rights Missions*. A Study of the Fact-finding Practice of Non-governmental Organizations. 1986 ISBN 90-247-3364-2
8. H. Hannum: *The Right to Leave and Return in International Law and Practice*. 1987 ISBN 90-247-3445-2
9. J. H. Burgers and H. Danelius: *The United Nations Convention against Torture*. A Handbook on the Convention against Torture and Other Cruel, Inhuman or Degrading Treatment or Punishment. 1988 ISBN 90-247-3609-9
10. D. A. Martin (ed.): *The New Asylum Seekers: Refugee Law in the 1980s*. The Ninth Sokol Colloquium on International Law. 1988 ISBN 90-247-3730-3
11. C. M. Quiroga: *The Battle of Human Rights*. Gross, Systematic Violations and the Inter-American System. 1988 ISBN 90-247-3687-0
12. L. A. Rehof and C. Gulmann (eds.): *Human Rights in Domestic Law and Development Assistance Policies of the Nordic Countries*. 1989 ISBN 90-247-3743-5
13. B. G. Ramcharan: *The Concept and Present Status of International Protection of Human Rights*. Forty Years After the Universal Declaration. 1989 ISBN 90-247-3759-1
14. A. D. Byre and B. Y. Byfield (eds.): *International Human Rights Law in the Commonwealth Caribbean*. 1991 ISBN 90-247-3785-0
15. N. Lerner: *Groups Rights and Discrimination in International Law*. 1991 ISBN 0-7923-0853-0
16. S. Shetreet (ed.): *Free Speech and National Security*. 1991 ISBN 0-7923-1030-6
17. G. Gilbert: *Aspects of Extradition Law*. 1991 ISBN 0-7923-1162-0
18. P.E. Veerman: *The Rights of the Child and the Changing Image of Childhood*. 1991 ISBN 0-7923-1250-3
19. M. Delmas-Marty (ed.): *The European Convention for the Protection of Human Rights*. International Protection versus National Restrictions. 1991 ISBN 0-7923-1283-X

International Studies in Human Rights

20. A. Bloed and P. van Dijk (eds.): *The Human Dimension of the Helsinki Process.* The Vienna Follow-up Meeting and its Aftermath. 1991 ISBN 0-7923-1337-2
21. L.S. Sunga: *Individual Responsibility in International Law for Serious Human Rights Violations.* 1992 ISBN 0-7923-1453-0
22. S. Frankowski and D. Shelton (eds.): *Preventive Detention.* A Comparative and International Law Perspective. 1992 ISBN 0-7923-1465-4
23. M. Freeman and P. Veerman (eds.): *The Ideologies of Children's Rights.* 1992 ISBN 0-7923-1800-5
24. S. Stavros: *The Guarantees for Accused Persons Under Article 6 of the European Convention on Human Rights.* An Analysis of the Application of the Convention and a Comparison with Other Instruments. 1993 ISBN 0-7923-1897-8
25. A. Rosas and J. Helgesen (eds.): *The Strength of Diversity.* Human Rights and Pluralist Democracy. 1992 ISBN 0-7923-1987-7
26. K. Waaldijk and A. Clapham (eds.): *Homosexuality: A European Community Issue.* Essays on Lesbian and Gay Rights in European Law and Policy. 1993 ISBN 0-7923-2038-7; Pb: 0-7923-2240-1
27. Y.K. Tyagi: *The Law and Practice of the UN Human Rights Committee.* 1993 ISBN 0-7923-2040-9
28. G. van Bueren: *The International Law on the Rights of the Child.* 1993 ISBN 0-7923-2221-5
29. L.A. Rehof: *Guide to the* Travaux Préparatoires *of the United Nations Convention on the Elimination of All Forms of Discrimination against Women.* 1993 ISBN 0-7923-2222-3
30. A. Bloed, L. Leicht, M. Novak and A. Rosas (eds.): *Monitoring Human Rights in Europe.* Comparing International Procedures and Mechanisms. 1993 ISBN 0-7923-2383-1
31. A. Harding and J. Hatchard (eds.): *Preventive Detention and Security Law.* A Comparative Survey. 1993 ISBN 0-7923-2432-3
32. Y. Beigbeder: *International Monitoring of Plebiscites, Referenda and National Elections.* Self-determination and Transition to Democracy. 1994 ISBN 0-7923-2563-X
33. F. de Varennes: *Language, Minorities and Human Rights.* 1994. ISBN 0-7923-2728-4
34. D.M. Beatty (ed.): *Human Rights and Judicial Review.* A Comparative Perspective. 1994 ISBN 0-7923-2968-6

This series is designed to shed light on current legal and political aspects of process and organization in the field of human rights.

MARTINUS NIJHOFF PUBLISHERS – DORDRECHT / BOSTON / LONDON